Teachers'
Professional Learning

GW00566812

Teachers' Professional Learning

Edited by
James Calderhead

 The Falmer Press

(A member of the Taylor & Francis Group)
London • New York • Philadelphia

8·95

UK The Falmer Press, Falmer House, Barcombe, Lewes, East Sussex, BN8 5DL

USA The Falmer Press, Taylor & Francis Inc., 242 Cherry Street, Philadelphia, PA 19106-1906

First published 1988

Library of Congress Cataloging in Publication Data is available on request

ISBN 1 85000 388 2
ISBN 1 85000 389 0 (pbk.)

Jacket design by Caroline Archer

Typeset in 11/13 Bembo by
Imago Publishing Ltd, Thame, Oxon

Printed in Great Britain by Taylor & Francis (Printers) Ltd, Basingstoke

Contents

Contents

Introduction

James Calderhead

Amidst much recent public concern about the quality of education in our schools, attention has inevitably been directed to the adequacy of teachers' preparation for the classroom and to their ongoing professional development. In England and Wales, a national review of first year teachers (HMI, 1982) highlighted several alleged weaknesses in teachers' training. This led to various recommendations for the improvement of pre-service training courses (DES, 1983), the establishment of new accreditation procedures for the evaluation of courses, and more detailed monitoring of teacher education and the prescription of good practice (HMI, 1987). In addition, nationally-proposed changes in in-service funding have, at the same time, led to modifications in the kind of advanced professional training that is available to teachers.

Similarly, in the United States, the Carnegie Foundation (1986) recently raised questions about the quality and appropriateness of higher education in general, and has prompted some radical thinking about the role of colleges and universities in American society. With a more specific focus, the Holmes Group report (1986), produced by an influential consortium of teacher education institutions, expressed doubts about existing teacher education practices and proposed new structures for the training of 'career professional teachers'. In Australia and some European countries, the same dissatisfactions with education and the state of teacher preparation have led to reviews of current practice, and the formulation of policies for change.

Whereas teacher education has in the past been based largely on tradition, modified and adapted by the craft wisdom of the teacher educator, it has currently become much more influenced by national policies, which acclaim the importance of high quality professional training and attempt to map out its characteristics. But where do these

policies come from? On what ideas about teaching and about professional learning are they based?

Unfortunately, there is little hard evidence or sound theoretical
understanding from which policy can be derived, and therefore it is
often influenced by the prevailing views of good practice and the
common-sense reasoning of policy-makers. Not surprisingly, the
ideas about teaching and teacher education that are implicit in such
policy are sometimes quite unsophisticated. A frequent policy response to improve the quality of pre-service training, for instance, is
to demand higher entry requirements, increase the length of the
course, increase the time spent on the study of subject matter, extend
the time spent on school practice, and increase the involvement of
practising teachers. These quantitative recommendations, however,
presume very simple relationships amongst the student, the training
input and students' eventual classroom practice, leaving out of
account, for instance, the nature of the knowledge that informs teaching action or the potentially conservative effects of a greater involvement of classroom teachers in the training process.

There are indeed many questions which need to be tackled about
the nature and effects of professional training and its relationship to
classroom practice. Learning to teach involves complex cognitive,
affective and behavioural changes, and research into this complexity
has only recently acquired momentum. This research clearly promises
to be of value in informing current policy and the practices of teacher
educators.

The chapters in this book arose from a conference on Teachers'
Professional Learning, sponsored by the British Educational Research
Association (BERA), and held at the University of Lancaster in July
1987. The principal purpose of the conference was to bring together
researchers from several countries who were pursuing research on
teachers' learning, with the aim of exploring both empirical research
findings and tentative theoretical frameworks, and of considering
their implications for both the pre-service and in-service education of
teachers. The chapters therefore address theoretical and conceptual
issues and also the practical issues concerning how teacher education
courses might best be structured and the rationale for such structure.

It was clear from the conference, which in fact attracted not only
researchers but teacher educators, and some teachers and local education authority advisers, that there was a need for a much better
understanding of the processes of professional learning and a pooling
of available knowledge. Through a greater appreciation of the processes involved in acquiring teaching competence, those involved in

teachers' professional development might be able to make their efforts more constructive, and meaningful policy might eventually be derived.

Organization of Chapters

The chapters in this book are variously interconnected in terms of the issues that they address, and the theories and research methods they utilize. Consequently, they could have been sequenced in several alternative ways, maintaining a variety of coherent themes and arguments. The sequence eventually adopted, however, was that of the teacher's career. The first five chapters, therefore, focus on student and beginning teachers and issues associated with learning to teach. The next two chapters are concerned with research-based innovations in pre-service education, and the remaining five chapters concentrate on the nature of teachers' knowledge and skill, means of facilitating its development, and impediments to continuing professional growth.

In the first chapter, Russell questions the relationship between theory and practice as it is generally conceptualized in pre-service training. He points out how the college-taught element of teacher training is typically regarded as providing theory, for instance of child development and subject methodology, to be later implemented by student teachers in their school practice. However, in a series of case studies of teachers with varying levels of experience, he discovers that theory is often meaningless to teachers until they have mastered practice. In the case of experienced teachers, he finds that it is only after they have become competent in the classroom that they are able to criticize and question their performance and start to relate theory to their own actions. Similarly, he finds that the student or beginning teacher needs to acquire routines to operate in the classroom before they can begin to think about theory and relate college experiences to their own teaching.

Russell argues that the typical 'theory into practice' perspective might generate considerable confusion and dissatisfaction amongst student teachers. As students struggle to find the relevance of college-taught theory they may resort to dismissing it in favour of unreflective practice and the imitation of observed classroom routines. In contrast, Russell suggests that student teachers might more profitably be encouraged to understand theory through experience. Once they have developed confidence in classroom routines, they might be encouraged to reflect upon their actions and come to understand the relevance of theory, examining their practice in the light of theoretical knowledge.

The role of reflection in teacher education is an issue examined in chapter 2 by Korthagen, who investigates student teachers' experience of a Dutch teacher education course designed to promote reflective teaching. In a questionnaire and interview evaluation of the course, it was found that not all students seemed to benefit from a reflective teacher education approach. Some possessed what Korthagen terms an 'external orientation', in that they expected to be told how to teach and for others to evaluate and direct their teaching. For students to engage in professional growth through reflection, on the other hand, seems to require an 'internal orientation' in which students employ their own knowledge and values to examine and evaluate their practice. For some students to benefit from a reflective teacher education course may therefore require efforts to be directed at developing an appropriate learning orientation and for students to become aware of, and take control over, their approach to learning. Such preparation for reflective teaching seems particularly important since Korthagen found that tutors on the course generally assumed that the students learned to teach with an internal orientation and failed to appreciate that students might approach professional learning in other ways.

In chapter 3 the reflective processes involved in teacher education are viewed as a repertoire of metacognitive skills — ways of thinking about one's own thinking. It is argued that the knowledge that is delivered in teacher education courses is qualitatively different from that which guides teachers' practice, and it is through the use of various metacognitive skills that the two can be related. Research on teachers' practical knowledge suggests that it can be best conceptualized in terms of images, routines and rules of practice. For instance, teachers frequently hold images at different levels of abstraction — an image of an ideal teacher, of how a practical science lesson is taught, and of what a class of 9-year-olds is typically like — all of which influence teachers' classroom action. It is suggested that the development of teachers' practical knowledge involves the acquisition, comparison, evaluation and synthesis of images, and that a greater understanding and awareness is required of how different types of knowledge might relate to classroom practice and of the metacognition skills that are needed in the generation and manipulation of teachers' knowledge.

The following two chapters report empirical research on the developing thoughts and reflections of student and beginning teachers, attempting to trace aspects of the professional learning process. In a content analysis of interviews with student teachers about their planning and post-lesson reflections, Borko and her colleagues found four factors that appeared to be related to patterns of student teachers' thinking: the extent of their subject matter knowledge, the subject matter area, the number of times the lesson is taught, and the extent to which students feel in control of classroom events. For example, students, particularly those teaching in secondary schools, planned lessons in more detail when they were unsure of the subject matter, and students who felt in control of classroom events more often took steps to remedy weaknesses in their own practice. Borko points out that a sense of control over classroom events frequently coincided with those students who were judged by others to be very effective teachers, and she speculates, interestingly, that this may be an important component of classroom competence. This notion may have some similarities with Korthagen's concept of internal orientation, though it is impossible of course, given the available data, to identify its relationship to judgments of effectiveness. For instance, does a student's sense of control encourage analysis, reflection and the motivation to succeed, or does success in the classroom lead to student attributions of self-effectiveness? One might well expect both of these processes to be operating to some extent.

Busher, Clarke and Taggart's research focusses on secondary teachers in the early stages of their careers. Using interview, observation and teachers' commentaries on videotapes of their lessons, they similarly find that teachers vary in the extent to which they feel empowered to influence classroom events or alternatively feel constrained by external factors, such as the syllabus and the expectations of parents and senior teachers. Their research also demonstrates how early conceptions of teaching, learning and subject matter can strongly influence what a student teacher extracts from teacher education and their experience in classrooms. In addition, they indicate how inconsistencies in these conceptions lead to dilemmas, as in the case of a young science teacher who views science as a process of experimentation and creative thinking but who also views teaching as a process of information delivery and acquiring correct responses from the children. Such incompatible views led to much frustration and feelings of ineffectiveness. Busher, Clarke and Taggart emphasize the value of confronting objective evidence on one's own practice, as they describe how video feedback enabled this teacher to begin to examine and resolve the contradictions in his beliefs and actions.

The chapters by McIntyre and Wood are concerned with drawing upon research on teachers' knowledge to inform initial teacher education practices. McIntyre describes the development of a new teacher education course which aims to take account of some of the difficulties that beginning teachers experience in learning to teach. In particular, McIntyre is concerned with developing a course framework in which student teachers can unthreateningly explore and critically appraise a variety of professional knowledge and practice. He distinguishes the different areas of expertise of the supervising teacher and the college tutor, the differing criteria each of these groups uses for the assessment of knowledge and practice, and describes a course structure in which teacher and tutor can adopt roles to facilitate students developing their own understandings of practice and in which they can encourage students to test out and reflect upon alternative practices as their knowledge of, and competencies in, teaching grows.

Wood, on the other hand, is concerned with constructing an expert tutoring system to help student teachers analyze their classroom teaching. By examining the conversations of teacher-tutors with their students, she builds a computer-based model representing teachers' understandings of classroom processes. Such a task clearly demonstrates the enormous complexity of teacher knowledge and a computational model can only amount to a crude representation of teachers' real working knowledge. Nevertheless, Wood demonstrates how such a model can be used in a tutoring system, both as a heuristic for the development of reflective skills in student teachers, and as a means of exploring the structure of teachers' knowledge.

The remaining chapters examine the nature of experienced teachers' expertise and consider the difficulties involved in its further development. Anning explores experienced teachers' conceptions of learning and learners in the primary school, using stimulated recall, interviews and repertory grid techniques. Although she finds many similarities amongst the teachers in the kinds of information about children they appeared to seek in the classroom, the teachers were found to possess a variety of theories or images of teaching and learning which influenced how they structured tasks and used the information they perceived. The teachers' conceptions of children's learning would, for instance, stress the importance of active involvement in the task, an emotionally secure environment in which failure is non-threatening, or the exploration of open-ended activities through one's own trial and error, and such conceptions would lead to quite different types of classroom activity and teacher-pupil interaction. Anning demonstrates that teachers, as a result of years of experience, have accumulated their own theories about teaching and learning, though they often have difficulty explicating these, and researchers need to work closely with teachers in order to gain access to them.

Leinhardt, in a very detailed study of one teacher, examines how a teacher's approach to the teaching of subtraction has been influenced through her experiences of mathematics teaching over thirty-five years. Leinhardt illustrates how experience of different methods and texts might be selectively synthesized resulting in knowledge which is highly specific to a particular situation. This 'situated knowledge' enables teachers' actions to become automatic and highly efficient, but its complexity and context-specificity may also be major factors in explaining why teachers encounter great difficulty in changing their practices or adopting new ones.

The following chapter by Johnston explores how two teachers attempt to change their classroom practices in the teaching of science. The teachers are committed to a conceptual change approach to science teaching, which takes account of students' prior ideas and attempts to modify them through active involvement in the learning situation. Detailed observation of teachers' lessons and interviews with the teachers suggest that although they espoused a strong commitment to the conceptual change approach, the teachers' practice frequently took a more didactic form. Teachers' pre-existing views of teaching, learning and the nature of science were firmly embedded in their practice which had become adapted to their particular school context. Like the beginning teacher described in Busher, Clarke and Taggart's study, Johnston demonstrates that producing fundamental change in teaching and learning in classrooms may be a slow, experimental process, in which teachers need considerable help to identify the mismatches between their espoused theories and theories-in-use, and to think through the implications of new theories for their own particular practice and school situation.

The knowledge that teachers acquire in the process of professional development can be of many different forms and can be acquired in various learning situations. This point is well made by Eraut who proposes a typology of knowledge, based on an analysis of teacher management training experiences. By distinguishing different types of knowledge, Eraut demonstrates how the knowledge informing teachers' actions can often be complex, interrelated, partially tacit and situationally adapted. He also indicates how different types of knowledge are developed in different ways, necessitating alternative tasks in professional training. For instance, knowledge of educational practice might be enhanced in group situations, enabling teachers to exchange and probe one another's experience, whereas conceptual knowledge, useful in the analysis of practice, may be more readily developed in a more structured setting in which tutors provide concepts and case studies in which particular concepts can be examined and their significance appraised. Mapping out the knowledge of teachers in this way is seen by Eraut as providing a guide to the design of management training courses, but the distinctions in knowledge bases that he suggests may well provide a heuristic for thinking about professional learning in general, increasing teacher educators' awareness of the complexity of teachers' knowledge and the alternative means by which it might be developed.

The final chapter returns to the theory-practice issue, and draws upon notions of empowerment and reflection to explain some current difficulties in professional development and educational change. Based on a series of biographies, obtained through in-depth interviews, Rudduck suggests that teachers, in order to cope with change and take control over their own professional development, need to explore the personal meaning of their own situation. Experienced teachers have generally been socialized into a role that they have never seriously and critically questioned. By identifying the theories, assumptions and values that underlie their own practice, and considering their significance to themselves as people as well as professionals, Rudduck argues that teachers may acquire an analytic purchase on their situation as well as a sense of control over changing it. Rudduck does not underestimate the difficulties that teachers may encounter in this task, but suggests that examples of teacher biographies might well provide the stimulus for other teachers to start questioning their practice, producing the initial, enquiring discontent that frequently accompanies the beginning of change.

Teachers' Professional Learning

Looking across the chapters of this book, a number of recurring themes and issues concerning teachers' professional learning are raised and explored. First of all, several of the chapters highlight the sophistication and complexity of the teacher's knowledge base. Teachers' practical knowledge may be qualitatively different from systematic academic knowledge, being acquired principally for the purposes of guiding action rather than understanding events, though the two may well, on occasion, be related. Teachers' knowledge spans diverse content areas, and takes several different forms, and teaching tasks typically draw upon multiple areas and forms of knowledge. The nature of teachers' knowledge is not well understood, but its complexity, and the ways in which different types of knowledge are developed, are clearly crucial to explore in our efforts to understand and improve teacher education.

Secondly, theory and practice are frequently regarded as separate entities in teacher education, sometimes the former being viewed as primarily the responsibility of the college which aims to build the theoretical knowledge of the student and the latter the responsibility of the school, where expertise is developed under the supervision of the experienced teacher. However, in several chapters it is argued that this is a false dichotomy. Theory is implicit in practice, and the relationship between theory and practice in teacher education is not one of implementation — theory being translated into practice — but a continuously interactive one. With assistance, students, as they acquire competence in classroom teaching, can begin to identify the theory that is implicit in their action, compare this to other theory and thereby begin to evaluate their practice, considering alternative directions in which it might develop. Theory can provide the analytic and conceptual apparatus for thinking about practice, while practice can provide the opportunity for the testing and assimilation of theory.

Thirdly, practice in schools is clearly an important starting point for learning to teach, but not in the sense of providing models for students to imitate. Student teachers require knowledge or images of teaching before they can experiment, analyze and evaluate. Discussions of teaching may seem fairly meaningless without a sound grasp of what teachers in fact do. Wide experience of observing and working with teachers may provide the essential basis for any attempt to develop reflective teacher education.

Fourthly, reflective teacher education has been argued on several grounds. It enables self-directed growth as a professional. It facilitates the linking of both theory and practice in education. It helps to explicate the expertise of teachers and subject it to critical evaluation. It enables teachers to take a more active role in their own professional accountability. But the term reflective teaching is described and operationalized in different ways in different teacher education courses. Exactly what is the process of reflection? It might be defined in terms of the critical evaluation of one's own teaching in the light of alternative models of the nature, purposes and context of teaching. But this begs questions concerning the kinds of knowledge and skills that are needed in reflecting and how these are acquired. For instance, reflective teaching seems to take for granted the ability of teachers to stand back from their teaching and look upon their actions objectively, yet this ability of looking upon one's behaviour 'in the third person', separating oneself and one's own emotional commitments from practice, is often itself a difficulty for both student and experienced teachers. Research is needed to enquire into what exactly the processes of reflection involve and how they might be developed.

Fifthly, teacher education courses have sometimes conformed more to a certification process than a genuinely professional learning process. Student teachers have learned to demonstrate a narrow range of contrived competencies in order to be favourably assessed and certificated as a teacher. Similarly, courses of advanced professional study for teachers have frequently assessed particular areas of competence which may have little bearing on professional practice. A teacher's completion of a dissertation, for instance, says nothing about their practice in the classroom. There are many constraints within the academic and professional environment that will continue to pressure teacher education courses into producing certification rather than learning experiences. Several of the chapters point to the source of these pressures and begin to suggest ways in which the structure of teacher education must change in order to counter these effects.

Lastly, a theme addressed by several of the chapters is the role of a sense of empowerment in teachers' professional learning. Several authors have argued that if teachers do not feel in control of classroom events, and in control of their own practice, they will tend not to engage in those processes of analysis, reflection and experimentation that result in change and improvement. This may be an important factor to consider in the development of educational policy relating to classroom practice. In Britain, for instance, there is a growing level of external control of the school curriculum, assessment procedures and teaching methods. Whilst the intention may be to improve the quality of classroom practice, such policies may risk some adverse effects. Practices imposed from outside might change the ways teachers view their work, lessen the responsibility they undertake for their own professional development, possibly leading to a decline rather than improvement in the quality of teaching and learning.

How teachers learn to teach, the nature of that learning, how it is developed and how it is influenced by the context in which teachers work are clearly important questions to investigate in the quest for educational improvement. The research in this volume has begun such investigations and has started to unravel and describe the complex processes involved. In doing so, it suggests some tentative answers to existing problems which will be of interest to teachers, teacher educators, advisers, policy-makers and others concerned with education.

But the research also raises many other issues to discuss and investigate further. Given our current state of knowledge, there is much that future research on teachers' professional learning can contribute to our understanding of the development of classroom practice.

References

CARNEGIE FOUNDATION (1986) *A Nation Prepared: Teachers for the 21st Century*, Hyattsville, MD, Carnegie Forum on Education and the Economy.

DES (1983) *Teaching Quality*, London, HMSO.

HMI (1982) *The New Teacher in School*, London, HMSO.

HMI (1987) *Quality in Schools: The Initial Training of Teachers*, London, HMSO.

HOLMES GROUP (1986) *Tomorrow's Teachers: A Report of the Holmes Group*, East Lansing, MI, The Holmes Group Inc.

1 From Pre-service Teacher Education to First Year of Teaching: A Study of Theory and Practice

Tom Russell

Introduction

'Theory into practice' is a familiar phrase in education. Teacher education programs in Canada and the US are organized on patterns consistent with the idea that what one learns in a university classroom, one later puts into practice in a school classroom at the appropriate grade or subject level. Indeed, most schooling is organized on a 'learn first, practice later' perspective, and beginning teachers would have little reason to see 'theory into practice' as an assumption requiring attention in relation to their learning to teach. There is at least one flaw in the situation, however, and that concerns the contrast felt by preservice teachers between their education courses and their practice teaching experiences. Many are quick to report that the practice teaching experience is the most significant aspect of their teacher education program. This should not be particularly surprising, as the practicum provides essential opportunities for beginners to perform the actions of teaching and to receive relatively immediate commentary, in a one-to-one relationship, from a teacher with some experience.

Schön's (1983) *The Reflective Practitioner* draws a contrast between 'technical rationality' and 'reflection-in-action' as perspectives on the nature of professional knowledge and how it is acquired. Technical rationality is the familiar scheme that pervades our schools and universities and that sustains the image of 'theory into practice'. Schön's point in drawing the contrast is not to put one perspective as superior to the other but to point out that there may be an entire range of issues and assumptions relevant to learning the practical knowledge of a profession that are unnoticed and neglected without the 'reflection-in-action' perspective. Even though Schön's examples from teaching are few in number, the perspective he draws evokes many questions about our present patterns of teacher education.

This chapter reports data from a program of research at Queen's University, Kingston, Ontario. We are studying how teachers learn the practical, professional knowledge of teaching. Data collection presently focusses on interviews of teachers immediately following a period of classroom observation; interviews are spaced at monthly intervals, when possible. The fifteen participants include teachers in a pre-service teacher education program, teachers in their first year of teaching, and several teachers with a number of years of experience.

We are particularly interested in the concept of 'seeing as' applied to teachers' views of their work: the process of perception is regarded not as observation followed by selection and interpretation but as a unified process in which observation *is* interpretive. Individuals vary in their ways of interpreting classroom events and in their awareness of possible alternative interpretations. Thus we are interested in the occurrence and significance of metaphors in teachers' accounts of their practical knowledge (Munby, 1986). We are also interested in the changes that occur in teachers' perspectives on their work, over time, during, and as a result of events of practice. Here we draw on Schön's (1983) account of 'reflection-in-action' as a process in which professionals reframe practical problems in response to puzzles and surprises. This perspective has already proven valuable in studying the experiences of student teachers and beginning teachers (Russell, 1986).

During pre-service programs, beginning teachers expect substantial amounts of on-campus course work and, at least initially, they can be expected to take it for granted that the content of courses will transfer directly and unproblematically to the in-school practical setting where they begin to act as a teacher. As experience accumulates, particularly in the first years of teaching, the fundamental puzzles of professional education take on more and more meaning as the beginning teacher realizes that much course work seems 'irrelevant' from the perspective of practice. Schön (1983) argues that the tension between on-campus rigor and in-practice relevance is a fundamental characteristic of the present state of education for the professions. This chapter examines specific features of this tension as it occurs in the professional education of teachers.

Reporting pre-service and first-year teachers' statements to illustrate their perspectives on the practice-theory relationship can be organized in several ways. One approach would be a developmental one, beginning with the views of pre-service teachers and continuing on with views of first-year teachers. An alternative approach is taken here, showing first the contrast between two teachers, one with ten years of teaching experience and one in her first year. Once that contrast has been drawn to provide a framework, the views of four other teachers are discussed; two were interviewed during their pre-service program and two others were interviewed during their first year of teaching. Thus there are two main sections to the chapter. The first section describes two teachers individually and in some detail — Diane as an experienced teacher and Nancy as a first-year teacher. The second section presents excerpts from interviews with Lynn and Carol (first-year) and Ann and Sandra (pre-service); the excerpts are organized around themes rather than around the individuals, to facilitate making comparisons relevant to the issue of how theory and practice are related. A final section draws comparisons across all six individuals and summarizes the interpretations.

One goal of the chapter is to call attention to the potential value of assisting beginning and experienced teachers in understanding and coping with the puzzling tension between theory and practice as they work to improve their own practices. As we study the accounts of teaching experience given by these and other teachers, we are increasingly convinced that the image one holds of the relationship between theory and practice *can significantly influence understanding of the personal learning process* at every stage in one's development of the professional knowledge of teaching. The data provided here are intended to illustrate the potential importance of direct and explicit attention to the 'theory-practice' relationship from the earliest phases of formal pre-service teacher education programs.

Views of Theory and Practice: An Experienced Teacher and a Beginning Teacher

An Experienced Teacher — Diane

Over a period of ten years, Diane has taught in grades 7 and 8, in kindergarten, and presently at the grade 1 level; her school is located in a semi-rural area near one of the larger cities in eastern Ontario. Diane adapted quickly to the experience of being interviewed about her work, and most of the quotations that follow are taken from her third interview. Her ability to recall clearly her personal development as a teacher contributed significantly to the richness of her comments about the relationships between theory and practice.

The earliest summer courses she attended provided her with techniques of teaching, techniques that she valued considerably but that did not challenge her to think through the 'Why?' of her teaching. She suggests that there may be no other way to begin to teach than to accumulate and develop 'techniques that work.' (Italicized speeches are those of the person interviewing Diane.)

> Instead of taking a [course that ran over] three summers, I took phys. ed. one summer, math the next, something different. So that I tried to grow strong in everything instead of being more narrow. And then when I knew a lot of methods, I felt it was time to consider why I was doing what I was doing.
> *So your first courses were ... basically methods courses?*
> It's just a quick fix. Monday morning ... what do I do Monday morning. Some of them were very good. But they don't get you to think through why you are doing it, what are your objectives. They say, 'Here's a package; It'll probably work.'
> For a beginning teacher, maybe that's the only way you can start is to have really sound methods. I don't know.

As Diane continues, she shifts to describing how she began to 'feel uncomfortable' about the teaching techniques she was using.

> With me it was usually, 'Why do I feel uncomfortable teaching kids this way?' Most of the things that I felt uncomfortable with were ... I was imposing things on the children rather than ... us telling them what they had to learn, how they had to learn, when they had to learn it ... and I had to use really tough discipline to get them to sit down long enough to do all the things I wanted. And I don't like being really hard on kids. I mean it's nice to have a classroom where they are very quiet and scared to death of you, but I didn't like that. I got uptight teaching that way.

Thus it appears that Diane accumulated and used new techniques across a range of subject areas but found herself becoming increasingly uncomfortable about the fact that she was making all the decisions about the learning process, with little or no involvement of her students in those decisions. Enrolling in a Master of Education program provided the avenue Diane needed to make progress in understanding why the techniques she had mastered at the level of practice made her uncomfortable at the level of theory. She indicates in the following statements that she gained support for her discomfort and she began to learn of alternative techniques of practice.

> So when I started to go ... into the master's degree ... that was the best thing that ever happened because we got to go and look at how children learn how to read, how do they learn how to write. You know, how does one type of instruction not suit certain types of students. And it was really what I was looking for. I knew what we were doing before wasn't right for kids, for a lot of kids ... But I didn't have anything to replace it with. I didn't have a methodology. Even when they started talking about centres [groups] ... a lot of people taught centres the same way they taught them when they were in rows. They just moved it to a table. It still wasn't getting at what I needed. I needed to know, really know especially in the primary, really know how they learned how to read so that you could give it to them easy. I didn't like teaching them the phonics and all that. It was too hard for them. They didn't like it. You had to threaten them or they wouldn't learn it and when they did know it, they didn't know what to do with it. So I had to know a lot more about the subject. And then when the centre idea came along at the same time, then it all sort of fit in.

Diane suggests that the development of alternative practices and the development of a coherent framework supporting the practices went hand in hand. She is brave enough to admit that she is not certain how much her practices changed, but she found it very important to develop a personal philosophy. 'Easy learning' is an intriguing notion.

> So I don't know whether I really changed. I just found more ... I felt better about the things I was doing and ... you know because they suited what I had studied about reading or math and they went along with my philosophy of learning, you know, what I call 'easy learning': Let the child lead you. And if he's not happy, then you're doing something wrong. You're getting in his way or you're going too fast or some-thing like that. I don't think children are lazy. And they won't fight you if you can just find their path ... almost all of them. Everything sort of ... when it matched my philosophy, the type of instruction, I kept on with it and I gradually. ... even now I eliminate things that I am not comfortable with.

Diane has concentrated on theories of reading in her studies, and it is important to her that practices of teaching reading have theoretical support. At the same time, she continues to attach importance to knowing that her children like the experience of learning to read. Diane displays a clear understanding of how difficult it can be for teachers to assess or modify gaps between their theories and their practices. She also acknowledges that knowing more about theory can stimulate the frustrating process of self-criticism, yet it seems unlikely that she could ever view her practices any other way. She refers to new math textbooks as 'old math' because of the theory of mathematics learning on which they are based. Diane also speaks critically of the tendency of some teachers to use a 'new' math program mindlessly. She is very clear about the importance of teaching practices that suit how children learn *and* that can be supported at the level of theory by the teacher.

> Every once in a while you think when you're teaching . . . it is so complex when you start to look at it, if you didn't know the theory, you might be better off. It can get in the way. You see you start to question, you criticize . . . I've got books in my room that are not two years old that are what I call the old math, where the children learn 'two plus one equals three' and there are no counters. Two hundred pages for them to write in. Well if you didn't have any theory about how children learn math and you weren't the type of person to question anything at all, you would just hand them the book and they would have to do it. And the parents love it. And the thing is if you give them a standardized test, they'll do just as well as any other group. That's because the test is wrong. It's made for the book. And it's the same way with *Math Their Way* [(Baratta-Lorton, 1976)]. People take that and they use it straight gospel, from page one to the end with no thought given to whether they are interested. I mean the lady who wrote that did a tremendous service to the people who were using the old math because they were looking for a method; they knew they were uncomfortable with the old way.

As Diane continues to comment on the math program that interests her, she speaks of learning the program 'really well' at the level of practice in order to be able to assess it at the level of theory. She reports her personal interest in studying the learning of math just as she has already studied the process of learning how to read. Diane also admits to a degree of uncertainty about how math should be taught.

> The time isn't there to reflect and say, 'What could we do better?' and you need your universities for that. Maybe they have the time to do that. But now we have to learn the *Math Their Way* really well so we can step aside and say, 'Hey, where does this fit into the theory?' I don't really think I had much of a theory about Math and that's why it's taken me so long to really inspect the *Math Their Way* approach. I didn't have much to tell me what's right. I know that children need to learn through things that are relevant and that they need a lot of concrete stuff and that they have to be out of their seats and active or active in their seats, whatever, and at the same time you have to have certain objectives for them to reach. They are not going to discover math on their own. I think that maybe they could more or less discover reading, but they are not going to discover that 'six plus four equals ten'. Maybe it would take them five years. They just don't seem to do that. At least they wouldn't get to our objectives. I would like to have some sort of really good theory about math ... or maybe what we're doing with them in *Math Their Way* is good. See I'm not sure.

Earlier in the interview, Diane had given a similar indication that she sees a teacher beginning by mastering a program at the level of practice, then moving from *comfort with* practice to *criticism of* practice, using theories acquired by studying how subjects are learned. The overall impression from Diane's interviews is that of an experienced teacher who has thought carefully about her practices in the classroom. Diane seems aware of her own mastering of routines of practice, and recalls that 'comfort' provided both the stimulus to question practice and the basis from which practice could be criticized in terms of theory.

Diane displays confidence in her professional knowledge and an acute awareness of how that knowledge developed over time and in relation to experience. If Diane ever did feel that she lacked 'theory', she no longer gives any signals to that effect. She presents a striking account of the importance of acquiring routines and mastering their use *as a basis for* moving on to consider theory and ask questions about one's practices. She distinguishes clearly between courses that offer a 'bag of tricks' and courses in a Master of Education program that offer theories and questions about the 'Why?' of teaching. Diane speaks of becoming comfortable with practice and *then* moving on to theoretical issues associated with questioning and criticism of practice. She admits that theory 'can get in the way', yet it is apparent that she cannot stop herself once she begins to ask questions about practice. The cycle that she has completed with respect to the teaching of reading is one that she now feels ready to begin with math, and she would like to follow that cycle with a similar analysis of how science is taught. Diane's accounts of how she began to teach and of how her professional knowledge continues to develop provide a distinct contrast to the 'theory into practice' image of learning.

A Beginning Teacher — Nancy

Nancy was identified as an articulate representative of the first-year teachers who are presently participating in our study. She is quick to tell us, openly and frankly, that she did not learn the things she needed to learn in her classes at the Faculty of Education last year, during her pre-service program. She is teaching a class of grade 2 children in a school in a rapidly growing community in southern Ontario. For the first two months of the year, she and her class were allocated space in one area of the school library. The move into her own classroom with four walls and a door brought a welcome change in November. But that event did not remove the dilemmas of professional practice for this first-year teacher, and the first quotation makes it apparent that this is a thoughtful beginning teacher. Nancy indicates an awareness of how much she is learning from her practice; she also suggests that what little free time she has would not be spent reading 'how to' books. She puzzles about what it means to be 'professional' and about the adequacy of her 'professional knowledge'. She speaks of 'theory' as something to have and then apply, and this suggests the familiar perspective that Schön (1983) terms 'technical rationality'. (Italicized speeches are those of the person interviewing Nancy.)

> I've been thinking of something else for the past few weeks. I feel that I'm not ... my professional knowledge is not good. *Why?* Because, I mean, I'm just learning to cope in the classroom. I'm learning to establish a routine, establish a trust, and all those types of things. And I haven't ... that my time is not free ... when it is free I certainly don't want to pick up a book on 'How to Teach ... How Children Learn to Spell'. Maybe I'm not being as professional as I could be. But I think in a

couple of years, once I get myself feeling that way, maybe then I'll pick up some books on the theory of 'why'. You see it shouldn't be that way, I should have all that theory and then be able to apply it.

In one of her first interviews, very early in the school year, Nancy spoke of the pressure to set rules and routines, and saw herself as 'just trying to get through'. She also criticized her pre-service education because it did not provide specific practices and procedures. These are familiar criticisms: teacher educators often want their clients to understand what they will be doing in classrooms with children, yet those clients yearn for specific practices that will enable them to perform successfully the activities of teaching.

> As a beginning teacher, you're just trying to get through the curriculum. You need to establish your rules, you have to set your routine, things that I think I learned [last year] from talking to teachers ...
> [At the Faculty of Education] they emphasized things that I don't think needed to be emphasized and instead left out the important nitty-gritty stuff. Yet I look back at the things I did at [the Faculty of Education] and I wonder how much I really am going to use ... not a lot.

What Nancy does value, at the level of 'practical knowledge', are the techniques suggested at conferences and professional meetings; the contribution of her pre-service teacher education program seems to have been minor. She makes first mention of a significant professional puzzle: the tension between 'child-centred' and 'teacher-centred' approaches. Here, then, is an immediate concern that has consequences at the level of 'theory'.

> Certainly I know about inventive spelling and I know about things that I learned from the 'Reading for the Love of It' conference, and things that I learned from professional activity days. And a few minor things from [the Faculty of Education] and the trend in education. But I don't really know the meaty things that I feel that I should know. Over the last few weeks I haven't been doing centres. And that's because I obviously have them more at my fingertips when they're not in centres. And I mean you hear all about being a child-centred rather than a teacher-centred educator. And I'm totally for that and I hope that's the way I run my classroom. However, at first I do want **not** to have control of them. I want them to be responsi-

ble to think on their own, but at the same time ... I don't
think it's a contradiction ... but I want to be able to feel like I
know where they're at.

It is not surprising to find that Nancy is attentive to what she learns
and does not learn from other teachers in her school and to their
comments about her teaching. When one teacher expressed particular
surprise that Nancy was 'doing centres', Nancy defended her practice
to herself by noting that it was the only approach she knew well.

The other teachers are willing to help me if I go and bang on
their door, but as far as coming and saying, 'Well look, here's
what we're doing. Would you like to do this?', they don't.
One of them said to me, 'You're doing centres in your first
year?' And I felt like saying, 'Well it's the only thing I've ever
been taught to do. I wasn't taught to run off dittos [work-
sheets]!'

Nancy also realizes that she is learning more and more about how
children think at a particular grade level. What she is learning about
individual differences is telling her that there are no absolute rules, and
this suggests that no one 'theory' can guide a teacher's practices across
a group of children. Theoretical positions are here characterized as
'traditional' and 'modern'.

Like right now I'm learning what a grade 2 ... how they
think. I don't know how educators can say that you should
never sound out words, or that you should never do this or
that. You can't. If you're getting children at their individual
needs, you have to realize that kids learn differently. I feel
there is such a friction between the traditional way of doing
things and the modern way. And I think there's a balance
between the two. I'm finding with some of these kids that
there are some I'd love to give centres to. And they could
work independently. But the majority of them can't. And if
they don't have the basic skills, I'm not going to give them
things independently to do that they are struggling with, that I
can't teach a group lesson about.

Nancy is comfortable with the 'theory' of using centres in classrooms
at the grade 2 level, and she has practical experience using centres.
Now the practical difficulties of using centres with the particular
group of children she is teaching are generating concerns about the
theory she would like to adhere to in her practice. She indicates that

she is finding it easier to think about her work, and she could be said to be learning about 'theory' in two interactive ways: as she teaches, she comes to understand the full meaning of a particular approach, and she also learns how different children respond to an approach.

> I'm more confident about reflecting on what I've done. I can look now at what the kids are doing and say, 'No, I'm going to have to modify that.' And I know how I'm going to modify it. I'm getting to know them better.

As we work to draw a composite sketch of Nancy's views of theory and practice, we see a strong emphasis on the importance of practical information. She was not 'given' enough practical informa-tion but she would 'give' such information to others were she in a position to do so. Nancy is aware of issues at the level of 'theory', particularly the issue of modern versus traditional approaches and the tension between child- and teacher-centred classroom routines. She seems to know that theory and practice relate in some way, but just how is not yet clear. Even though she speaks in the familiar language of 'having theory to put into practice', it appears that her real starting point was routines that would enable her to conduct lessons in her first classroom. Routines enable her to acquire teaching experience and thereby to find out whether children can learn what she wants them to learn.

Here, then, is a strong similarity to the process of professional learning suggested by Diane. What was heard and discussed in a university program seems restricted and inadequate beside the im-mediate and personal nature of accumulating classroom experience, and experience functions in several significant ways. There is *no other way* to establish routines in one's teaching behaviours. Experience also *gives meaning* to written and spoken statements which may range from advice to 'theory'. The beginning teacher may not realize that *the ability to relate advice to practice changes and develops rapidly* as experience in one's own classroom accumulates.

Views of Theory and Practice: First-Year Teachers and Student Teachers

The accounts provided by Diane and Nancy provide perspectives on the 'theory-practice' issue that can guide the interpretation of state-ments by four additional teachers. Lynn and Carol are first-year teachers, while Ann and Sandra are student teachers in a pre-service program. Lynn is teaching science; Carol teaches a split grade 2–3 class. Ann and Sandra are both preparing to teach science at the secondary level. Again, italicized speeches are those of the interviewer.

In this portion of the argument, data are organized within three broad categorizations of statements that were judged to be indicative of how individuals learning to teach were viewing the relationship between practice and theory. The first section presents statements in which the participants emphasize that they learn from experience, and only from experience. The second section presents statements related to the issue of whether one can be 'told' theory, while the third section presents statements illustrating the tension between covering material and using desirable teaching strategies.

Only Experience Can Teach One How to Teach

This section introduces each of the four beginning teachers who, with Diane and Nancy, make up the total of six included in this report. Sandra, a pre-service student teacher, indicates the trust she puts in her own experience rather than in formal theories. She also discusses her impression that some of her courses were repetitive, while her extended practicum has been scheduled at a time when courses for other students are dealing with topics of immediate concern to her practice. She seems to suggest that she would prefer to have experience that would prepare her to make sense of 'theory' presented in courses. Ann, also a pre-service student, speaks as one of a group of students who explain that course work provides ideas to think about, but experience is 'the real teacher' in the process of learning to teach.

Sandra's pre-service perspective

Theme: Theory, practice, and personal experience

The practice itself generates questions, and I'm almost getting the impression that there's another world somehow separated from this world, where people do have questions arise, but . . . [theory] doesn't seem to be the answer to it.

Do you know what I think about [theory-practice] and the other world . . .? I did all the theory things, and I was always very interested . . . like, for instance, exceptional children and all the psychology and the sociology . . . and I took it all in. All these people were credited with all these brilliant ideas . . . you know, sociology and psychology, and a lot of them, to me, were every-day things. Things that people should naturally realize! They weren't some brilliant idea that should be credited to this one individual. It wasn't ... you know, it's not his thought ... it never was! And I'd go back to the practicum, and you'd see that sort of thing ... that other empty space. I see that. I see myself relating more and more to ... my common experience and things like that. I don't call on Freud or somebody!

You find yourself referring back to your own experiences?

I trust it more, too. You know it's easier to trust something that you've experienced.

Theme: Course work, experience, and program sequence

Given what you've been up against here, what could have gone on at [the Faculty of Education] in the fall term? It may be that the gap can't be addressed. It may be that ... it's a gulf that can't be crossed. But, if you were to rewrite the scheme of things there ...

You know what I think the main thing would be, as a Concurrent student, is that I would prefer to do these four months September–December [before taking most of the course in education]. I'm not sure about the logistics of it all but, as far as relating to the theory, it [course work] was a repeat [of my introductory courses in education].

So you felt that you had already covered a lot of the ground?

Yeah. And just when we were starting to get into things. Like, right now I ... doing all those labs, and things like that. Things that I really **need** [I don't get because] I'm **here** [in the school, not at the Faculty of Education]. I don't resent it, but I kind of feel slighted. You know, there was a period when there was nothing going on as far as relating to me, and now there's things that are going on [in the courses that continue for consecutive students] that are really interesting, and I'm here. And they're there. I don't know. I agree with you. I don't know that you can bridge that gap. Because experience is something that's dependent upon each individual, and how you look at it, and how you relate to it.

Ann's pre-service perspective

Theme: Only experience can teach you how to teach

The following comments are made by several science students in a group that included Ann. These students have been in concurrent arts and science education for three years prior to this year, the comments were recorded shortly before the four-month internship that concludes their pre-service program.

But how do you see that relationship between the curriculum courses and the practice teaching experience in terms of how you learn to become a teacher?

You don't learn how to be a teacher, at least in chemistry and math, just examples of what to use to make it more interesting for the kids. But that's not teaching you how to teach. The only way you'd know how to teach is to be in the classroom and hands-on experience.

Yeah. During the summer I thought, 'How are these people going to teach us how to teach?', and they don't really. And that's good.

They give you lots of ideas though, but not how.

It's good you get lots of ideas.

Lots of ideas and you've got to learn how to teach on your own.

The statements from a pre-service perspective can be contrasted with statements from a first-year perspective. Carol suggests that when one begins to teach, a great deal of imitation of former teachers is involved, until one has developed routines. She also suggests that making decisions about how to teach requires direct, personal experience of teaching. Lynn suggests that nothing could be done in a pre-service program that would prepare her to teach as experience has this year been teaching her. She illustrates her point by describing her efforts to explain concepts as well as experienced teachers seem to be able to.

Carol's first-year perspective

Theme: Not theory into practice but imitation and learning routines

It depends on the person rather than experience versus novice. I would bet there's an awful lot of novice teachers who are doing things because they saw their associate teacher last year do them. Or that's the way they were taught or they haven't thought about it, they're just doing them ... But also I didn't realize the need for some of the routines until I taught for a while, because I hadn't done this before. Also there were things I thought were going to work but didn't.

I don't think you can make informed decisions about what you're going to do unless you have some familiarity with ... you have to have some familiarity to make the choices. I really wish that I had seen a class that was organized more like this school is, ahead of time, so that I could have seen the things that you have to watch out for and the things that really work well and the things that don't, and to see somebody really do a good job with it. I never did, and now I have nothing to shoot for? I don't know what happens or how you know if it's working right.

Lynn's first-year perspective

Theme: Only experience can teach you to teach

Challenge. [Pre-service education] doesn't prepare you for it! Well, [it] was a year for ... another year of university for personal growth. I don't think I've used anything from [the Faculty of Education]. Well, if I used a percentage of what I learned [there] it would be very small, very small. So really I guess you'd have to say it doesn't prepare you for teaching. Well, I don't think anything would ... Only the experience of teaching.

Theme: The problem of time and the challenge of explaining concepts well

I just ... I skimmed over the ideas too quickly, I think, and I don't think I taught the unit as well as it could have been taught ... I still haven't learned how to present an idea that well. Other teachers can present an idea in a class, maybe two, and the unit's over. And for me, it takes me so much longer to present ideas. I'm behind all the other teachers. Not that it's bad ... it's just that I wish that I had a technique that I could explain it better. And I think that just comes with experience ... learning the subject.
Is that a frustration you feel during class?
No. Usually after! I sit down and say, 'Oh, did I get anything done that period ... do I think they gained anything from that class?' ... and there are some days when, no, I don't think they did gain anything. They do an experiment, and I would like to review it ... and you just ... time is such a precious commodity that you just ... and I seem to waste it by ... I don't take the time to explain some of the things. I show them, and then I don't reinforce it. I don't explain it again. And that's something I need to do. So, I present the idea ... and this is in grade 10 ... they

do an experiment on it ... and, maybe a week later, I decide to go back and explain the experiment and by then it's too late.

Relating Theory and Practice: Can Theory Be Told?

Like so many pre-service teacher candidates, Ann seems confident that one can be told theory, and that one should be told so that the option to use it is available to each individual learning to teach. In contrast, Lynn suggests that what was presented in her pre-service program would have been more successful with individuals who already had some teaching experience. She illustrates with the example of learning how to write tests, wishing she had received 'hints' but quickly making it clear that she found assistance from another teacher in her school. Lynn finds it very difficult to relate theoretical points in a setting so different, and she regrets the lack of time to think about her own teaching. Carol and Nancy discuss the difference between being told to use progressive teaching approaches and actually teaching children whose diversities reveal the limitations of any single teaching approach.

Ann's pre-service perspective

Theme: Can 'theory' be told?

The dilemma that intrigues me ... it **seems** *like you can tell people things ... We have this tension between what you can be told and what you do in the classroom.*
You can be told something, and it's up to you whether you want to adopt it, modify it, or ignore it. But still, it should be presented to you so that you have that opportunity.

Lynn's first-year perspective

Theme: What (if anything) did I learn in pre-service training?

There's just so much to learn. And basically the things that you have to learn right away are the things they don't teach you at [the Faculty of Education]. They don't teach you how to teach, and those are the first things you have to learn here. Some of the techniques in how to teach.

Could they teach you at [the Faculty of Education]?
I think they should give you some hints. I think there are possibilities there.
What sorts of things?
More about test writing. For example, I gave my grade 9s a test on Monday. And that one class ... I'm marking one class now, they're a better class, so they're doing all right. The one class ... they're quite noisy. They're good kids but they talk too much, they fool around too much. They did lousy so I 'belled' their mark up five marks. And I hate to do that, but it's either do that or count it as less percentage in their final report card. It doesn't matter which way you do it. And I asked [a colleague], 'Am I writing my tests wrong? Should I be asking them more on straight recall?' Because I was looking at [a friend's] sister's notes. I have some of her grade 9 notes which we're doing in grade 10 now. And the teacher has tested almost straight recall. They've done the homework and it's repeated. And to me that's not teaching but I asked him if that's what I should do. And he asked me, 'Can your slowest kids pass the test just on what you have for recall?' And I said, 'No, because I don't ask enough recall. Am I asking for too much thinking?' And he said, 'Well grade 9s just haven't developed that much in order to do too much thinking.' In terms of conceptualizing something. So I think I'm writing my test too hard for this particular ... maybe I could ... I'm thinking maybe I should write two different tests.

Theme: Relating theory and practice is so difficult

I think what they're saying [at the Faculty of Education] is being wasted on first-year teachers. For teachers that are more experienced, it's good to go back and reinforce their idea and get away from the curriculum but, for first-year teachers, it seems to ... it goes in, it goes out ... because they get to school and they find out ... 'Jeez, did I really learn anything at [the Faculty of Education]? Because this institution is doing something completely different, and I've got to follow the new rules!' And you forget about what happened back there.
Or at least you can't relate it.
You can't relate it, because we don't have time to think about it. And that's the problem that I find, is that to look back, to go back through all my things from last year that we did, I just haven't had the time. And that was all good stuff! And being able

to reflect. And who has ... you don't have time to reflect! It's really too bad, because it's something you should do. For some people, things come back really easily. For me, I really have to sit and take time to think about what's gone on, and make something of it, whereas [a friend] ... he just ... snap, snap, snap ... he comes up with ideas, no problem!

Or, it looks like that.

It looks like that, anyway! I think if we had more time to **think** about our style of teaching, and to think about what we're giving the kids ... A good example is professional development days: you get a lot of information, and it sounds so ideal, and then you go back to your old routine. You get the information but you don't implement it.

A first-year perspective — Carol and Nancy

Theme: We are told to be 'progressive'

Nancy: The theory is that we have to show that we're progressive and when the Academic Resource Teacher drops in we should have our centres, but there's an undercurrent of, 'Are centres really the thing that we should be doing?' For writing, yes, but there's just an undercurrent of, 'We were from the old school, and we're trying to get out of it, but we really believe that there are some things back there that we should try and hold onto.' But probably when we are teaching for twenty years, centres will be out. We will sit around at the staffroom table and somebody will say, 'Oh yes, centres are out now. In England now they're doing something else; they're doing it totally different.'

Carol: I think there are fads in education, but I think as time goes on, teachers are becoming more diverse. They're not throwing out one thing altogether and adopting something new.

Nancy: There's a balance and a mixture.

Carol: They are getting to use ... to find out what works and use something from this and something from that ...

Eclectic? And understanding more that every child is different ...

Carol: And I don't think people will move backwards in that, but I can see them getting a new word for centres or a new concept or something like that. But I can't see them abandoning the whole thing. I think this individualized stuff has made an important contribution.

Relating Theory and Practice: Covering Material vs.
Taking time to Use Desirable Teaching Strategies

Ann, who has only a few brief formal teaching experiences so far, anticipates the dilemma of deciding whether to cover the curriculum or take the time to use teaching strategies that motivate students and help achieve understanding. Carol has enough experience that she can put the matter more forcefully, illustrating the very real differences between 'coverage and exposure', and finding out what individual students have understood from her teaching.

Ann's pre-service perspective

Theme: Time, motivation, and covering the curriculum

In addition to the fact that you don't feel you're using much of them, are there things that you think contradict what you find you have to do? You mention the things that haven't been discussed, and you said the classes have discussed things that you don't use, but are there contradictions?
I don't know if it's as much a contradiction. [One professor] has a lot of ideas of motivational techniques and little things to play with and make it real. I really question whether you can do that on a day-to-day basis and still get the material covered. The same thing with [two other professors]; it's nice to have all these demonstrations and toys and games, but are you actually going to get the material covered? I was at a department meeting here, and one man actually stood up and said, 'Well, according to the guidelines, I'm three units behind.' The new guidelines actually say what you are supposed to do if you're using all these things. You're going to be sacrificing something, and it's going to be content. I think that is a contradiction. They should bring these a little more down to earth for us in the sense of practical terms, the things we are going to be faced with.

Carol's first-year perspective

Theme: Covering and exposing material vs. achieving understanding

And it's fine to say, 'The curriculum guide says that you have to cover this,' whatever that means, and so you expose kids to it and who knows what the real understanding of it is. You can get kids doing pretty sophisticated things I think, without necessarily

understanding it ... so I wonder how important it is to teach
kids if [a word] ends in 'f' or 'fe'.
*Whereas it's more important to get at the fundamental concept of learning
to read so that you can apply what you read into your own writing and
so on.*
I don't know. People from the 'whole language' school would
say, 'No, you never do anything like that.' But then the people
who don't agree with that would say 'How do you make sure
that the kids know what to look for and are exposed?' And I wish
I knew the answer to that.

Discussion: The Role of Theory and Practice in Learning to Teach

The excerpts from interviews with Nancy and Diane were selected for
their potential to reveal how two teachers, one beginning and one
experienced, see 'theory' and 'practice' in the context of their thoughts
about their teaching and their experiences of learning about how to
teach. The picture that emerges in each instance suggests that learning
to teach is *not* a two-step process of (i) learning theory; and (ii) putting
theory into practice. Yet our culture in general and our universities in
particular use the phrase 'theory into practice' so easily and freely that
it would be surprising if those electing programs of teacher education
did not *see their own learning as* a two-step process.

The statements selected from interviews with two pre-service and
two other first-year teachers indicate that the issue of how theory and
practice relate to each other is both significant and problematic. The
individuals who have shared their thinking with us emphasize the
very significant role of experience in the process of learning to teach,
and they also suggest that experience is significant in learning the
'theory' of teaching. Theory and practice are also portrayed as difficult
to relate to each other. The first-year teacher has little time to reflect
and finds it difficult to shift from the university to the school context.
*It is difficult to take in the full meaning of theory without experience, and it is
difficult to resolve at the level of practice the tensions between teaching in the
best ways possible and teaching to cover the prescribed curriculum content.*

Is it possible for teacher educators to deal with theory in a way
that conveys to beginning teachers significant details of the process of
professional development that awaits them as they develop confidence
in their classroom practices? *Is it possible* to shift beginning teachers'
unexamined assumption that they are involved in a process of 'putting

theory into practice'? A colleague has provided an indication of an important shift in her perspective as teacher educator:

> I forget that many of these young people still do not know how to teach when I work with them, and I often share things which I as an experienced teacher *know* they need, but they, lacking the experience, are not receptive because experience has not yet taught them that it is needed. (D. Bull, personal communication, 27 February 1985)

Research on inservice education of teachers in the last two decades — including research such as that reported from the PEEL Project in Australia (Baird and Mitchell, 1986) — has produced important new insights that have not yet been used as perspectives for recasting the initial professional education of teachers. The data provided by Nancy, Carol, Lynn, Ann and Sandra encourage one to continue to listen to the pre-service candidates one teaches, to help them examine and reshape their assumptions about theory and practice, to heighten their awareness and enhance their interpretations of their own experiences of learning to teach. The following two assumptions provide one type of summary of the messages about theory and practice in the comments of the teachers we have interviewed:

1 Experience, including one's present teaching practices, *shapes the meaning* that we read into research, theory, and other sources of recommendations for changes in practice.
2 The relationship between theory/research and practice can be one in which the two are alternate phases *of a single activity*, not two independent domains linked by a tenuous act of faith. (Russell, 1987, p. 130)

As our research into teachers' professional knowledge proceeds, we will continue to examine participants' interviews for further insights into their understanding of the relationship between theory and practice. A statement made in the introduction may take on new meaning in view of the data reported from several pre-service and first-year teachers: *We are increasingly convinced that the image one holds of the relationship between theory and practice can significantly influence understanding of the personal learning process, at every stage in one's development of the professional knowledge of teaching.* There seems to be considerable promise and potential for research that tracks the theory-practice perspective through the broad range of pre-service and in-service teacher education activities. Making sense of the very significant differences between university courses, which are interpreted as dealing with 'theory', and personal teaching experiences, which are clearly designated as 'practice', is an important concern for those who are learning to teach. The data reported here suggest that very important developments occur as one moves from a pre-service program to the first year of teaching experience. To the extent that in-service education of teachers is designed for the experienced teacher, for whom the theory-practice tension may no longer be problematic, we may be overlooking very important opportunities to contribute to the development of the beginning teacher.

Note

This chapter reports data drawn from a study of 'Metaphor, Reflection, and Teachers' Professional Knowledge' funded by the Social Sciences and Humanities Research Council of Canada. Phyllis Johnston and Charlotte Spafford provided valuable assistance in the preparation of this chapter; Hugh Munby is co-investigator.

References

BAIRD, J.R., and MITCHELL, I.J. (Eds) (1986) *Improving the Quality of Teaching and Learning: An Australian Case Study... The Peel Project,* Melbourne, Monash University.

BARATTA-LORTON, M. (1976) *Mathematics Their Way,* Menlo Park, CA, Addison-Wesley.

MUNBY, H. (1986) 'Metaphor in the thinking of teachers: An exploratory study', *Journal of Curriculum Studies,* 18, pp. 197–209.

RUSSELL, T.L. (1986) *Beginning Teachers' Development of Knowledge-in-action,* paper presented at the annual meeting of the American Educational Research Association, San Francisco, April.

RUSSELL, T.L. (1987) 'Re-framing the theory-practice relationship in inservice teacher education', in NEWTON, L.J. FULLAN, M. and MACDONALD J.W. (Eds), *Re-thinking Teacher Education: Exploring the Link Between Research, Practice, and Policy,* Toronto, Joint Council on Education, University of Toronto/OISE, pp. 125–34.

SCHÖN, D. (1983) *The Reflective Practitioner: How Professionals Think in Action,* New York, Basic Books.

The Influence of Learning Orientations on the Development of Reflective Teaching

Fred A.J. Korthagen

Introduction

During the past decade most reports on the effect of teacher education programmes on actual teaching practice have not been very optimistic. Many authors refer to the phenomenon known as the *transition shock* (for example, Corcoran, 1981; Veenman, 1984): beginning teachers work under considerable emotional pressure and in general they make a quick shift from progressive to utilitarian perspectives on teaching (Lacey, 1977; Goodman, 1985). Even practice teaching during pre-service teacher education was mentioned in this respect (for example, Zeichner, 1980; Tabachnick and Zeichner, 1984). Student teachers often see practice teaching as unrealistic; they feel like guests in the domain of their supervising teachers and have little opportunity to develop their own teaching style.

The search for a solution to these problems has resulted in new paradigms of teacher education, in which reflective teaching is the basic principle: preservice teacher education should promote the ability of prospective teachers to reflect on their teaching as a means of directing their own growth and development in the teaching profession. The question of *how* to respond to a given classroom situation must be related to questions about the *why* of the situation: why do pupils act as they do, why does this make me feel uncomfortable, why do I react in a particular way, etc. More important, teachers must examine the whole context in which learning and teaching take place: 'the moral, ethical and political issues, as well as the instrumental issues, that are embedded in their everyday thinking and practice' (Zeichner, 1983).

For many years the Mathematics Department of the Stichting Opleiding Leraren (SOL), a teachers' college in Utrecht, The Netherlands, has based its programme on the reflective teaching principle. It is a four-and-a-half-year pre-service programme comprising a combination of mathematics and one other subject (physics or geography, for example), plus one year of professional preparation which is spread over the entire programme.

The present chapter opens with a description of the main characteristics of the programme, followed by the results of an evaluative study. These results compelled us to question whether a programme based on the promotion of reflection is equally suitable for all prospective teachers. This led to a longitudinal study on the development of prospective teachers during pre-service teacher education. We discuss the results of this study, which show that the concept of *learning orientation* is crucial to an understanding of the effects of the programme on different students. Finally, this concept helped us to formulate suggestions for the improvement of teacher education programmes.

The goal of this chapter is to fill in a number of gaps in the present research into reflective teaching; there is, for example, a lack of programme descriptions and almost no reports are available on the outcomes of these programmes. Moreover, little is known about the thinking and behaviour of teacher educators and about interaction processes in teacher education.

The Basic Principles of the Programme

The programme is based on the assumption that it is impossible to prepare prospective teachers for each and every professional situation with which they may be confronted during their careers. However, the programme can train them to reflect on their experiences and on the manner in which they function as teachers and to strive for a conscious awareness of their own professional development. Consequently the supervision proceeds from the subjective perception of reality on the part of the prospective teacher, with regard to, say, some particular lesson. Later the teacher will have only this subjective perception to fall back on, and it is this upon which the students are asked to reflect. It is for this reason that the programme attaches such importance to the reports or logbooks in which the students describe and reflect upon their experiences. Students are taught to trace the various phases which make up the cycle in figure 1. Phase 5 signals the start of a new cycle, so that in effect we are talking about a spiral model, which we call the ALACT model, after the first letter of the five phases.

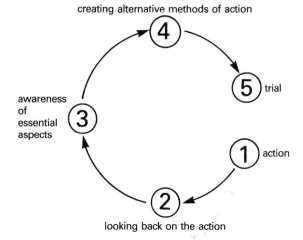

Figure 1

creating alternative methods of action

awareness of essential aspects

trial

action

looking back on the action

The final goal is that the student teacher learns to proceed through the spiral model without the help of the supervising teacher educator and to make use of *internal feedback* based on his or her own experience and *external feedback* from pupils or other teachers, adjusting where necessary their own subjective view of reality.

The First Year: Reflection on Experiences Within the Teacher Education Institute

The ALACT-model starts with an action phase. These experiences need not be limited to classroom experiences, for as Zeichner (1981) notes: 'Reflection which is directed toward the improvement of practice does not necessarily need to take place within the boundaries of the classroom to have an impact.' Small task groups of student teachers working together (for example on mathematics) have many opportunities for reflection: on learning processes, on the processes of helping fellow students and of being helped, on the process of co-operation within the group, and on the ways in which problems can be solved.

Moreover, there is a special first year practicum in which the student learns to reflect on his or her own thoughts, feelings, attitudes and actions in everyday relationships with others at the SOL. Activities such as role-playing, games and discussions are used in this reflection practicum, which gives students an opportunity to develop their empathic understanding, to learn to express their feelings, and to become more proficient in dealing with problems of cooperation.

The process involved in learning mathematics is also used as an object of reflection. At regular intervals, students are asked to hand in written reports on the way they set to work on a particular mathematical problem. In this way not only the mathematical *product* is stressed, but also the mathematical *inquiry process*: 'It is a not so new but still rarely fulfilled requirement that mathematics is taught not as a created subject but as a subject to be created' (Freudenthal, 1978). At secondary school, pupils are often given the impression that the important thing in solving math problems is coming up with the right answer. It is for this reason that the teacher educators prefer problems to which more than one solution is possible, or for which no cut and dried solution exists. This makes it more interesting to compare solutions and the ways in which the various students tried to tackle the problem.

As regards the students' reflection on their working and learning methods, the programme does away with the myth that mathematics is primarily a mental exercise. Feelings and attitudes quite naturally come to the fore in such aspects as the fun of problem-solving, an aversion to a particular problem, the experience of sinking one's teeth into a problem, the pleasure of working together and the excitement when something finally 'dawns'. It is extremely important for prospective teachers to recognize the significance of the more emotional aspects of the learning process.

Throughout the programme there are several points at which students are allowed a choice. On the pedagogical and didactical side, for instance, they have a say in the general curriculum, and in the mathematics courses they are often given a choice of material. There is a close link between learning to reflect and learning to choose: pondering the past or future choices compels the students to reflect on their own goals and attitudes. Individual interviews and the students' logbooks, to which the supervisors add their comments, encourage students to reflect on the various choices open to them, and help them to develop their own style of teaching.

In this description of the programme two aspects are particularly noteworthy. First of all, learning to reflect is not limited to the pedagogical component of the programme. It is also a recurring principle on the mathematical side. Students are encouraged to reflect not only on the subject content, but also to consider the way in which they help or cooperate with others, as well as their awareness of feelings, attitudes and personal goals. Thus *the mathematical side of the programme and the specific professional preparation are closely linked*.

A second major aspect of the programme is that *reflection is stressed even before students embark on their practical teaching*. The idea behind this is that student teachers can be armed against socialization into established patterns of school practice. The student teacher must first gain some idea of who he or she is, of what he or she wants, and above all, of the ways in which one can take responsibility for one's own learning. The first period of student teaching can be one of extreme stress, in which the prime concern is simply to 'get through'. This is not an auspicious moment for learning the art of reflection. Prospective teachers must already have at their disposal sufficient powers of reflection to enable them to evaluate the influence of these personal concerns on the way in which they themselves function in the classroom.

The Phasing of Practice Teaching

It is not until the second year that students actually become involved in practical teaching. The first stage is helping individual secondary school pupils. This eliminates the problem of controlling a whole class and gives the student teacher a chance to devote his full attention to individual learning processes and didactic procedures. Here, too, the use of the logbook and college-based supervision are important in stimulating student reflection.

The first classroom experience takes place at the end of the second year. A primary school class (11 to 12-year-olds) is divided into three (or two) groups. During a period of six weeks each student teacher works with his or her own group of about eight children for one to one-and-a-half hours a week. The cooperating teacher is not present. The group of two or three student teachers who teach children from the same class is supervised by the teacher education institute. This supervision is based on the students' logbooks and the supervisor does not visit the school, which means that the student teachers are given a large measure of freedom and responsibility. This helps the prospective teacher to find his or her own personal style of teaching and, more important, it stimulates reflection on personal style and growth. Again an essential aspect of the experience is that the problem of controlling the class is not dominant.

In the third and fourth years, the students work with whole classes at secondary school level and are supervised by cooperating teachers. To provide effective supervision these teachers must first acquire specific helping skills, the most important of which is the ability to set aside their own beliefs about teaching and to help the student teachers to develop theirs.

The Professionalization of Teacher Educators

This brings us to one of the most important elements of a preparation programme based on reflective teaching. This type of programme places no small demands on the skills of teacher educators and supervising teachers. For several years intensive courses were held to teach them how to stimulate reflection, and how to supervise student teachers without actually observing them in the classroom. An important aspect of this process of professionalization is the development of a reflective attitude of the teacher educators and co-operating teachers themselves.

However, according to present government regulations, cooperating teachers no longer receive a remuneration, and this has resulted in a considerable decline in the number of well-qualified cooperating teachers.

The First Evaluation of the Programme

An initial evaluation of the programme in 1982 was based primarily on a questionnaire, which was sent to 116 former students of the Mathematics Department of the SOL and to thirteen students who were approaching graduation. The most important (open) questions were:

1   What have you learned during your teacher preparation?
2   What do you think was missing in your teacher preparation?

A categorization of these *learner reports* by two independent researchers showed that more than 50 per cent of the respondents had experienced important learning effects in the field of reflective teaching and directing one's own growth, in spite of the fact that there was nothing in the questionnaire or in the accompanying letter to suggest that this was a main issue in the research. Examples of reflection-oriented responses were:

— *I have learned to reflect on my teaching. I think this is important because I think it can be helpful when I am teaching on my own. How can I correct myself? What did I do well? What did I do wrong? What was the cause? I think that this capacity can be important in problematic classroom situations.*

— *I have learned to have confidence in myself, to develop a notion of what I am good or reasonably good at and to accept what I am not very good at without simply resigning myself to it.*

— *I have learned to learn, as best I can, from my experiences.*
— *I have learned to take note of my mistakes and to improve myself.*
— *I have experienced that it helps, and that it is necessary, to keep asking myself why I do things in a certain way.*
— *I have learned to evaluate myself. A central issue during the preparation was to give your own opinion about how things went, for example, if you thought it went well, you had to say why; what went well? The same applied when you thought things had gone wrong, so that you became critical of your own teaching. Terribly important for school practice!*
— *I think the most important thing I've learned is to look at myself, to be able to solve problems myself, or at least to know the ways toward solutions.*

On the negative side many teachers reported that they had been insufficiently prepared to handle problems of discipline and motivation. In particular those teachers who were working in lower vocational schools noted a gap between teacher preparation and teaching practice. They expressed disappointment about the impact of practice teaching, due to the fact that they were not given complete responsibility for the classes they taught. However, other elements in the programme, especially the first-year reflection practicum were seen as very important by the respondents. To quote a former student:

> The first-year reflection practicum was a revelation to me. I began to see that I was capable of standing back and looking at my own actions and their impact on others. That one year brought about an enormous change in my attitude and behaviour and in the way I thought about them. The same point was brought home later on, in an optional course on expressing one's feelings. In fact this was something that kept coming up in my logbooks and in supervision sessions.

Differences in Learning Orientations

It became clear from a further study of the individual reports that the respondents could be placed on a continuum with at one end those who stressed the acquired ability to reflect, and at the other end those who felt the need for more directions for teaching practice. In order to study this difference between the respondents more thoroughly, five former students representing both ends of the continuum were interviewed. Summaries of these interviews were published in Korthagen

(1982). We concluded that student teachers differ in the degree to which they prefer to learn via reflection. We call this learning by *internal direction* and we use the term *internal orientation*. Other students have an *external orientation*, that is, they prefer to learn through external direction, from a supervisor or a book, for instance. They want structure and guidelines from outside (cf. Hunt, 1979). These differences in learning orientations may be caused by the *belief systems* and *implicit theories* which students have about learning. The so-called Göteborg group showed that people can differ considerably with regard to their *conceptions of learning* (cf. Säljö, 1979).

The evaluation gave rise to some doubt as to whether a preparation programme in which reflective teaching is a basic principle, is equally suitable for all students.

A Longitudinal Study: The Research Questions and Method

This prompted our decision to start a longitudinal follow-up study, based on the following research questions:

(a) How do students with different learning orientations develop during this teacher education programme based on reflective teaching?

(b) What is the impact of the programme on that development of students with different learning orientations?

In this longitudinal study, which is still in progress, we examine eighteen prospective mathematics teachers during their preparation programme at the SOL. We use the following research model (figure 2):

Figure 2

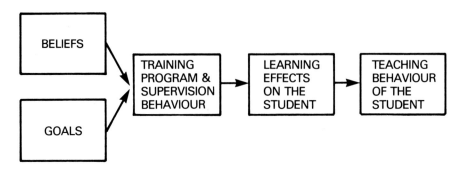

The process variables are the beliefs (and explicit goals) of the thirteen *teacher educators* and their supervision behaviour, while the product variable consists of the learning effects on *students*. The following instruments and research methods were used:

1   *Standardized interviews with the teacher educators*, focussing on their goals, on the way they try to implement these goals in the programme and on the results they observe. On the basis of the largely qualitative analysis of these interviews, we drew up

2   *A questionnaire* in which a number of statements about the fundamentals of teacher education could be scored on a scale from one to five.

3   *Kelly's repertory grid* (Kelly, 1955) enabled us to make explicit the categories used by the teacher educators in assessing their students. Kelly speaks of *constructs*.
     Examples of such constructs are dependent/independent, certain/uncertain, etc. In this RepGrid-method the teacher educator is given three cards with the names of three students. He is asked to mention one quality (construct) in which one of the students differs from the other two. Then, by assigning a score from on to five, he rates each student for all the constructs mentioned.

4   *Interviews with the students*. Twice a year the students in our study were interviewed about their opinion of the programme, learning results, points of criticism, the characteristics of the programme as seen by the students, and their learning conceptions, in particular their attitude towards reflective teaching.

5   *The I.E.O.-test*. In attempting to develop a test for evaluating learning orientations of prospective teachers, we discovered that it is impossible to classify students according to the degree of preference for reflection without taking into account the various areas on which learning has a bearing. Sometimes students appear to have an internal orientation in one area and an external orientation in another. From our interviews with students we derived the following areas or *domains* upon which learning can have a bearing (table 1):

Table 1

Domains of learning of students in the initial stage of the teacher education programme	1 the prospective teacher him(her)self 2 the fellow students 3 the subject matter (mathematics) in the programme.
Domains of learning of students after practice teaching	1 the prospective teacher him(her)self 2 the pupils in the schools 3 the subject-matter (mathematics) at school 4 the school

On the basis of this classification of domains we devised two versions of a questionnaire, called the I.E.O.-test for internal/external orientation. One version is designed for students in the initial stage of their training, while the second is for students who have experienced classroom teaching. In the case of the SOL Mathematics Department this means third and fourth-year students. For purposes of this chapter we will confine ourselves to the version designed for the students in the initial stage of the programme, as the data obtained by the other version of the I.E.O.-test are not yet available. This I.E.O.-test consists of three groups of items, corresponding to the following domains: the prospective teacher him(her)self, fellow students and subject matter (mathematics) in the programme. For each domain there is a scale designed to measure to what extent students have an internal learning orientation in this area and another scale which measures to what extent they are externally oriented. Thus there are six scales in all, each consisting of two types of items. One type asks the students to rate themselves on a five-point scale according to the extent to which a certain statement is applicable to their way of learning. On the other type they are to indicate how frequently they do something. An example of the latter type of item is: I reflect on the question 'who am I'.

To assess its reliability the test, consisting of sixty-one items, was administered to 138 first and second year students from three teachers' colleges. Cronbach's alpha ranged from .77 to .87, a good score for scales consisting of about ten items.

Results of the Longitudinal Study

Although the longitudinal study has not yet been completed, we are already in a position to report some important findings.

The *interviews with the teacher educators* and the *questionnaire completed by these teachers* showed a homogeneous 'team view'. Reflective teaching does indeed appear to be a fundamental goal. The teacher educators also mentioned concrete areas of knowledge which in their opinion students should master. These were concerned with such matters as the process of mathematics learning, didactic principles and the field of interpersonal contact (listening, cooperation, etc.). When the students entered the second year of the programme, the teacher educators placed more emphasis on acquiring skills in these fields.

The *RepGrid* showed that in considering individual students the constructs which the teacher educators had in mind differed considerably from the reflective/non-reflective construct, which was mentioned by only one teacher educator in the RepGrid. Many constructs had a bearing on qualities that could also have been mentioned as characteristic for one's personal functioning outside the college, such as shy, spontaneous, cheerful. The most frequently mentioned were: reserved (6×), inventive (5×) and industrious (4×).

Looking into the relationship between these qualities of students and the strategies followed by the teacher educators to reach the programme goals, we found that these goals were often abandoned or that the educators were sometimes at a loss to know how to attain the goals with certain students. In many cases the teacher educators decided to moderate their educational demands for fear that increased resistance would prevent the student concerned from learning anything at all. This spontaneous differentiation in strategies was based on all sorts of beliefs and implicit theories. There were no explicit theories about differences in learning orientations, and certainly not on the part of the entire team of teacher educators. On the basis of the interviews we arrived at the hypothesis that teacher educators only understand the way reflective students learn, possibly because they themselves have a reflective style. This was further investigated in two consecutive years by asking two of the educators who had been teaching an intensive educational course in a second-year group, to complete two questionnaires containing statements about ways of learning. One questionnaire was to be completed as the teacher educator thought that the student designated by him as 'most reflective' would have done, and the other questionnaire as if he were the student he considered 'least reflective'. Next the p.m. correlation was calculated between the predicted scores and the real scores (on a five-point-scale) for thirty-four different statements. The results are shown in table 2. These data support the hypothesis that the teacher

Table 2

p.m. corr. between predicted and real scores	teach.ed.A (1984)	teach.ed.B (1984)	teach.ed.C (1985)	teach.ed.A (1985)
most reflective student	0.73	0.53	0.78	0.66
least reflective student	−0.16	−0.13	−0.24	0.04

educators only understand the learning orientation of reflective students.

It is impossible to include here all the qualitative results from the *student interviews*. However one interesting point was the comparison we made between the eight students from the experimental group who left the programme after the first year and the ten who remained. The most important points of criticism put forward by the drop-outs may in fact be interpreted as indications of a clash of belief systems or, more specifically, of underlying learning conceptions:

— there is too much you have to find out for yourself.
— it should be clearer what you are supposed to learn, when something is good enough, what is right and what is wrong.
— those teachers are always asking questions.
— you have to keep telling them what your opinion is, what you are thinking or feeling.
— there is little opportunity to do things your own way
— it is an unnatural situation and there is too much coercion.
— you *have* to take part in everything, and you *have* to have fun.
— too much has to come from the group, and there is not enough explanation.
— there is no structure.

Because the teacher educators are more or less of one mind, the students feel that there is a strong pressure to conform to certain ways of learning. Most of the drop-outs considered these pointless, or at most foreign to their own ways of learning.

Among the students who stayed on after the first year there were those who were enthusiastic about practically everything the programme had to offer, others who were moderately enthusiastic, and still others who were critical of the programme, but who had nonetheless stayed on. Critical remarks about the teacher educators were sometimes repressed in an effort to 'play the game'.

It is noteworthy that those who stayed on voiced hardly any

criticism of the programme in the interviews which took place during the second year. On the one hand this has to do with the fact that the students with learning orientations that did not fit in, had already dropped out, while on the other hand we assume it was also the result of a learning effect at the meta-cognitive level. To quote a second-year student: 'What I found difficult to get used to, coming from secondary school, was that you have to learn in an entirely different way. In the beginning, because it was all so new, I wished I could do things the same way as in secondary school. It seemed much safer. Whereas now I see that we work in an entirely different way. Much more practical. You start to see that it is really a better way of doing things.'

How do you learn now?

'Now you reflect on the way in which you learn and the way in which you have learned something.'

What extras are in it for you?

'I think that it is very important, because you can fall back on old things you already know and use that as a basis for your present work.'

With regard to the value of reflective teaching as a fundamental training goal, the essence of the programme seems to lie in this *development and shifting of learning orientations.*

These qualitative findings were supported by quantitative results from the *I.E.O.-test*. Of the eight students who gave up, three of them left at such an early stage, that the I.E.O.-test could not be administered. The remaining students (five drop-outs and the ten who stayed on) completed the test in their first year. There were no significant differences noted for each separate scale, but the sum total of the scores on the three internal scales was clearly lower for those who gave up their studies (p=.07, in a one-tailed t-test).

Conclusions and Suggestions for the Improvement of Teacher Education Programmes Based on Reflective Teaching

We may conclude from the above that the teacher educators of the Mathematics Department of the SOL take a rather explicit view of the goals of teacher education in which reflective teaching occupies a central position. In practice, however, the actions of the educators are governed to a high degree by their perceptions of individual students and the strategies which the educators have at their disposal. In general they do well with students who prefer to learn in an active and reflective way, while the existence of other learning orientations is barely acknowledged.

Fundamental changes take place with regard to the learning orientations of students, a phenomenon which has its positive as well as its negative side. On the one hand our results indicate that the teacher educators in our study clearly promote the development of internal learning orientations, no doubt as a result of their own pronounced views. We must add, however, that part of the effects we found may be explained by assuming that externally oriented students disappear from the teachers' college through a process of self-selection. This is the negative side of the picture: this preparation programme based on reflective teaching shows a clash between the learning conceptions of the teacher educators and those of a number of the students. This may lead students to drop out or to simulate learning behaviour (*quasi-adaptation* to the conceptions of learning of the educators). This may well be a danger inherent in all teacher education programmes based on reflective teaching. As teacher educators, we must consider the plight of the less-reflective students. Do we want them to stay in the programme and be given a chance to gradually alter their learning orientation? If so, then there must be no obstacles which can only be surmounted by those students who already have an internal orientation. If programmes based on reflective teaching are to be effective, it is of fundamental importance that supervision strategies take differences in learning orientation into account.

We would like to put forward two suggestions. First, externally oriented students should be allowed to learn the art of reflection gradually. This is called a *strategy of gradualness* (Korthagen, 1985). Otherwise the fear of these students that the programme will be of little use to them may become a self-fulfilling prophecy. The teacher educator can help externally oriented students by not expecting them to be able to figure everything out for themselves right from the start. He can give them concrete instructions, offer them choices and provide sufficient feedback. It might be wise to provide the student logbooks with a written commentary, thus adapting the supervisory procedure to the needs of the individual student.

'Make haste slowly' is the watchword here. Within the SOL programme, for example, first-year students start out by holding practice lessons for their fellow students. Short lessons of about ten minutes appeared to be more effective than half-hour sessions. As they reflect on the method for solving a particular mathematical problem, first-year students are being prepared for the time when they will be asked to reflect on their learning processes during practice teaching and throughout the courses.

Secondly, we believe that students should be made explicitly aware of the problem of different learning orientations. Many authors believe that stimulating people to reflect on their own learning processes is an excellent means of developing adequate learning orientations (for example, Brown *et al.*, 1981). Gibbs (1981 and 1983) propagates a structural method in which students reflect on their conceptions of learning processes and study tasks, and then discuss their views with the rest of the group. We believe that this approach could have great advantages for teacher education programmes. The effect is twofold: it operates on the level of the processes of learning and teaching during the programme itself, as well as on the level of the school where the students will ultimately be teaching. It is essential for prospective teachers to realize that their pupils, too, will have different learning orientations, which will be influenced to no small degree by the education which they receive.

Acknowledgements

I would like to express my thanks to Bas van de Brink, Erik Ellinger, Marco Swaen, Hildelien Verkuyl and Theo Wubbels for their contributions to the research project and to this chapter.

References

BROWN, A.L., CAMPIONE, J.C. and DAY, J.D. (1981) 'Learning to learn: On training students to learn from texts', *Educational Researcher*, 10, 2, pp. 14–21.

CORCORAN, E. (1981) 'Transition shock: The beginning teacher's paradox', *Journal of Teacher Education*, 32, 3, pp. 19–23.

FREUDENTHAL, H., (1978) *Weeding and Sowing, Preface to a Science of Mathematical Education*, Dordrecht, Reidel.

GIBBS, G. (1981) *Teaching Students to Learn — A Student-centered Approach*, Milton Keynes, Open University Press.

GIBBS, G. (1983) 'Changing students' approaches to study through classroom exercises' in SMITH, R.M. (Ed.), *Helping Adults Learn How to Learn*. San Francisco, CA, Jossey Bass, pp. 83–96.

GOODMAN, J. (1985) 'Field-based experience: A study of social control and student teachers' response to institutional constraints', *Journal of Education for Teaching*, 11, 1, pp. 26–49.

HUNT, D.E. (1979) 'Learning style and student needs: An introduction to conceptual level', in *Student Learning Styles: Diagnosing and Prescribing*

Programs. Reston, VA, National Association of Secondary School Principals, pp. 27–38.

KELLY, G.A. (1955) *The Psychology of Personal Constructs Vols I and II,* New York, Norton.

KORTHAGEN, F.A.J. (1982) *Leren Reflecteren als Basis van de Lerarenopleiding,* 's-Gravenhage: Foundation for Educational Research (Dissertation, Dutch)

KORTHAGEN, F.A.J. (1985) 'Reflective teaching and pre-service teacher education in the Netherlands', *Journal of Teacher Education,* 36, 5, pp. 11–15.

LACEY, C. (1977) *The Socialization of Teachers,* London, Methuen.

SÄLJÖ, R. (1979) 'Learning in the learner's perspective. I: Some common sense conceptions', *Reports from the Institute of Education, University of Göteborg 76.*

TABACHNICK, B.R. and ZEICHNER, K.M. (1984) 'The impact of student teaching experience on the development of teacher perspectives', *Journal of Teacher Education,* 29, pp. 28–36.

VEENMAN, S. (1984) 'Perceived problems of beginning teachers', *Review of Educational Research,* 54 pp. 143–78.

ZEICHNER, K.M. (1980) 'Myths and realities: Field-based experiences in pre-service teacher education', *Journal of Teacher Education,* 31, 6, pp. 45–55.

ZEICHNER, K.M. (1981) 'Reflective teaching and field-based experience in teacher education', *Interchange,* 12, 4, pp. 1–22.

ZEICHNER, K.M. (1983) 'Alternative paradigms of teacher education', *Journal of Teacher Education,* 34, 3, pp. 3–9.

3 The Development of Knowledge Structures in Learning to Teach

James Calderhead

What kind of knowledge is acquired by student teachers in learning to teach? How is this knowledge structured and used? How is it imparted or developed in students to promote the growth of their classroom practice? In current efforts to design teacher education courses which well equip students for the task of teaching and which also promote continued learning, these are important questions to explore and to attempt to answer. This chapter aims to address these questions, drawing on available evidence from recent research on teachers' professional learning. In particular, examples are drawn from two studies in which the author has been involved. One focussed on student primary teachers' planning, teaching and assessment of children, investigating the ways students employed their own subject matter knowledge in teaching (Calderhead and Miller, 1986). The other examined the kind of thinking and evaluation that took place in student field experiences and the roles of teachers and tutors in fostering student teachers' learning (Calderhead, in press). Based on this evidence, the chapter aims to promote further enquiry and debate by offering some speculation on how the professional learning process might be conceptualized and on the implications of this for teacher education.

Research on Learning to Teach

From the research literature, some interesting and related observations can be abstracted concerning students' experience of learning to teach.

Early Conceptions of Teaching

Student teachers begin their teacher training with some general conceptions of the teachers' task. The long 'apprenticeship of observation' (Lortie, 1975) undertaken as a pupil at school, has equipped them with a knowledge of what teachers' work is like. Several researchers have suggested that these formative impressions of teaching are a powerful influence in shaping the beginning teacher's classroom practice (for example, Lacey, 1977; Tabachnick and Zeichner, 1984). The exposure to teaching as a pupil may also partly explain the unquestioning confidence with which some students initially approach teaching. For example, Book, Byers and Freeman (1983), in a survey of American student teachers entering professional training, found that students frequently viewed teaching as an extended form of parenting, and 24 per cent began their training confident that they could teach without much development of their professional knowledge. The extent to which this view persists may depend upon the student and the kinds of experiences they encounter in schools. In our experience, a few students do seem to survive a one-year postgraduate training course relatively unaffected by it, whilst others quickly realize the patchiness and generality of the knowledge they have acquired from their childhood observations. Such observations may have equipped students with a few strategies and routines, which are adopted when no other alternatives seem available, but their limitations are often appreciated.

It would appear that students' contacts with school as a pupil are potentially powerful influences on their developing practice, but their effects may vary considerably across different students and situations. Nevertheless, one of the basic challenges facing teacher education may be persuading some students that there is much more to be learned in becoming a teacher.

Learning How to Learn

Although students at the beginning of their training have some general ideas about what teaching involves, they appear to have much cruder notions about how they are going to develop and implement those ideas. Questions such as 'how am I going to learn to teach?' and also to some extent, 'what have I got to learn in order to teach?' are questions which beginning teachers rarely ask themselves and have great difficulty answering when they do. Although in learning to teach, many student teachers encounter problems of classroom management, role conflict and uncertainty concerning teaching strategies, they do not appear to have any clear conception of how their learning might be involved in the resolution of these difficulties. Frequent probing of student teachers on these issues has generally resulted in answers which emphasise practical experience — 'You learn from experience.' or 'That's the sort of thing you eventually pick up in the classroom.' — but which don't articulate the actual process of how experience helps. Such answers, together with students' frequently expressed preference for placement in the classroom as opposed to theory and college-based activities in their training (for example, HMI, 1982) clearly indicates how students value classroom experience in the process of learning even if the process itself seems, for one reason or another, to be beyond description.

Teachers' Views of Professional Learning

This apparently unproblematic view of learning to teach is often supported in the culture, or taken-for-granted values, of schools. Teachers have generally been found to attribute little worth to professional training (Lanier and Little, 1986), and teachers often regard classroom competence as largely a matter of personality. It is typically believed, for instance, that teachers are born, rather than made (see Jackson, 1968); they may acquire particular strategies, tips, and routines but these are refinements rather than the basis of teaching and they are acquired on the job, rather than through pre-service or in-service training. As a headteacher in one of our studies claimed: 'We can't *make* a good teacher. We can tell when students first come to the school who's likely to be a good teacher and who isn't. And you can put them alongside another teacher and hope they pick up the practical side of things. But they've either got what it takes or they haven't. Some have it and some don't.' This may well not be a universally held view, but it is one which seems to be strongly voiced in schools, and may well discourage student teachers from developing any understanding of the processes of learning to teach.

Images of Teaching

Although students' conceptions of teaching and of the process of learning to teach may be vague and undifferentiated, student teachers start their pre-service training with some specific images of teaching in mind. Sometimes these are ideal images of the kind of teacher they would like to be, based on recollections of teachers who had taught them at school, sometimes on one particular teacher who has been influential in their lives and who acts as a model for teaching. Occasionally, student teachers have negative models derived from teachers they have encountered that they definitely don't want to be like, such as distant authoritarian figures. These images, either positive or negative, seem to be quite powerful influences on students' developing practice. For instance, student primary teachers in our studies were sometimes found to hold ideal images of teaching which emphasized the role of teacher as guide, confidant, and friend which directed their attention to the development of good classroom relationships, sometimes at the expense of any detailed consideration of teachers' instructional role. In other cases, the image students had of a teacher led them to think of teaching as a process of enthusing children about the subject matter. In one case, a student teacher's experience in the Scouts had equipped him with images of real-life collaborative problem-solving as a basis for thinking about his own role in the classroom.

Practical Knowledge

The nature of teachers' practical knowledge — the knowledge that is directly related to action — is qualitatively different from academic, subject matter or formal theoretical knowledge. We know relatively little about teachers' practical knowledge, but it has been described in terms of such concepts as images, scripts and routines or rules of practice (for example, Elbaz, 1983). It is knowledge that is readily accessible and applicable to coping with real-life situations, and is largely derived from teachers' own classroom experience. The term 'image' has been particularly useful in attempting to describe practical knowledge. 'Image' has been defined at different levels of abstraction revealing perhaps something of the structure of teachers' knowledge. For instance, Clandinin (1986) and Connelly and Clandinin (1985), in a series of intensive case studies, describe images at a very high level of abstraction. One infant teacher is described as having an image of 'classroom as home', a powerful metaphor that shapes her thinking about teacher-pupil relationships, classroom 'atmosphere' and organisation, and which frequently enters into her thinking about her own classroom practice and professional problem-solving. An image, at this level, has strong affective connotations, and is associated with powerful beliefs and feelings of what are 'right' ways of teaching, rooted in past life experiences.

At a lower level of abstraction are the images that student teachers possess, as mentioned earlier, of an ideal teacher or of different types of teaching.

At a still lower level are images relating to particular lessons or activities (Morine-Dershimer, 1979). These are the images teachers have in mind of how lessons typically run. For instance, teachers can have an image of a mental arithmetic lesson, spelling lesson or practical science lesson which typifies the way in which the lesson would be conducted, the necessary preparation and organization, what the children would do and how they are likely to respond.

The term 'image' can also refer to the snapshots of perception that continually enter into teachers' thinking, the largely visual memories that teachers have of particular children, incidents or behaviours that come to mind as they plan or teach (c.f. Schank and Abelson, 1977).

How these images at different levels of abstraction interact with one another requires further exploration, but the term image seems a potentially useful one to describe the repertoire of influential models, cases, typifications and incidents that act in the mind of the teacher as exemplars, metaphors and guides for action.

The contrast between this practical, action-related knowledge and academic, theoretical knowledge can perhaps best be illustrated if we consider a teaching situation. Suppose, for instance, that we are asked to teach a friend to drive a car, and we have a short time to think about how we are going to perform the task. It seems unlikely that in either planning or executing the task we would consider our 'academic' knowledge of advance organizers or theories of motor skill development, and if we did, thinking through their implications in terms of teaching someone to drive might turn out to be a very time-consuming process. On the other hand, what is perhaps more likely to come to mind and to be useful in this situation is a store of practical knowledge about driving a car and of how we ourselves were taught. We might, for instance, remember our own first lesson, particular techniques of the driving instructor, we might analyze our own experience to decide what the task of driving a car actually involves, or perhaps recall negative images of impatience, intolerance and strained relationships when being taught by a friend, providing us with an instructional model to be avoided. Such images may be much more readily recalled and more easily related to action than any body of systematic, general, theoretical knowledge.

Developing Practical Knowledge

In their early experiences in classrooms, observing teachers and experimenting with their own teaching, students appear to accumulate and assemble various images at different levels of abstraction. Sometimes their existing higher level images shape the development of images at a lower level. They notice actions that seem 'good', 'appropriate', 'desirable' or that fit their general images of what teaching is about. For instance, one student in our studies noted the particular strategy of a teacher in assembling and dismissing the class at the end of the day. She praised the pupils who had tidied things away and were ready to go, and this produced an infectious conformity with the others in the class, who hurriedly copied the approved behaviour. This was in contrast to other teachers who, he recollected, responded to the same type of situation by nagging the children to get ready. The former appealed to him as being much more in line with his own very child-centred conception of what teaching ought to be like, and was an example of practice that he felt was important to remember and to imitate.

However, the images of teaching that students develop are not necessarily consonant with one another at different levels, and that dissonance can sometimes be quite alarming to students. In our studies, some students were conscious of, and occasionally concerned by, the difference between their own ideals for teaching and the need to adopt survival strategies in the classroom. Others commented on the sharp contrast between their own, usually quite liberal, ideas about teaching and the practice of their seemingly more authoritarian supervising teachers, but the students adopted many of their teacher's strategies because the students could see that they worked.

Learning to teach might involve the accumulation and use of these images, but the process of learning to teach cannot be explained purely in terms of modelling, or image accumulation. Models, or images, are probably valuable to student teachers struggling to cope with a complex task, as indeed they are to experienced teachers faced with the task of changing their classroom practice or implementing a new curriculum. As Doyle and Ponder (1977) suggest, innovations which have high practicality, which can be seen to be relevant and applicable by teachers to their own situation, are more likely to lead to classroom change. But models of teaching are not universally applicable — they have to be selected and possibly adapted for particular classes or situations, or changed in view of the beliefs and general ideas about teaching that a teacher possesses. This introduces the importance of higher order cognitive processes, or meta-cognition, in thinking about, evaluating, structuring, comparing and developing images of practice for particular individuals, situations and contexts. One could, in fact, hypothesize a series of metacognitive skills that structure experience to make it instrumental and applicable for action.

Utilizing Academic Knowledge

Student teachers have other knowledge bases which they bring to teacher education and which are sometimes specially developed in teacher education with the intention that they will inform classroom practice — subject matter knowledge, for instance, psychological theories of learning, theoretical knowledge about curriculum develop-ment, etc. But these knowledge bases are not readily translated into classroom action. In fact, student teachers with a well developed subject matter knowledge base have been found when planning and teaching in this subject area, still to draw upon the observed practices of their supervising teacher rather than their own store of subject matter knowledge (Calderhead and Miller, 1986). Similarly, it seems somewhat unlikely that the psychology graduate will be able to apply their expert knowledge of children's learning to their own practice in the primary classroom. That is not to say that these other knowledge bases cannot inform teaching, but it is more difficult and time-consuming, and students, coping with immediate time constraints, may rely more on readily available images than a distant and abstract knowledge base. The translation of subject matter knowledge into practice requires interaction between this knowledge and other knowl-edge such as that concerning children or teaching strategies. And it seems likely that those interactions are highly complex (see, for exam-ple, Wilson, Shulman and Richert, 1987). Interestingly, in discussions with several teacher educators who organize courses for curriculum coordinators in the primary school, it has been claimed that a good science teacher, for instance, or a good science coordinator, is not necessarily a teacher with a strong science background, and that a teacher with a lot of art and craft or drama experience can sometimes come to grips more readily with the creative processes of teaching and learning primary science. A possible explanation for this may be that the art and craft or drama teacher is better equipped to cope with the open-ended activities of hypothesis generation and designing experi-ments, which are the areas of great weakness identified by the APU science surveys and which are frequently stressed in in-service science courses. In contrast, the scientist with a large store of subject matter knowledge, perhaps much of it taken for granted, may find it difficult to foster experimentation and enquiry at the primary school child's level. The scientist's knowledge may also sometimes be associated with images of teaching and learning quite contrary to those appropriate for the primary school. The non-scientist, on the other hand, although having a comparatively low level of subject matter knowledge, may have other knowledge and skills — readily available images of how open-ended activities are organized and managed and the routines with which to enact these — that enable them to teach science to better effect. Similarly, the skills of working with other adults in an instructional situation may enable a science coordinator with relatively little subject matter knowledge to carry out their coordinating task more effectively than the teacher whose major asset is a store of specialist subject matter knowledge.

Such anecdotal evidence must obviously be regarded with some scepticism. What these teacher educators define and assess as being good practice is not clear — is the management of the open-ended activity being valued more highly than the children's learning, for instance? Are those two factors necessarily related? At the same time, such examples draw attention to the complex ways in which subject matter knowledge might inform practice, a process whose complexity seems frequently to be underestimated. The employment of subject matter knowledge in teaching is clearly dependent on other knowledge bases, together with some sophisticated metacognitive skills in orchestrating them to produce knowledge relevant to, and able to guide, practice.

Conceptualizing the Professional Learning Process

Implicit in the design of teacher education courses are certain assumptions about the nature and content of knowledge that is of value and about how this is to be acquired and utilized. In many courses, and in much current teacher education policy, it is assumed that there are particular vital knowledge bases that must be developed in student teachers — knowledge on subject matter, curriculum, materials, teaching methods, and children, for instance. However, the processes by which these knowledge bases inform classroom action is both unarticulated and unexamined. The linking of knowledge to action is sometimes regarded as mostly the student's responsibility, it is expected to occur as the student acquires experience in the classroom, but the means by which it happens, or the help that may be needed to facilitate its development is unstated. This model of professional learning is represented diagrammatically in figure 1.

It can be argued that what such a model fails to acknowledge are the differences between formal, academic knowledge and practical, action-related knowledge, the role of metacognition in processing knowledge, and the influence of learning conceptions on metacognitive processing. The possible interrelationships of these factors are noted in figure 2.

Figure 1: A model of knowledge use in teaching, implicit in teacher education

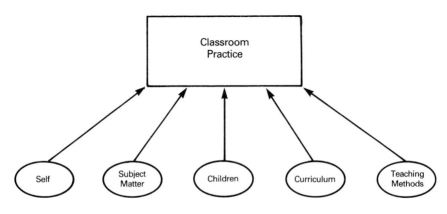

Figure 2: An alternative model of knowledge use in teaching

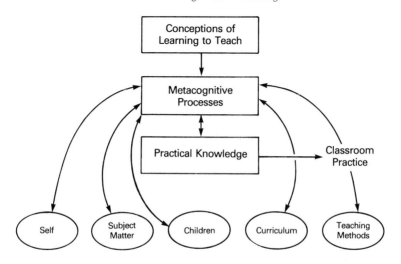

The term 'metacognition' has been adopted by Brown (1978) to denote the controlling processes of human cognition. In the case of learning to teach, it seems an apt term to apply to the processes of abstraction, comparison, analysis, and evaluation that operate on different images of practice or on a variety of knowledge bases to generate usable practical knowledge.

These metacognitive processes play an important role in learning to teach, but their significance is frequently left out of account in teacher education courses. For instance, we commonly require student teachers to plan a scheme of work before they embark on teaching practice. It is often the case, however, that once into teaching practice they realize how inappropriate their schemes of work are. They have misjudged the children, or not allowed for the available resources or the accepted practices within the school. In order to plan a scheme of work, students need to draw upon a wide range of knowledge about children, the curriculum,· teaching methods and school practices, and need access to particular types of knowledge. Although students might have accumulated theoretical knowledge about child development, and knowledge about individual children, planning a scheme of work requires other, for instance typificatory, knowledge about children. Planning for a class of 11-year-olds requires some conception of what a class of 11-year-olds is generally like, what range of abilities, interests, and spans of attention they might have and how they typically react to different types of material or situations. In order to plan a scheme of work for a class, a teacher has to have accumulated a considerable amount of knowledge about children and to have abstracted from that knowledge typifications, or exemplars, of what children and classes are like. These processes of abstraction are what might be included in the term 'metacognitive skills' which act on different knowledge bases to generate practical knowledge or images that are useful in the context of teaching.

Similarly, the process of using a store of subject matter knowledge in planning is not, as suggested earlier, a straightforward implementation task. In fact, planning may rely upon several metacognitive skills which enable different knowledge bases to be compared and contrasted. Planning might start with an idea which is gradually elaborated into a formal plan or mental image of a lesson, drawing on knowledge of subject matter, pupils, teaching strategies, material context etc, which are all compared and contrasted in a series of decisions about what form a lesson will take. An initial idea may be abandoned when consideration is given to the likely noise level it will generate, for example, or an adaptation made to enable an alternative form of classroom organization to be tried out. The process of drawing upon one's knowledge in lesson design is an experimental and interactive one in which different areas of knowledge are orchestrated to inform practice.

Students may also be dependent on metacognitive skills in the processes of evaluating their teaching, and improving upon their practice. Evaluation may involve the comparison of alternative images of practice, comparing, for instance, one's real performance with an ideal. Subject matter knowledge or knowledge of theories of children's learning might also be used to evaluate teaching performance, considering the appropriateness of particular activities or how one's teaching compares with particular teaching principles. For example, various learning theories or research findings might be used to evaluate a particular lesson and consider how the teaching approach might be changed to improve the quality of learning in that area (e.g. analyzing a maths lesson in terms of its demands for instrumental or relational understanding, Skemp, 1976). Such processes require metacognitive skills to abstract from and compare alternative knowledge bases.

Over and above the metacognitive skills that student teachers possess, one might hypothesize a further organizing structure which has some influence over how knowledge is developed and used. This is the conception that students have of the process of learning to teach. They may not always have a clear conception of this, and it may be largely implicit in their approach to learning, but students' conception of how teachers learn seems likely to influence the type and extent of metacognitive skills that are employed. For instance, it has been found that student teachers who come to view learning to teach as a process of performing certain behaviours which will count well towards their assessment on teaching practice, tend to identify and perform what they believe to be 'proper' teaching actions — insisting on silence when the teacher addresses the class, circulating when the children are working, etc. — even in situations where such actions might be considered inappropriate. Similarly, one might expect those students who conceptualize the task of learning to teach in terms of a theory-practice link to develop metacognitive skills which attempt to interrelate their theoretical and practical knowledge. On the other hand, those viewing learning to teach as a process of modelling may develop few metacognitive skills, adopting fairly uncritically the actions of their supervising teacher. Whatever view is adopted of learning has implications for how knowledge is developed and used.

The link between one's conception of learning to teach and metacognition may at times be tenuous. Student teachers could clearly develop and use metacognitive skills which are not wholly in accordance with their explicit conception of learning to teach, but to consider the possible relationship between the two may be of value in teacher education in drawing attention to the potentially constraining effects of some conceptions of professional learning.

Implications for Professional Training

Recent research on student teachers tends to suggest that their teaching relies heavily on the images of practice that are acquired from past and current experiences in schools. These images can be taken and implemented uncritically. The evaluation of practice might remain at a superficial level and knowledge bases which could potentially inform practice be little utilized. Furthermore, the school, and sometimes college, ethos might support a conception of teaching which does not encourage and may even impede an analytical response to one's own teaching, leading in some cases to opinionated or self-defensive approaches to professional learning. As a result, student teachers' learning could quite quickly reach a plateau where teaching has become routine, conservative and unproblematic.

It is tentatively suggested that some of these difficulties in learning to teach might be attributed to particular models of professional learning which have become implicit in teacher education and which fail to acknowledge the nature and use of knowledge in teaching. It is suggested that they especially fail to address the division between academic knowledge and practical knowledge, the role of metacognitive skills in the generation, structuring and use of knowledge, and the influence of learning conceptions on metacognition.

It is argued that there is a need for models which more accurately represent these distinctions and their interrelationships. One is proposed in this chapter, though it must be recognized as a first speculative attempt to depict the process of professional learning and has many shortcomings in itself. To represent subject matter knowledge as a single, discrete entity, for instance, is an oversimplification, when it is often acquired in different contexts for different purposes and is at times clearly interwoven with other knowledge.

Nevertheless, the proposed model and its rationale raise a number of issues concerning practice in teacher education. It provides a basis for both students and tutors to think about the process of learning to teach, directing attention to the types of knowledge that are required and how they might inform practice. For tutors, an awareness of the complex processes involved in learning to teach might enable them to facilitate learning further and to consider critically what kinds of tasks in a teacher education course are likely to develop practical knowledge, what kinds of roles, relationships and common language need to be established amongst teachers, tutors and students to discuss practical knowledge and promote metacognitive skills, what role academic knowledge might fulfil in a teacher education course and how it is best presented, and what kind of course structure and assessment is likely to facilitate professional growth. For students, an awareness of the processes of learning to teach might enable them to analyse their own experiences in professional development, to identify those areas of knowledge and skill that must be built up, and to recognize the potential of professional learning for their own practice.

Research on teachers' learning can help us further understand the structure of teachers' knowledge, how it is developed and how it informs classroom practice. Such an understanding can enable us to examine critically our current teacher education practices and to build teacher education courses which equip student teachers not only with basic classroom competence but with the knowledge, skills and confidence to continue learning.

References

Book, C., Byers, J., and Freeman, D. (1983) 'Student expectations, and teacher education traditions with which we can and cannot live', *Journal of Teacher Education*, 34, 13, pp. 9–13.

Brown, A.L. (1978) 'Knowing when, where and how to remember: A problem of metacognition' in Glaser, R. (Ed.) *Advances in Instructional Psychology*, Hillsdale, NJ, Erlbaum.

Calderhead, J. (in press) 'The contribution of field experiences to student primary teachers' professional learning', *Research in Education*.

Calderhead, J. and Miller, E. (1986) 'The integration of subject matter knowledge in student teachers' classroom practice', Research Monograph, School of Education, University of Lancaster.

Clandinin, D.J. (1986) *Classroom Practice: Teacher Images in Action*, Lewes, Falmer Press.

Connolly, F.M. and Clandinin, D.J. (1985) 'Personal practical knowledge and the modes of knowing: Relevance for teaching and learning', in Eisner, E. (Ed.) *Learning and Teaching the Ways of Knowing*, 84th Yearbook of the NSSE, Chicago, University of Chicago Press.

DOYLE, W. and PONDER, G.A. (1977) 'The practicality ethic and teacher decision-making', *Interchange*, 8, pp. 1–12.

ELBAZ, F. (1983) *Teacher Thinking: A Study of Practical Knowledge*, London, Croom Helm.

HMI (1982) *The New Teacher in School*, London, HMSO.

HMI (1987) *Quality in Schools: The Pre-service Education of Teachers*, London, HMSO.

JACKSON, P.W. (1968) *Life in Classrooms*, New York, Holt, Rinehart and Winston.

LACEY, C. (1977) *The Socialization of Teachers*, London, Methuen.

LANIER, J.E. and LITTLE, J.W. (1986) 'Research on teacher education', in WITTROCK M.C. (Ed.) *Handbook of Research on Teaching*, 3rd edn, New York, Macmillan.

LORTIE, D.C. (1975) *School Teacher*, Chicago, University of Chicago Press.

MORINE-DERSHIMER, G. (1979) 'Teacher plan and classroom reality: The S. Bay Study, part 4', Research monograph, Institute for Research on Teaching, University of Michigan.

SCHANK, R.C. and ABELSON, R. (1977) *Scripts, Plans, Goals and Understanding*, Hillsdale, NJ, Erlbaum.

SKEMP, R.R. (1976) 'Relational understanding and instrumental understanding', *Mathematics Teaching*, 77, pp. 20–6.

TABACHNICK, B.R. and ZEICHNER, K.M. (1984) 'The impact of the student teaching experience on the development of teacher perspectives', *Journal of Teacher Education*, 35, 6, pp. 28–36.

WILSON, S.M., SHULMAN, L.S. and RICHERT, A.E. (1987) '150 different ways of knowing: Representations of knowledge in teaching' in CALDERHEAD, J. (Ed.) *Exploring Teachers' Thinking*, London, Cassell.

4   Student Teachers' Planning and Post-lesson Reflections: Patterns and Implications for Teacher Preparation

Hilda Borko, Carol Livingston,
Joseph McCaleb, Linda Mauro

Little is known about the process of learning to teach (Feiman-Nemser, 1983) or the thinking and actions of novice teachers (Tabachnick and Zeichner, 1984), though the growth of research in these areas seems highly promising. Shulman and Feiman-Nemser, for example, are currently each studying the development of subject matter knowledge and pedagogical knowledge in preservice teachers (for example, Feiman-Nemser and Buchmann, 1986a and 1986b; Shulman, 1986; Wilson, Shulman and Richert, 1987). The research programs of Berliner and Leinhardt contrast cognitive skills of expert and novice teachers (for example, Berliner, 1987; Leinhardt and Greeno, 1986). While all of these programs are still under way results to date confirm the importance of research in these areas for increasing our understanding of learning to teach. As Berliner (1987) notes based on initial findings in his research program, 'experience as a classroom teacher leads to changes in cognition — in perception, memory, and thought — in ways that seem more sophisticated, more efficient, and more useful' (p. 76).

The present study, and the research program of which it is a part, were designed to add to this growing knowledge base about the development of pedagogical expertise. This study focussed primarily on how pre-service teachers think about instruction. In particular, we sought to describe participants' planning for, and reflections after, lessons taught as part of the student teaching experience, and to identify factors that influenced these aspects of their teaching. We selected participants to enable comparisons on three dimensions which research suggests may impact teacher thinking and the process of learning to teach: grade level, content area, and type of teacher preparation program.

Several researchers have suggested that secondary teachers may plan very differently than elementary teachers and that their planning may be strongly influenced by the nature of the content they are teaching and methods and activities appropriate to teaching that content (Calderhead, 1984; Smith, 1984). Yet the vast majority of studies of teacher planning are conducted in elementary classrooms, usually focussing on reading and/or mathematics instruction. Participants in this study, in contrast, were preparing to teach in a range of grade levels and content areas.

In an attempt also to examine the relationship between teacher preparation programs and student teachers' thinking, we selected participants in this study from two programs at the University of Maryland: the traditional teacher preparation program and the Masters Certification Program. The traditional program is a four-year undergraduate program which includes coursework in human development, educational foundations, and general and content-specific methods; field experiences associated with several of the courses; and a semester of student teaching. The Masters Certification Program is an alternative teacher preparation program implemented for the first time during the 1985/86 academic year. It enables adults who hold Bachelor degrees with strong liberal arts and academic emphases to earn a Masters degree and certification in a single calendar year of intensive preparation. Key features of the program include: a teacher education curriculum which is theory and *research* based; an emphasis on teacher problem solving and *reflection*; and carefully planned and integrated campus-based and school-based experiences aimed at providing the beginning teacher with a *repertoire* of teaching strategies. We thought these key features — often referred to by program participants as 'the three Rs' — might be reflected in the student teachers' planning for, and reflections after, lessons. (For additional information about the Masters Certification Program see McCaleb *et al*, 1987.)

Participants

The participants in our investigation were twelve prospective teachers from the University of Maryland who student taught during the spring semester, 1986. Each student teaching placement was in a county school system in suburban Maryland.

To accommodate the three contrasts (grade level, content area,

Table 1:   Student Teachers' Placement and Preparation

Student teacher	Grade level[a]	Content area preparation	Content area observed	Program[b]
Laurie	2	elementary	reading	MCP
Joan	2	elementary	reading	trad
Lana	4	elementary	lang arts	MCP
Ben	4	elementary	mathematics	trad
Jack	hs	mathematics	geometry	MCP
Bob	hs	mathematics	elem algebra	trad
Sandra	10	English	literature	MCP
Conrad	9	English	literature	trad
Danny	9	speech	literature	MCP
Lou	hs	speech	speech	trad
Katie	hs	theater	theater	MCP
Leslie	hs	theater	theater	trad

[a] hs = range of grade levels in high school
[b] MCP = Masters Certification Program; trad = traditional teacher preparation program.

and teacher preparation program), student teachers were selected in pairs. Two student teacher pairs were in elementary school placements: one pair in primary grades and one in intermediate level classrooms. The four pairs in secondary school placements represented a diversity of content areas: mathematics, literature, speech, and theater arts.[1] One member of each pair was enrolled in the traditional teacher preparation program and one was in the Masters Certification Program (see table 1). Because students in the Masters Certification Program differed from the 'typical' student teacher with respect to age and grade point average, participants in each pair were matched on these variables as well.

Data Collection

Each student teacher in the study was observed teaching on two consecutive days and interviewed following each observation. Consecutive observations and interviews provided us with the opportunity to investigate the influence of classroom events and the student teachers' reflections about these events on subsequent planning and teaching.

Our primary data sources for this chapter were transcripts of the audiotaped interviews. Open-ended interview questions focussed on the student teachers' planning for the lessons and their reflections after teaching. Questions about planning directed them to discuss how they planned the lesson, what they thought about as they planned, and what factors influenced their plans. Questions about the lesson re-quested that they discuss its prominent features (what stands out), strengths and weaknesses, changes from plans, reasons for those changes, revisions proposed for future lessons, and reasons for the proposed revisions. The interview transcripts were supplemented by the student teachers' written lesson plans and researchers' fieldnotes.

Data Analysis

The procedures used to analyze interview protocols were designed to ensure systematic, reliable coding of participants' responses to inter-view questions, as well as to capture our holistic impressions of the interviews and identify particularly representative remarks. As a first step, the two principal researchers developed a coding form with categories derived from our research questions and an initial reading of interview protocols for one secondary and two elementary partici-pants. The coding form consisted of three major sets of categories: preactive decisions, changes in plans, and reflections after teaching.

In the second step of the analysis, we coded the interview pro-tocols of the twelve participants. Interviews were coded by placing a check mark on the coding form for each category of information that was mentioned at least once in the interview protocol. We coded one set of interviews together, to arrive at consensus for category descrip-tors and coding conventions. We then independently read and coded four sets of interviews, and compared our codings to record agree-ments and disagreements and reach consensus. Using a conservative approach in which only categories checked by one or both coders are used in the calculation, intercoder agreement for these interviews was .80 (Holsti, 1969).

Based on the coding of these four sets of interviews, we revised the category system by adding, deleting, and combining categories to more accurately reflect the participants' responses. Also, despite the fact that our level of agreement is considered adequate for this type of data analysis (Warner, 1986), we decided to continue the process of independently coding each interview and then discussing disagree-ments to achieve consensus. Since most of our disagreements reflected ambiguities in participants' responses which called for judgments about which category more accurately captured the participant's meaning, we felt this procedure would increase our confidence in our coding decisions. Inter-coder agreement for the entire set of interviews was .79.

While coding the interviews, we simultaneously kept records of several types of information not captured by the codes. We summarized the essence of student teachers' responses to the interview questions, identified quotes that were particularly representative of their expressed thoughts, and recorded our holistic impressions of each interview and any insights about possible patterns and themes which were emerging for individuals and across cases. We also consulted fieldnotes and written plans to clear up any ambiguities and uncertainties in our understanding of the student teachers' comments.

As a final analysis step, we compared the coded data, holistic impressions, and representative comments for all twelve student teachers. We first summarized the coded data by computing, for each information category, the number of interviews in which that category was addressed by four groups of participants: elementary Masters Certification students, elementary students in the traditional program, secondary Masters Certification students, and secondary students in the traditional program. We then searched for patterns of similarities and differences in the responses that might be explained by grade level, content area, or teacher preparation program.

Results

The student teachers in this study attended to similar elements of classroom teaching and learning during planning and post-lesson reflections. However, there were differences in the nature of their comments and in the relative emphasis they placed on these classroom elements. These patterns of similarities and differences in participants' comments are presented below. We first report elements of the lessons to which the student teachers attended. We then examine the nature of their comments. This examination is organized according to four factors which we found to be associated with patterns in the comments: subject matter and pedagogical knowledge, content area influence, the opportunities presented by teaching multiple sections of the same course, and student teacher responsibility and control.

Elements of Teaching and Learning Addressed

An examination of coded interviews revealed that student teachers attended to similar aspects of classroom teaching and learning when planning lessons, regardless of the grade level or content area of the class or their teacher preparation program. For example, in describing their daily planning, all student teachers mentioned attending to lesson content, student activities and teacher activities. Goals and objectives, organization and management of instruction, and materials were mentioned in over half the interviews. Also, in at least one interview, each student teacher mentioned planning for contingencies or building flexibility into plans to allow for the unexpected.

Student teachers also focussed on similar elements of classroom teaching and learning in their reflections about lessons, with the exception of one pattern associated with grade level and one associated with teacher preparation program. Students were the major topic of reflections after teaching. In almost every interview, student teachers mentioned each student attribute we coded: affect, effort or participation, understanding, learning outcomes, and behavior. Each of the lesson attributes we coded — accomplishment of goals, quality or appropriateness, and timing or pacing — was mentioned in over half of the interviews. Two of the teacher attributes, affect and instructional effectiveness, were also mentioned over half the time.

The one difference in focus associated with grade level was on the teacher attribute, classroom management effectiveness. This attribute was mentioned in half the interviews with elementary student teachers, but only one-fourth the interviews with secondary student teachers.

Students in the traditional teacher education program mentioned contextual factors such as administrative requirements, paperwork, classroom interruptions, and institutional scheduling more frequently than did students in the Masters Certification Program. For example, in half of their interviews student teachers in the traditional program indicated that institutional scheduling of activities such as assemblies and cancellations or delays due to weather influenced their lessons. Participants in the Masters Certification Program never mentioned such schedule changes as influential factors in their lessons, despite the fact that several of them, like a number of student teachers in the traditional program, were observed on days immediately following cancellations due to snow.

Subject Matter and Pedagogical Knowledge

There were clear differences in student teachers' subject matter knowledge and confidence in their knowledge, which were associated with differences in their planning and teaching. In general, when student teachers had strong content area preparation and confidence in their knowledge of course content, they planned in less detail and were more responsive to students while teaching. Katie (all names used in reference to this study are pseudonyms), who had previously taught theater at the college level, felt very confident in her knowledge of the theater arts course content. As she explained:

> I feel so secure in this content area that, in terms of planning for today, I really had three things in mind. I mean I didn't really structure that discussion ... We solve problems around something specific that you can see. I find that I'm very quick on my feet about figuring out what it is we need to do to fix it and how I can make sure that they understand.

Sandra was confident in her knowledge of the literature her class was reading. 'I mean I know the book and so, I just was able to talk about it with them.' Because of her familiarity with the readings, 'This class has been a real easy one for me to just come into.' And, with respect to her teaching, 'I felt comfortable switching things around. I felt comfortable doing something that I hadn't done the same ways before.'

Lou and Bob both spoke of differences in their planning across courses due to differences in subject matter expertise. Their comments provide vivid, within-person illustrations of the role of content knowledge in teaching. For Lou, the contrast was between his speech class and an advanced directing class. In the directing class:

> If I wished to do so, I could come without a lesson plan at all, because I happen to have a fairly intimate knowledge of what we are working on ... But I'd never do that in this [speech] class. There's just no way. I would be deathly afraid and then I would be stumped ... I just don't know my material well enough.

His goal was to know all of his courses as well as advanced directing. 'I wish that I knew my subject so well that I never had to write lesson plans. That I would just write five words on a piece of paper and know exactly what I had to do.'

Bob contrasted elementary algebra and analytic geometry:

> In elementary algebra, I'm fully at ease. Now, this analytic geometry course which I hope to pick up soon, that's a different matter ... I have been reading the first section of chapter 2 several times. I guess that is what I hadn't anticipated about

teaching high school math — I really have a single amount of time to put into just understanding the material. So in elementary algebra I do tend to spend less time in planning than in other courses.

One student was placed in an English student teaching assignment when his expertise lay in speech and political science. (He initially indicated a desire to become certified in English, but changed his mind. Later in the semester, after observations for this study, he was moved to a speech placement.) Danny was familiar with neither the content nor the pedagogical strategies in English, and his student teaching and personal evaluations reflected this lack. He commented about a lesson in which the pace dragged, 'I've never led a discussion on a novel before and I'm not all that familiar with some of the techniques that need to be used in order to speed things up.' The negative impact of this placement was apparent:

> I really am not an English certification candidate. I'm a candidate for speech certification, and I'll be looking forward to that and quite probably could be certified in social studies also, but I'm quite a few credits away from English and I may not be all that interested in it ... I find that it would take an awful lot of work for me to be confident enough to really lead four sessions of English and I don't feel that's what I want to do. To be frank, it's a turnoff.

In contrast to these clear differences in subject matter expertise and confidence, almost all of the student teachers discussed their limited pedagogical knowledge and its impact on their teaching. Several spoke of the process of learning to present content in a way that would be appropriate for the students. For example, Jack addressed the issue of pacing:

> I found myself initially, when I started, covering more than I really should have because I felt the subject matter was easy, not realizing that I'm teaching it to people who are learning it for the first time. So I find myself now slowing down ... I have to concentrate on teaching this to the people who have not had it before.

Inexperience was also reflected in limited repertoires of teaching strategies and routines. Ben felt he was spending too much time checking mathematics homework in his fourth grade class. He had tried several homework-checking routines, but had not found one which gave him immediate feedback without conflicting with his pedagogical beliefs:

> Most of my thought was spent on how I'm going to get them to check homework ... I have a feeling this group will tune out if I read out answers. And I'm not sure that does them as much good. So I'm still trying to experiment with ways that will get them involved in checking without just a, you know, 'Yeah you, what's the answer?'

Similarly, Conrad was unable to plan a good introduction to his Shakespeare unit:

> Last Monday I gave them an introductory lecture. I didn't want to do it, but I don't have the experience of teaching something like this before. I didn't know how else to do it. And I talked to them for most of the period. And I lost them about, you know, maybe about halfway through, if I got that far.

Content Area Influence

For the secondary student teacher, patterns in planning and lesson reflections were related to their subject matter specializations. In particular, their thinking seemed to be influenced by the extent to which course content and structure were determined by a prescribed curriculum and/or the hierarchical nature of the content. The subject area specializations of participants in our study can be arrayed on a continuum of structure, with mathematics at one end, theater arts at the other, and literature and speech classes in the middle.

In the highly structured mathematics curricula, textbooks played a central role in planning. Jack described long-range planning for his geometry classes as follows:

> In general, there's a textbook that's used. And we go essentially by chapters, with some chapters either covered at a later time or an earlier time. I discussed with my cooperating teacher in what order does he want to treat the chapters (sic). And I discussed essentially how long I felt I would take on each one ...

His daily planning consisted primarily of selecting problems and examples, rather than making decisions about content to be covered.

Like long-range planning, daily planning was strongly influenced by the text:

> OK, I took a book, the math book we're using . . . and looked at some of the samples. I had some other textbooks like Jacobs and some other authors. I looked at how they presented their data. I do this every time I plan a lesson, how they presented, what they saw for suggestions, or some teacher guide sections, how I think I could modify something to bring about what I want to reinforce in them. And by putting all this together, just come out with some problems.

Theater classes represented the opposite extreme of the continuum. For both student teachers we observed, there were no assigned textbooks to drive the curriculum. The student teachers relied to a much greater extent than the mathematics student teachers on personal knowledge, interests, and experience in designing both units and individual class sessions. Leslie commented that she was 'pretty much given free rein' regarding what to teach. She felt that she needed experience presenting information in a lecture format, so she asked her cooperating teacher if she could teach a unit on musical comedy. Leslie selected musical comedy because 'I have this big collection of musical records and it's always been an interest of mine.' Her decisions about unit objectives and content were based on this record collection and her own familiarity with various composers and their work. This flexibility and freedom was not without its drawbacks. Leslie noted: 'The hardest thing about being in a drama class is there isn't a lot of rigid set curriculum like there is in an English class or something.'

Literature and speech classes fell between mathematics and theater arts on the continuum of curriculum structure. These classes were similar to theater arts in that units were the central focus of planning. Unit plans, in turn, had a strong influence on daily planning. Lou's description of the role of his unit plan was typical:

> I have a unit plan that is taken from knowing what I have to do in the curriculum, knowing that, for instance, I have a personal narrative speech to deliver; knowing that I want to cover delivery, I want to cover all of these points in the lecture. Then I determine how much time I have to space them out. The unit plan is basically a general overview of what I have to get done in the next two weeks. Then I take my daily plans from that.

As Lou's comment indicates, unit planning for his speech classes consisted of identifying a set of objectives based on curriculum guidelines, and then selecting materials and activities to achieve those objectives. Sandra's description of planning for a unit in her secondary literature class illustrates a similar process:

> This unit is really the only full unit that I'm teaching these kids, and so I really had to decide what my objectives were and then what pieces of literature would best satisfy those ... And then, primarily ... I like to allot time for good activities, good discussion, that kind of thing.

For both literature and speech classes, the influence of textbooks on the curriculum was less than in mathematics classes but more than in theater arts. Lou explained that there was a textbook for the speech class. However, like his cooperating teacher, he decided not to give it to the students. 'He gave me the option and explained to me his reasons for not using it and I agreed with him.' Lou consulted the textbook, as well as other speech books, when planning lessons. 'I draw the information from a text, almost always. At least one, but I don't have a set text. I have several speech texts, two of them from here and several of my own.'

Novels, plays, and other readings served as the textbooks in the literature classes we observed. Once selected, they played a central role in planning and instruction. In Sandra's class, discussions focussed on the novel they were reading. To prepare,

> I kind of wrote some outlines of questions, and wrote a few questions as possibilities ... I made a lot of notes on my own copy ... I did a lot of underlining and put notes in the margins and I wanted to draw their attention to some things.

Teaching Multiple Sections

Another contrast among secondary student teachers was in the way they approached teaching sections of the same course several times ('common preparations'). Seven of the eight secondary student teachers taught sections of the same course twice or more. (For elementary student teachers, there was no comparable experience.) All seven talked about this situation in their interviews. As their comments indicate, they differed in the extent to which they used the opportunity presented by the situation to think about and improve their teaching.

Three of the student teachers, Danny, Jack and Bob, discussed differences between the sections they taught, but did not indicate that these differences affected their instructional strategies. Danny explained:

> I have another period of this same class, sixth period, and I think they'll probably get into it more than this group did. It's later in the day and those students, after lunch they're restless and generally do tend to participate more in terms of discussion and so forth, so maybe they'll be a little livelier.

Jack was concerned primarily with keeping his two geometry classes together: '... we try to look at how we can get all the groups together so that they're adequately prepared for the test'. This task was made more difficult during the observation times because of snow days and cancelled classes.

Bob's situation was slightly different, as the algebra class we observed was two weeks behind the 'on-level' class. His only comment was that this situation enabled him to use exercise sheets created two weeks earlier by the cooperating teacher for the 'on-level' class.

Leslie, Conrad and Katie talked about differences in the instructional strategies they used when teaching the same lesson to different classes. Changes in their teaching were motivated primarily by two factors: the belief that instruction should be tailored to the unique characteristics of individual classes, and the desire to use insights from lessons taught earlier in the day to improve their instruction in later lessons.

Conrad and Katie both talked about modifications they made to accommodate unique characteristics of the students and classes. Conrad reported, 'Each class is different and I make mental notes to myself, you know, how am I going to approach this with this class.' With respect to management, for example, 'I will treat talking in the third period class a lot differently than I will in the sixth period class.' Similarly, Katie explained, 'I want to accomplish exactly the same thing, but the interaction will be different and my responses will be different because the students are different.'

All three of these student teachers spoke of adjusting plans for later lessons in light of what happened earlier in the day. For example, when asked about differences in the lessons for her theater arts classes, Leslie reported that she 'just cut down on the number of songs' and 'changed the wording (of her stories) just a little bit, depending on the reaction'. When stories worked well, 'I made a special point to make sure that I included that, almost in the same way, in each period.'

Conrad used the opportunity to teach multiple sections of the same course in a similar manner:

A lot of times I come in here and I'm not sure whether I've got enough material or not. So, it all depends on, if it runs well in the first period, I know I'll be OK. Otherwise I make adjustments. Good thing about having to teach it to three classes. By the last time you've got it down pretty good.

Katie's comment that when she taught her first period theater arts class, she thought about how to tailor the lesson to her more rowdy fourth period students, represents a combination of the two factors. As she noted on one occasion:

Anything that could go wrong that didn't go wrong today could more likely go wrong in fourth period. I just think it's a fabulous dress rehearsal for me to teach first before I teach fourth, because things that I notice that aren't as smooth in terms of transitions, I'll know I've got to be extra careful to anticipate that for them.

Sandra took the initiative to ensure that teaching multiple sections of her high school literature course would be a learning experience by enlisting the aid of her cooperating teacher:

I asked [my cooperating teacher] to come in first period and observe and give me some feedback, and she did, and I made some changes based on it. And so it sort of is amazing how just a few little things, a few little bits of clarification make a huge difference.

Responsibility and Control

Student teachers also differed in the extent to which they perceived themselves as responsible for, and in control of, classroom events. And, these perceptions were associated with differences in their teaching. Participants who expressed attitudes of responsibility and control more frequently took active steps to correct problem situations and to improve their teaching.

Statements by Ben and Laurie are illustrative of the sense of empowerment some student teachers felt. Ben clearly accepted responsibility for a pacing problem in his fourth grade mathematics lesson:

> We spent the beginning time talking, going over homework
> and . . . I dragged that out a lot longer than I expected to. And
> I think it was more my doing than the kids.

When confronted with the restlessness and inattention of her weaker
second grade readers, Laurie problem-solved to come up with an
alternative instructional format for her next lesson:

> Well, I tried to think really concretely. You know, things that
> I could bring and things that they could do that would be
> really concrete and individual, like working with the little slate
> board. That was something that each of them could do.

Most of the comments reflecting attributions to external factors
focussed on the student teachers' inability to 'make students learn'. As
Leslie explained, 'Learning only takes place when they *want* to learn.
You can't *make* someone learn.' Lana expressed a similar set of beliefs:

> Some of the kids just don't like learning. They really don't like
> being here and there's nothing you can do. You know, you try
> everything to draw them into the learning scene, but this is
> not what they are interested in.

Conrad's comments about his English class reflect a resignation that
frequently seemed to accompany external attributions:

> Some of them didn't really feel like being serious today. That's
> something you just don't know until you come into the room
> and see how they're behaving . . . We did manage to get
> through most of it. Can't have everything. [Sigh]

Responsibility and control is the only one of the four factors
associated with patterns in student teachers' comments for which we
found differences related to teacher preparation program membership.
In addition to mentioning contextual factors less frequently in their
reflections about lessons (as we reported earlier), Masters Certification
Program students less frequently attributed instructional or management difficulties to contextual elements outside their control than did
student teachers in the traditional program. They also used a problem
solving approach to planning more frequently, actively modifying
their plans based on their own self–evaluations and their cooperating
teachers' suggestions. Lana was the only Masters Certification student
to make statements which clearly attributed successes or failures to
circumstances beyond her control. In contrast, three of the six participants from traditional programs commented on aspects of classroom
life which they perceived to be outside their control.

Discussion

We began this investigation expecting to find differences in student teachers' planning and post-lesson reflections associated with grade level, content area, and teacher preparation program. These expectations were only partially confirmed. Specifically, our data clearly support a relationship between content area and planning. We did not, however, find systematic differences in the planning or lesson reflections of elementary and secondary teachers. And the only clear difference we found between student teachers in the two teacher preparation programs was that the Masters Certification Program participants were less likely to attribute classroom successes and failures to external factors. They seemed to have a greater sense of control over classroom events than did student teachers in the traditional program.

Our analysis of qualitative differences in student teachers' comments revealed three factors which, in addition to content area, were associated with differences in planning and post-lesson reflections: subject matter and pedagogical knowledge, variations in the use of opportunities presented by teaching multiple sections of the same course, and sense of responsibility and control. These four factors and their implications for preservice teacher preparation are discussed below. First, however, we explore possible reasons for the lack of differences associated with grade level and teacher preparation program.

It may be that differences exist in the thinking of elementary and secondary student teachers, but in aspects of planning or post-lesson reflections not addressed by this investigation. For example, elementary teachers' planning for core curriculum areas such as reading and mathematics may be similar to the planning of secondary teachers, while their planning for subjects such as science, social studies, or art (not examined in this study) may be very different. Further research is necessary to explore this issue.

Master Certification students' greater sense of control over classroom events may be related to the experimental nature of the program. The Masters Certification Program underwent many revisions during its first year, and students participated actively in the change process. Through their role in program revisions, they may have come to perceive that they did have control over, and responsibility for, their professional preparation experiences. We do not know why other differences between participants in the two programs were not found. It may be that the two-day data collection period was insufficient to reveal differences. Or differences which exist in day-to-day teaching may have been masked by the special effort all participants put into their lessons, because of the researchers' presence. Again, additional research is necessary to examine these possibilities.

Patterns in Planning and Post-lesson Reflections and their Implications for Pre-service Teacher Education

Some participants in this study entered into student teaching with adequate preparation in their content areas; others were adequately prepared for some teaching responsibilities but not others; and some were inadequately prepared. These differences in content area preparation, both within and between student teachers, were related to the amount of time and effort required for daily planning, the focus of attention in planning (for example, learning of content, planning of instructional strategies), flexibility in planning and teaching, and self-confidence as a teacher. In contrast to these variations in adequacy of content preparation, all student teachers indicated a need to improve their pedagogical skills. Like novice teachers in other studies (for example, Borko, Lalik and Tomchin, 1987; Leinhardt and Greeno, 1986), they had not yet developed repertoires of routines for class-room management and the organization of instructional activities characteristic of expert teachers. The student teaching experience is the component of pre-service teacher education designed for, and uniquely suited to, developing and practicing teaching strategies and routines. To maximize this learning opportunity, preservice teachers should enter the student teaching experience with strong content preparation and should be placed in classes within their areas of content expertise. In this way, their time and energy can be devoted to the learning of pedagogical skills, rather than the learning of content.

Differences in planning related to content areas confirm Calderhead's (1984) hypothesis that lesson planning will differ by content area. For example, the more central role of textbooks in planning for the highly structured mathematics curriculum, contrasted with a greater reliance on personal knowledge, interests, and experience in planning for theater arts adds further evidence to Smith's (1984) finding that one of the strongest influences on secondary teachers' curriculum planning was their '. . . perceptions of the subject they were teaching, the types of knowledge it represented, and the methods and activities appropriate to teach it' (p. 605). However, our data also support the viewpoint that there are commonalities in planning across grade levels and content areas. Combined, these findings suggest that the argument over generic versus content-specific pedagogical preparation should be resolved (as it now is in many programs) by including both components (for example, general and content-specific methods courses) in a teacher preparation program. All student teachers can benefit from an introduction to the cognitive skills of teaching and assistance in developing instructional routines and schemata for planning and teaching (for example, planning nets, cf Leinhardt and Greeno, 1986). In addition, they need assistance in developing what Shulman (1986) has labeled pedagogical and curricular content knowledge.

The value several student teachers derived from teaching repeated sections of the same course suggests to us that teacher preparation programs should systematically incorporate this type of opportunity into the student teaching experience. Further, the opportunity should be structured to maximize its potential to foster reflection and action based on that reflection. As was the case with Sandra, the student teacher's and cooperating teacher's schedules should include time between the sections for feedback. The student teacher should then have time to revise the lesson based on the feedback before teaching it again. For this type of student teacher/cooperating teacher relationship to work best, the cooperating teacher must have the expertise and commitment to observe the student teacher and provide constructive feedback. Yet, as Feiman-Nemser and Buchmann (1986b) note, cooperating teachers do not always have the expertise to be teacher educators. They 'need time and commitment to develop the necessary understandings, skills and orientations and schools must broaden the scope of what teachers do and what they are rewarded for to include teacher education' (p. 43).

Finally, patterns in the data lead us to speculate about the importance of an attitude of responsibility for teaching and learning, and a belief in one's control over classroom events. The student teachers differed in the extent to which they held these beliefs. Our ideological position is that the sense of empowerment associated with internal attributions and personal responsibility for classroom successes and failures is an important characteristic of effective teachers. While we did not systematically gather information about student teacher effectiveness, several sources of anecdotal evidence suggest that participants who held these beliefs were more successful student teachers than those who did not.

As one example, the researcher in Leslie's class indicated in the comments accompanying her fieldnotes that she considered the observed lessons to be rather weak. As evidence for this assessment, she noted the high level of off-task behavior in Leslie's class and the fact that Leslie did not attend to this behavior in either her actions in the classroom or her comments during the interview. Leslie also appeared unconcerned when over half of her students did not return to the classroom following a fire drill. Lana, another student teacher who expressed external attributions for classroom events, experienced difficulties the following year as a first-year teacher. As a result of these difficulties, her principal decided not to renew her contract for the next school year.

In contrast, the cooperating teacher and principal with whom Laurie worked reported to the director of the Masters Certification Program that she was one of the strongest student teachers they had encountered. Katie was hired by her principal to replace her cooperating teacher, who took a different teaching position. And, Ben's success in the traditional teacher preparation program is evidenced by his selection as the College of Education's Outstanding Graduating Senior for the Class of 1986. While by no means conclusive, these and other similar anecdotes suggest that internal attributions and personal responsibility for classroom events are related to successful teaching. The systematic investigation of this hypothesized relationship between personal responsibility and control, and success as a student teacher, is an important focus for future research. Another important question for teacher educators and researchers is how best to help student teachers develop internal attributions and personal responsibility for classroom successes and failures.

Note

1 The study was originally designed with sixteen students. However, because of tape transcription difficulties, data from four student teachers — two in elementary placements and two in secondary science — could not be analyzed.

References

BERLINER, D.C. (1987) 'Ways of thinking about students and classrooms by more and less experienced teachers', in CALDERHEAD, J. (Ed.) *Exploring Teachers' Thinking,* London, Cassell Educational Limited, pp. 60–83.
BORKO, H., LALIK, R. and TOMCHIN, E. (1987) 'Student teachers' under-

standings of successful and unsuccessful teaching', *Teaching and Teacher Education*, 3, pp. 77–90.

CALDERHEAD, J. (1984) *Teachers' Classroom Decision-making*, London, Holt, Rinehart and Winston.

FEIMAN-NEMSER, S. (1983) 'Learning to teach', in SHULMAN, L.S. and SYKES, G. (Eds) *Handbook of Teaching and Policy*, New York, Longman, pp. 150–70.

FEIMAN-NEMSER, S. and BUCHMANN, M. (1986a) 'The first year of teacher preparation: Transition to pedagogical thinking?', *Journal of Curriculum Studies*, 18, pp. 239–56.

FEIMAN-NEMSER, S. and BUCHMANN, M. (1986b) *When is Student Teaching Teacher Education?* (Research Series No. 178), East Lansing, MI, Michigan State University, Institute for Research on Teaching.

HOLSTI, O.R. (1969) *Content Analysis for the Social Sciences and Humanities*, Reading, MA, Addison-Wesley.

LEINHARDT, G. and GREENO, J.G. (1986) 'The cognitive skill of teaching', *Journal of Educational Psychology*, 78, pp. 75–95.

MCCALEB, J., BORKO, H., ARENDS, R., GARNER, R. and MAURO, L. (1987) 'Innovation in teacher education: The evolution of a program', *Journal of Teacher Education*, 38, 4, pp. 57–64.

SHULMAN, L.S. (1986) 'Those who understand: Knowledge growth in teaching', *Educational Researcher*, 15, 2, pp. 4–14.

SMITH, D.L. (1984) 'A study of teachers' curriculum planning and decision making, 1 & 2', doctoral dissertation, Sydney, University of Sydney.

TABACHNICK, B.R. and ZEICHNER, K.M. (1984) 'The impact of the student teaching experience on the development of teacher perspectives', *Journal of Teacher Education*, 35, 6, pp. 28–36.

WARNER, D.R. (1986) 'An exploratory study to identify the distinctive features of experienced teachers' thinking about teaching', doctoral dissertation, Armidale, University of New England.

WILSON, S.M., SHULMAN, L.S. and RICHERT, A.E. (1987) '150 different ways of knowing: Representations of knowledge in teaching', in CALDERHEAD, J. (Ed.), *Exploring Teachers' Thinking*, London, Cassell Educational Limited, pp. 104–24.

5   Beginning Teachers' Learning

Hugh Busher, Stephen Clarke, Laura Taggart

Our research tries to explore how beginning teachers in secondary schools learn about and make sense of their work in classrooms. This chapter describes our work and presents both general results to date and one particular study in depth.

In the hope of sharpening the focus of our research by working with teachers who were explicitly reflecting on their practices, we contacted teachers who were said to be 'effective'. The measure of 'effectiveness' was very crude, relying partly on what lecturer colleagues said of former students and partly on what teachers' schools said about who had made a 'successful start' to their teaching career. The nine teachers we observed have a range of experience of between less than one year and four years and all are still in the school in which they first gained full-time employment.

Teachers were observed with the same class on two or three occasions (though the choice of class and time of day of observation were deliberately left under the control of the teachers) and after each lesson teachers were asked for their reflections on the interactions of the classroom. Observers tried to encourage teachers to make explicit why they acted in the way they did, there being only one observer per teacher. This generated a lot of data about how teachers think about the teaching/learning process.

After the observational notes and post-lesson interviews had been transcribed, they were given back to the teachers to read through. Teachers were then interviewed, using an enriched interview, to try to elicit in more detail how they think about the interaction of the classroom.

After teachers' lessons had been observed on two or three occasions, a sample lesson was videoed. Some teachers had more than one video made of their lessons. Some, who felt that being videoed was too threatening, had none. It was hoped by this process that pupils would have become somewhat used to seeing the observer, so that the making of the recording would be less distracting to the pupils. This was another form of enriched interview.

During the course of an enriched interview the teacher was asked about how they learnt about and were helped to fit into their school. We thought that one significant aspect of beginning teachers' learning would be about their role in a school and about the constraints which expectations of a school as organization would place upon ways in which they could interact with pupils, possibly leading teachers to suffer cognitive and emotional dissonance — to borrow Festinger's (1962) concept — between idealized notions of how they would like to interact with pupils and how they were constrained to interact as a result of organizational constraints and pupil pressures. We expected that such dissonance would tend to provoke teacher reflection as they struggled to create a new entropy that more closely matched their experience of reality with their previously developed world view.

Before going on to describe how it seems that teachers think about their work, it is important to make clear the implicit and explicit conceptual frameworks of the research project. Central to this framework is the belief that teachers think in a complex manner about their work, gradually elaborating, as they progress in their careers, a theory of the teaching/learning process. This theory is constructed out of their reflections upon the disjunctions between their chosen aims, their enacted practices and the observed behaviours of other people including pupils. This overarching theoretical structure contains sub-routines, each one of which relates to the various interlocking aspects of a teacher's work.

It would be easy to place our conceptual framework within the traditions of action research. We are, after all, through participating in classroom processes, encouraging teachers to reflect on their own practices and are interested to notice what, if any, changes occur. But our intention has not been to provoke change. Whilst our understandings of teachers' approaches to their work must acknowledge the thinking of people like Elliott (1976–77) and Carr and Kemmis (1986), our research methodology does not have the same goals. We do not have the hidden messages or agendas about what to rectify or how to rectify it that McNamara (1980) complains underlies much of action research.

We cannot even claim to be naive phenomenologists, since our developing understandings of how teachers negotiate their roles with their schools and with their pupils necessarily have to take account of differences in the organizationally located power of different people and the consequent differing ability of one person to impose her or his definition of a situation upon another person. As Calderhead (1984) remarked, there are environmental aspects of a teacher's work which are completely or largely beyond the control of the teacher — such as the home background of pupils, or the configuration of the school buildings, or the headteacher's attitudes.

When we looked at the data from our cohort of teachers we found the teachers thinking about many facets of their work and hypothesising and generating theories-to-guide-action for many of these. Often these theories-to-guide-action created frameworks within which teachers could handle crises or take rapid decisions about future events.

Teachers seemed to believe that how they worked was heavily constrained by their environment, by the norms and expectations of the school, by the 'tyranny of the syllabus', and by the expectations of parents and the public about how teachers ought to teach and what pupils ought or needed to learn. In some cases, the expectations of the school were transmitted by heads of department or other more senior teachers wandering into teachers' lessons and then talking with them afterwards. As one of our teachers, Jan, put it:

> Why I know that I should be doing what I should be doing is because we actually have people come in to check on what we're doing, we have senior members of staff who come in … and walk around. And they come and check on our marking as well …

In other cases, the transmission of these expectations scarcely occurred at all, with beginning teachers being left to find their own way of relating to people in the classroom and to take advice from whoever was willing or able to help.

Teachers' theories-to-guide-action seemed to be wide ranging, but to revolve round conceptions of people. As Martin commented somewhat acidly:

> When you think about the amount of time spent [in training] on the technique of teaching your subject and yet really to get on with pupils at all, you really have to be able to handle them as people.

He went on to complain at the lack of training in communication skills for handling pupils' personal problems that he had received on his PGCE course. Jan illustrated the importance of knowing pupils individually very clearly when she said:

Depends on the individual ... I mean if Paul turns round talking, I know he hasn't got it down; Paul was one of the least able pupils in the class ... But if James did, then I'd know that he had got it down.

She went on in the course of the interview to give detailed examples of the different way in which each of the pupils in a class of twenty-three pupils behaved.

Connected with theories about the importance of understanding people were theories about managing oneself in the classroom and about self as a teacher which connect interestingly with the work of Nias (1986) on primary schools on being and becoming a teacher. Jan commented:

I ought to put in lots of effort to explain things clearly to pupils but there is a limit to what I can do — I give lower priority to pupils not taking the exam [a CSE] when several pupils need help at once.

Our teachers also seemed to be developing a theory about what is involved in the role of a teacher. This did not seem to be a normative theory about how all teachers ought to behave but rather a personal theory of how they wanted to and did act as a teacher. Christopher commented on the stress in teaching from having to be alert constantly to maintain control but also being caring about the needs of individual pupils.

It's tiring teaching ... When I'm talking to the class, if there's someone about to distract attention, I will look at him and consciously make sure he's looking at me and ... he realises that he's been caught ...

So I thought, I've got to hopefully help her, a pupil who found the work difficult ...

I'm keeping them behind 'cos you have to have home-work ... if I didn't I'd never get any books in and books would be lost.

Malcolm said about a classroom discussion that was task-focussed but somewhat noisy:

My concern was that it was uncontrolled. They couldn't do it in an orderly fashion ... the way they should have to in school.

He was worried that the pupil activity would not conform to school expectations, or even to the expectations of the subject department —

Malcolm suggested that norms varied between one area/course and another, to some extent.

As strongly emergent as the teachers' theories about people and about the role of the teacher, were theories about pupil learning. These seem to be made up of at least three interrelated strands about what is the pupil role in school, what motivates pupils to learn, and how subject knowledge can be taught efficiently in a lesson. The next two extracts refer to conceptions of what is the pupil's role. Christopher commented:

> You get two sorts; you get pupils that are actually needing help and pupils that need reassuring.

He knew which pupils fitted into which group from knowing the pupils individually and knowing their academic abilities.

Our teachers were also developing theories on what helped pupils to learn. Christopher suggested:

> Because if they don't see the relevance they don't see the point in learning and they have very little interest. That's why I chose that example ... It also put a basic concept over to them at a very simple level.
>
> If I speak quickly I don't get their attention ... and I use simple language ... 'cos they don't understand it unless I do.

Jan felt that some element of pupil control over the curriculum also helped and encouraged pupils to learn. Referring to a Maths problem:

> Whereas I might, if I'd not known that the pupils had worked it out by addition, I might have written it up as a subtraction and got into things ... which they wouldn't understand ... so we do it whatever way it works for them ... They're not going to use book methods, they're going to use whatever way they understand of solving their problems ... methods that are arithmetically correct but which seem kind of simple.

The advantages that she saw for this strategy were:

> They're more interested and they succeed.

Implicit in her notions of how people learn seem to be theories about how people should interact with each other in a learning process. She was willing to have pupils calling out answers, in the form of a class discussion, because she found it gave her immediate feedback on how the pupils were thinking and how they understood. She seemed to see learning as a cooperative venture in which she played a leading/guiding role.

Occurring in many of these theories about specific areas of classroom activity we seem to have found a repeated sub-routine that we have called a theory of repair. The theory of repair specifies how a teacher can move an interaction from an undesirable state to a more desirable state (from the teacher's point of view) and seems to have four stages:

1 The teacher has a prior criterion that defines what is acceptable pupil activity when an incident occurs.
2 The teacher manifests awareness to the pupils that they are not achieving this.
3 The teacher already knows of a range of tactics which can be applied to bring the unacceptable behaviour nearer to the chosen criterion of the first stage.
4 The teacher knows the circumstances in which particular tactics will be more or less effective.

The following example is an illustration of this. Christopher has been talking about how he gives low key reproofs to individual pupils that are focussed on that pupil and intentionally related to the task in which the pupil is supposed to be involved rather than to the pupil's personality. He believes that requests for pupil conformity to teacher-set norms are regarded by the pupils as most legitimate when the requests are connected with pupils' academic performance.

> I mean I've circulated, walked round the class. It's just being able to pick out when someone is slightly off task, I'm cueing into that straight away. Like someone turns round ... I know there's something wrong so I go across to him or her ... Ivan there would never ask me for help, he doesn't, so you have to pick up non-verbal cues that show when they can't do something. He justs lifts his head and looks around.

This theory of repair seems to be related to teacher theories of classroom control.

Other theories which our teachers were developing centred around the aims of schooling and the presentation and maintenance of authority.

One aim of our research has been to shed light on the practical value which new teachers place on their programmes of formal teacher-education, and those other sources from which they may espouse theory or on which they may uncritically model their own practices. The study of Martin, a one-time student of our department, was one of the most interesting not only because of the range and magnitude of the contradictions which he saw between his preferred aims in teaching and his actual practices, but also because he was so articulate. One of the contradictions he perceived was that although his headteacher considered him to be an effective beginning teacher, he considered himself to be a relative failure who could do nothing to resolve his problems but to work harder.

What we can learn from one case-study is limited, but it begins to shed light on the structure of the learning elements that shape the thinking of those who, new to the profession, have to bear the full responsibility for many pupils' progress.

The teaching that Martin has guided us to see and the reflections of his own critical mind on that teaching, bring into unusual clarity the contradictory nature of much that might be experienced by new teachers, who not only articulate their own dilemmas but dwell on them.

All of us experience gaps between what we hope to do and what we find ourselves doing, but in teaching, the possibilities of contradication are perhaps richer than usual, since the set of hopes that we carry into the classroom — let alone the combination of hopes and expectations — might not be composed with much internal coherence initially. Long-held notions about teaching might be overlaid by more recently acquired notions. This has not to do with a theory practice divide, but a divide, or a series of divisions, between competing theories or sets of theories. Some of these theories may look more like autobiographical assumptions than statements of systematic understandings at a principled level. In Martin's case we struck upon a rich articulation of deep assumptions which may hold the explanatory key to much of his behaviour in the classroom. It is at once an assumption *and* a highly persuasive item of theory about doing science and learning science.

Martin came into secondary school science teaching having previously been involved in a programme of university-based research that had enabled him to gain a PhD, but not to secure employment in higher education. After leaving the research programme he went to work in school for two terms before starting a PGCE course. Even then, in 1984, Martin chronicled the difficulties of teaching in the very earliest tutorials. The same difficulties were reported two years later when we went to interview him in school. These were:

[the] handling of classes in the formal situation of form teaching. I got very very poor help with [it] in any formal training sense on the PGCE course.

In his first interview, Martin tended to concentrate on what he saw as pressing practical difficulties. He felt that he had learnt little about class teaching — even though he had had a year's practice. Initially he said nothing about the part that his own subject played in his thinking. The key ideas at first seemed to be about organization, management and the ability to cope with children as strange beings — alien creatures who require a kind of tact that nobody, apparently, had trained him in.

Powerfully present also was that oft mentioned source of influence over new teachers, the expectations of the school. One would not be surprised to find that the expectations of the school, across a range of issues, had become, for Martin, both guides to action and constraints on his thinking. Martin was isolated, he said, within the school; nobody else wanted to talk about teaching and learning — they even rubbed blackboards clean lest he should see what they wrote, he said. This seems an interesting alternative conception of a common-place school policy that teachers should clean blackboards after use out of courtesy to colleagues who might want to use them next. Isolation, he felt, was an effective barrier to learning, which is why he thought that his teaching style and approach had changed very little since he began work. How he got better, how he was to improve in terms that would satisfy himself, remained puzzling. Meanwhile his view of working life led him to believe that the pupils:

get down the facts and information or whatever else it is that I've set myself as a target for them to achieve that day.

In other research, such as Russell (1986), it has been noticed that regular old hands grow sceptical at new teachers' attempts to establish open, liberal, enquiring classrooms. Martin gave no account of ever having tried and failed to do this. From the start he had wanted to fit in with the science department's philosophy (expressed in a syllabus) that so much content had to be 'done' by a certain date. His expressed attitudes certainly appeared consistent with a transmission paradigm of teaching and learning. Lessons we observed were characterized by phenomena that are consistent with a strongly subject oriented view of knowledge and learning. First of all, there were lectures delivered, usually at the start of lessons. Martin had been praised on TP for his ability to explain things in an interesting way. We speculate that this not only encouraged him to subsequently use this technique often, but it also seems to have constrained and channelled his conceptions of teaching into a transmission mode. Secondly, the subject was divided into clearly demarcated areas such as 'vitamins' or 'heat energy', as only so many lessons could be spared for any one topic. Thirdly, there was an insistance on the correct rituals — experiments had to be conducted thus or science would not be done. Fourthly, there was a high level of technical vocabulary deployed both in content material and in procedural explanations. Fifthly, those pupils whom Martin perceived to be in error were sharply reprimanded. Sixthly, question and short answer sessions were also common at the start of lessons and their function seemed to be memory tests of the previous week's contents.

If what we saw was typical of Martin's practice, then many of the lessons that he has learnt about teaching seem to have reinforced a previously conceived and subject-centred view about what science teaching ought to be like.

The crisis that arose upon coming into contact with large numbers of different classes in school was viewed by Martin as a crisis of personal limits. In the initial interview Martin saw his failures to achieve his ideal state in the classroom as having probably personal rather than professional origins. Were he to be a different sort of a person — less tense, warmer, better organized — then maybe the pupils would be keener, brighter, and more skilful when performing in the classroom.

In the enriched interviews we often saw Martin revalue the statements and actions of particular pupils, as he watched the video-recordings of his lessons. In nearly all cases this re-evaluation was upwards. He had not, during the course of the lesson, noticed how well pupils were tackling particular questions or certain aspects of the practical work. During the lessons themselves, however, we often saw a rush to judgment about individual and group actions by pupils and these judgments were evident in reproofs. That pupils did things wrong was not perceived by Martin as a function of their partial understanding so much as a reflection of failures on the teacher's part.

Where this is pointing to is to suggest that, with these levels of analysis, it would be hard to see what kinds of insight Martin could obtain that would change things for the better. Boxer's motto from *Animal Farm* 'I must work harder' could have been Martin's. Although he saw that harder work was a practical means of solving some problems, he felt himself to be up against the very limits of his own time and personal resourcefulness.

So far everything points to some very traditional forces at work in the shaping elements of Martin's learning to be a teacher. He has, from a previous career, derived status from identification with science as a subject (as a researcher); he has found work in a school that sees itself as being as closely modelled on its previous incarnation as a grammar school as possible; his TP school had a similar history to that of his present school; in his present job he is scrutinized but not supported, the internal examination system finding out how well he has taught his classes. Seemingly, then, Martin sees not too much being fundamentally wrong with the idea of teaching science in a way which creates for him the job of providing information and setting practical problems for the pupils to solve. His self-evaluation process was that if he had taught well then his pupils would reproduce the correct answers using the correct procedures.

It was only at a later stage that we discovered the complexity of Martin's background thinking as it applied to teaching in school. We have no idea yet whether giving him the opportunity to elucidate his dilemma to us will help him to solve any problems, but we were interested to note that when he saw the first video of himself teaching, he said that that was more helpful instruction than anything he had received in his PGCE year, which he didn't value very highly on a number of grounds. What we see as significant in his remark is the idea of the reflective practitioner gaining the opportunity to have a clear (uninterpreted) reflection of himself. We made no evaluations, but simply asked Martin and our other teachers for theirs.

When Martin saw the second video of himself at work, he began to get beyond previous levels of analysis — about individual pupils, for example. What emerged was the apparently extraordinary depth of his emotional attachment to the idea that doing science was creating science. Such was the intensity of his vision that even with lowish ability third year pupils he wanted to convey the idea that good science was aesthetically pleasing, and felt some kind of personal offence at seeing it done sloppily. Science was conceived by Martin as a kind of art — his word — in which aesthetically pleasing presentation of experiments and results went hand-in-hand with brilliant creative inductive thinking that handed the scientist the key to what no-one had understood before. When he had been a researcher he had had:

> the thrill, once every six months, of a feeling which people feel only once in a lifetime. I mean, the first time you fall in love, it was a bit like that, you know. The excitement, the sheer rapture of finding something that nobody else knew.

One of us asked:

Is that what you're trying to get across to the kids?

Martin replied:

Yes, but they'll never get it. I don't know why.

It is our contention that this intensity of vision about science is itself a prime cause of difficulty for Martin in the classroom. We speculate that certain aspects of Martin's approach to classroom teaching have their points of origin in these deep convictions.

In terms of looking at teacher thinking and learning, it is not so much that he teaches with great anxiety and force that concerns us, but that he is mentally locked into a conviction about science and science teaching that not only can lead a person to construct a teaching/learning model that resembles a transmission paradigm but, with certain environmental pressures of a school's expectations of teachers, does drive him to move into actually believing in and creating a transmission paradigm for his teaching that little can change at a superficial level. If Martin is to become the relaxed, effective teacher that he wants to be, then no advice about 'class handling' we think is going to get him there.

For Martin, the realization that his present deadlock — 'They'll never get it. I don't know why.' — is a productive starting point rather than a sticking point, and may be a way forward. Given that teachers construe what is going on in their classrooms from a theoretical base that is itself composed of a complex of beliefs, classroom encounters and other kinds of previous learning experiences, we might conjecture that helping them (and Martin) to cope with what they identify as difficult will, of necessity, involve them in a re-examination of their constructions to date.

Martin sees his pupils as 'difficult'. They are to him, but not in the customary sense of their being anti-social. Instead they are 'difficult' because they are not learning in what is to him the 'right way'. If Martin could come to realise that children learning through making mistakes (not getting something correct straight away) is in fact an effective learning experience rather than a personal or professional failure, he could move closer to one of his preferred aims for doing science and people becoming scientists, that of scientists being creative, theorising, experimental thinkers. This would then allow him to recognize that his conception of science is not necessarily congruent with a transmission paradigm of the teaching/learning process.

It is at this point that we face a difficulty methodologically. How do we encourage a re-examination without imposing a particular analysis? It would be tempting and easy to suggest to Martin our own view of why he is not the teacher that he wants to be, that we think that he needs to look more carefully at the learning attempts made by his pupils and mind far less that these attempts do not resemble the work of what he sees as serious scientists. To do this would be to remove from him the control of the agenda for his self-evaluation and to impose our own, presumably based upon some claim to expertise that may only be supported by our perceived status. Should we not be encouraging teachers to reflect on their experiences according to their own agenda in order to reconstruct their theories of action so that their perceptions of reality more closely match their own preferred paradigms? We are unsure what are the relationships between Martin's deeply held convictions and particular actions of his in the classsroom. We are unsure, too, of how best to help. On the evidence so far, we are encouraged in the belief that bringing to sharper consciousness aspects of his own thinking is a productive way forward. This approach may be as helpful to other beginning teachers trying to come to grips with their dilemmas as any other strategy that has been tried. Devices, such as video-recordings can act like questioning mirrors to allow teachers to face their own practices and other people's reactions to them through their own thought frameworks. It is a long way from the 'firm but fair' advice given by experienced teachers to raw beginners or from the invitation instanced by Martin, to a tea and sympathy chat about 'difficult' pupils. Reflective minds need un-clouded mirrors to encourage them to cope with the complexities of being active thinkers. Institutional programmes of help that recognize the complexity and individuality of teachers are long overdue.

Acknowledgement

This research was supported by funding from the School of Education, University of Leeds.

References

CALDERHEAD, J. (1984) *Teachers' Classroom Decision Making*, London, Holt, Rinehart and Winston.
CARR, W. and KEMMIS, S. (1986) *Becoming Critical: Education, Knowledge and Action Research*, Lewes, Sussex, Falmer Press.
ELLIOTT, J. (1976–77) 'Developing hypotheses about classrooms from

teachers' practical constructs: An account of the Ford Teaching Project',
Interchange, 7, 2.

FESTINGER, L. (1962) *A Theory of Cognitive Dissonance*, Stanford, CA, Stanford University Press.

McNAMARA, D. (1980) 'The outsider's arrogance: The failure of participant observers to understand classroom events', *British Educational Research Journal*, 6 (2), pp. 113–126.

NIAS, J. (1986) 'What is it to "feel like a teacher"?: The subjective reality of primary teaching', paper presented at the annual meeting of the British Educational Research Association, Bristol, September.

ORWELL, G. (1945) *Animal Farm*, London, Secker & Warburg.

RUSSELL, T. (1986) 'Beginning teachers' development of knowledge-in-action', paper presented at the annual meeting of the American Educational Research Association, San Francisco, April.

6 Designing a Teacher Education Curriculum from Research and Theory on Teacher Knowledge

Donald McIntyre

Introduction

This chapter is about a new PGCE programme at the University of Oxford. It seeks to outline and explain some of the ideas which have informed the planning of that programme. It is not intended, however, that this chapter should offer a comprehensive account of the programme or of the thinking which has shaped it: many important aspects of the programme are not discussed. What this chapter does attempt to do is to explain how the design of the new programme has been influenced by research-based thinking about teacher education.

The starting points for this account are two papers which happened to be published in the same volume in 1980. In the first of these, Harry Judge, then and now Director of the University of Oxford Department of Educational Studies (OUDES), argued that

> talk about attempts to professionalize teacher training conceals an ambiguity. There are two very different senses in which teacher training might in principle be rendered more professional, and the tension between these two senses and the policies in which they issue has become painfully obvious in the recent past. (p. 342)

On one hand, the aim of achieving professional status for teaching might most plausibly be attained by establishing professional schools in universities and by making entry to teaching dependent on academic study in these schools. On the other, the aim of ensuring the practical competence of entrants to the profession led to pressure for their training to be largely in the hands of practising teachers.

Judge argued, however, that university departments of education could do much to resolve this tension if they were both to give a high priority to their research and scholarly activities and also to demonstrate that

> they take seriously the practice of education and respect the practitioner. (*Ibid*, p. 347)

Furthermore,

> any school of education can demonstrate the sincerity of its respect for the practitioner by committing major tasks of training to him

and, as to their own reputation and credibility,

> schools of education will flourish by being scholarly, to be sure, but their scholarship must be related to the improvement of practice in the schools. (*Ibid*, p. 348)

It was no doubt this sense of university departments' obligation, need and power to resolve the ambiguity between the two senses of 'professionalizing teacher education' that led Judge to devise a new framework for the Oxford PGCE programme. By June 1985 he had persuaded Oxfordshire LEA and secondary headteachers of the desirability of this scheme; and they had agreed that twelve teachers would be seconded on a full-time basis during the 1986/87 session to collaborate with university staff in developing this new programme, so that it could be initially implemented from September 1987.

The scheme, as it will in practice operate, involves fifteen Oxfordshire secondary schools in immediate partnership with OUDES. It is not, however, an exclusive scheme, since the department sees its partnership as being with all Oxfordshire secondary schools which wish to be involved. It is expected that every few years some schools will drop out for a while to be replaced by others.

Those learning to teach are each involved in the work of one of these schools and of one subject department in it, throughout their training year. We signal the different position that this puts them in by calling them not students but INTERNS. One purpose of this arrangement is that interns should become thoroughly acquainted with the policies and practices of the schools and departments they are in, and also with classes and individual pupils. This, we believe, is the best way for them to acquire a contextualized understanding of the realities of teaching. This arrangement also makes it possible for one experienced teacher, called a MENTOR, to coordinate the classroom related learning experiences of each intern throughout the year. Mentors can give interns the protection and detailed guidance which they generally need at the early stages; and, as the year goes on, they can judge how to increase the responsibilities to be given to individual interns both so that they as learners can benefit and so that they can contribute to the work of the departments.

The 150 interns are attached to one or other of the fifteen schools, with a minimum of eight and a maximum of fourteen interns in each school. The interns in a school are in subject pairs, with each pair attached to a mentor in the relevant subject department. Within each school a member of staff is designated as the PROFESSIONAL TUTOR who has a coordinating responsibility for the full group of interns within the school. Attached to each school is a GENERAL TUTOR, a member of the OUDES staff responsible, in consultation with the professional tutor, for coordinating the work of the interns in that school and for those aspects of their work not directly related to classroom teaching. Interns' study and practice of classroom teaching are dealt with on a subject basis, with CURRICULUM TUTORS being responsible for the university-based aspects of the work and for coordinating the work of interns and mentors across schools.

The internship year starts with a brief orientation phase, but from October until the end of June interns spend two days of every week in their schools, except for a nine week period in the late spring when they are full time in their schools.

That, then, was the kind of framework initially negotiated; and it was a framework which gave scope for radical new initiatives which would not have been possible under the old system. Most centrally, the fact that interns were to be in schools and in the university on most weeks made a coherently integrated school-university programme quite feasible; and the relatively small number of schools and departments involved meant that programmes could be realistically planned and coordinated by subject teams of curriculum tutors and mentors, and by school teams of general and professional tutors and mentors.

What had yet to be decided, however, was the kind of programme that was wanted and, more fundamentally, the conception of teacher education which should inform it. The given framework was well suited to a number of very different approaches. For example, there could be strong arguments for a properly planned apprenticeship approach, with mentors as master-teachers and with day-release classes to fill in the broader and more theoretical background to teaching. In contrast, the very considerable strengths of the existing programme could be consolidated, with the new framework providing opportunities for it to be done much more effectively. That is, ideas of good practice could be presented, explained and justified at the university, with the interns then being sent into the schools to recognize these ideas being implemented by experienced teachers and to practise using these ideas themselves. Or the new structure could be used for an IT-INSET approach, with the curriculum tutor leading both interns and mentors in the exploration of new pedagogical and curricular ideas. There were many possibilities.

The primary purpose of this chapter is to explain the general approach which was decided upon by the staff of OUDES and endorsed by the collaborating Oxfordshire schools and teachers; and to offer, on the basis of research into teaching and teacher education, a rationale for this kind of approach.

An early version of the kind of approach adopted was outlined in the second of the two 1980 papers mentioned above. The remit of that earlier paper (McIntyre, 1980) was to consider what contribution research could make to quality in teacher education generally, not to think about the planning of a specific programme; and so the ideas outlined were of a schematic uncontextualised kind. These ideas have been well summarized by Alexander (1984) as follows:

> ... Learning to teach must be a continual process of hypothesis testing framed by detailed analysis of the values and practical constraints fundamental to teaching. The 'theory' for teacher education should therefore incorporate (i) speculative theory (ii) the findings of empirical research (iii) the craft knowledge of practising teachers, but none should be presented as having prescriptive implications for practice: instead, students should be encouraged to approach their own practice with the intention of testing hypothetical principles drawn from the consideration of these different types of knowledge. (p. 146)

Alexander characterized this approach as stage 7 in a seven-stage evolution which he discerned in the development over the last century of thinking about a theoretical basis for teaching in teacher education; but he rightly described this stage as one which remains a possibility rather than an actuality. It is this 'possible' approach which is being developed, tested and perfected in actuality in the new Oxford programme.

Before the main ideas of this programme can properly be explained, however, it is necessary to rehearse, re-examine and update some of the research-based thinking which can inform and justify these programmatic ideas.

Implications of Research for Teacher Education

Knowledge about Teaching

The question to be asked here is about the nature and quality of different kinds of knowledge which may be available for initial teacher education. In 1980, I concluded that

> there is not, nor can there be, *any* systematic corpus of theoretical knowledge from which prescriptive principles for teaching can be generated. (p. 296)

Classroom research, and especially research of a process-product kind, had demonstrated clearly that prescriptive generalizations about teaching *not* based on the study of classrooms, whatever their source, were dangerously untrustworthy. Such research had not, however, itself produced a body of knowledge which could be used to generate such prescriptive principles.

As Brophy and Good (1986), for example, demonstrate, there has in recent years been a great deal of valuable knowledge gained through process-product studies of high quality; and the coherence, quantity and quality of this knowledge is certainly such that it could not responsibly be ignored in initial teacher education. Nonetheless, my 1980 assertion remains valid, and on the same grounds. First, such process-product research is necessarily ideologically committed in its choice of process variables and, more especially, its choice of product variables; and this inevitably selective commitment is clearly reflected in the available research findings. Thus to use these findings as a basis for prescriptions about teaching would be to beg fundamental educational questions. Second, it is difficult to envisage ways in which such quantitative and comparative research can become sufficiently subtle and sensitive to take account of issues of the appropriateness of teacher actions to the specific situations and needs for which they are taken, or of the ways in which teachers generate these specific actions. Third, and most important, questions about the generalizability of findings across cultures and contexts, and the need to take account of so many possibly interacting variables, such as subject area and pupil characteristics, make unreasonable any aspiration to generate a scientific body of knowledge which student-teachers might be asked to apply in their teaching. Thus, for example, virtually all worthwhile process-product findings are either from outside Britain or relate to the primary age group: these findings *may* be highly relevant to teaching in British secondary schools, but this cannot be taken for granted.

If then we cannot rely on any systematic body of research-based prescriptive knowledge about teaching, what other kinds of knowledge about teaching are available for use in teacher education? In the 1980 paper, I referred with some enthusiasm to the aspirations of McNamara and Desforges (1978) to help student teachers to gain access to experienced teachers' craft knowledge. Their attempts to do this were apparently disappointing but since then Sally Brown and I have ourselves been engaged in a similar attempt in Scotland (Brown and McIntyre, 1986). In view of the difficulties encountered by McNamara and Desforges, we have approached the task much more slowly and cautiously. We have found that, if the agenda is clearly focussed on a particular observed sequence of teaching, if it also is concerned only with what the teacher views as the successful aspects of that teaching, and if the teacher is encouraged and helped by a skilled, sympathetic and mature researcher, many teachers — possibly most — are able to make explicit some of the very sophisticated thinking which is involved in their everyday teaching but which is usually only semi-conscious and not articulated. What teachers have been able to tell us has often surprised and excited them as much as it has excited us.

This research has convinced us that there is indeed a kind of knowledge about teaching which could be of great value to beginning teachers but which is not normally accessible to them. Amy McAlpine in Scotland and Hazel Hagger at Oxford are currently working with us to establish effective ways of helping student-teachers or interns to gain access to such knowledge, something which is not at all easy for them.

Intermediate between the objectified knowledge about teaching of the process-product researcher and the knowledge which is implicit in the teacher's classroom craft, there is, of course, a great deal of knowledge about teaching upon which teacher education can draw. There is in particular, the knowledge, common sense and wisdom of teachers and teacher educators.

The important thing which research can tell us about this kind of knowledge is that what concerns people, and therefore what they can talk most fluently and informatively about, tends to depend heavily on the position which they occupy. The wisdom of curriculum developers, advisers, inspectors and teacher educators tends to be concentrated upon understandings of good practice. These understandings draw on many sources, including their personal experience, their knowledge of what is happening elsewhere, and judicious 'raiding the disciplines' (Hirst, 1979) to help in developing, clarifying and justifying practical ideas.

In contrast, the wisdom of practising teachers tends to be focussed on issues of practicality, including organizational and resource constraints, the problems of time and expertise necessary to cope with the demands upon them, and especially to cope with suggested innovations. Practising teachers also very clearly depend upon and have available large amounts of knowledge about their specific contexts, including resources, organizational procedures, syllabuses and examination requirements, and especially the individual pupils whom they teach.

In planning a teacher education curriculum, then, there are several kinds of knowledge about teaching which can be made available to beginning teachers, each with their strengths and limitations. To decide what use to make of these different kinds of knowledge it is sensible to attend first to evidence about the knowledge which beginning teachers bring with them and to the ways in which they develop that knowledge.

Acquiring Knowledge about Teaching

In my 1980 paper I suggested that a crucial contribution of research to the planning of teacher education should be through the understanding it could provide of student-teachers' own ways of thinking about teaching, of the ways in which they coped with the demands upon them and of the ways in which their ideas about teaching developed. In essence I was saying that the agendas of the learner-teachers are the major determinants of what they learn; it is only through influencing these agendas and through responding to them that teacher educators can achieve their goals.

To exemplify such research I referred to the two best examples of it that I knew, that of Lacey (1977) and that of Macleod (reported in McIntyre, Macleod and Griffiths, 1977). Macleod's work showed how student-teachers in a microteaching context depended heavily on their own repertoires of concepts and criteria for construing and evaluating their teaching, only very gradually over time incorporating the concepts in terms of which they were being taught about teaching. It showed how they (like experienced teachers) evaluated their teaching primarily in terms of pupils' classroom activities, how they perceived their own behaviour quite accurately, and how they typically used hypotheses based on perceptions and evaluations of one lesson to guide their behaviour in the next. Macleod himself emphasized not only that the student-teachers had their own agendas, but even more that they approached the task of learning to teach with a high level of rationality.

Earlier research at Stirling had shown students' eagerness in the microteaching context to have as many different kinds of information as possible about their teaching; they were confident that they could select and use the information they needed. More recent research there has emphasized even more strongly the elaborate nature of the repertoires for thinking about teaching with which student-teachers start their courses, and the considerable, complex and continuing influence which these repertoires exert over their constructions and evaluations of their own teaching.

Lacey described, among other things, the various coping strategies which student-teachers used in relation to teaching practice, such as keeping their problems as much as possible to themselves lest they be judged inadequate, and displacing the blame for their apparent failures on to the system or the unsatisfactory pupils. One thing which I completely missed in 1980 was the extreme contrast between these defensive avoidance strategies and the rational attempts to learn about teaching which Macleod reported. Macleod even found that negative self evaluations in a lesson, far from being a cause for escapism, were highly correlated with the degree of success achieved in the following lesson in achieving the kind of interaction sought.

One has to be cautious in interpreting this contrast, but it seems at least plausible to suggest that the confident rationality of Macleod's students was due to the protected and simplified environment in which they were teaching, while in contrast the defensive escapism of Lacey's students was due to their exposed situations.

What I conclude then from our limited knowledge about how people learn to teach is, first, that they have their own extensive repertoires and their own agendas; and that we as teacher educators, if we are realistic, need to accept that we can only help them in their efforts, not define the enterprise in which they are engaged. Second, I conclude that even if we did believe that we had 'the answers', reliable knowledge about how best to teach, student-teachers would not accept it but would want to test it for themselves in various ways; we can probably exert more influence by encouraging this process of testing than by pretending it is not necessary. And third, we can have some confidence that if we do not put student-teachers into situations which overwhelm or seriously threaten them, we have good reason to believe that they will explore the problems of teaching with a high degree of objectivity about their own performances and rationality in their investigations.

Research into Problems of Teacher Education

Finally, in thinking about the research foundations for a new teacher education programme, I want simply to list some of the endemic problems which research has revealed within traditional forms of PGCE programmes:

(i) that student-teachers frequently find the 'educational theorizing' they encounter in their courses irrelevant to the practical tasks which confront them in schools;

(ii) that student-teachers sometimes find little opportunity or support in the schools for trying out even the practical advice they have been given in their courses;

(iii) that student-teachers generally do not learn much, although there is a great deal to be learned, from their observation of the practice of experienced teachers. This is because the student-teachers do not know what to look for and because the teachers often do not recognize how much there is to be learned from their own teaching;

(iv) that student-teachers frequently observe a wide range of practice in schools, and are not generally helped to subject this range to critical examination, and to understand the factors and considerations which shape it;

(v) that there is great variation in the extent to which supervising teachers are able to conduct systematic diagnostic appraisals of student-teachers' teaching or to conduct coherent and helpful discussions about their teaching;

(vi) that visiting tutors may have insufficient recent school experience to provide credible assistance, in that context, to student-teachers;

(vii) that visiting tutors, although generally seen as authoritative assessors, cannot visit student-teachers sufficiently often for their visits to be much more than tests for the student teachers to pass, sometimes with the collusion of the school staff;

(viii)   that student-teachers learn to view their situation as one of needing to meet the different criteria of school staff and of university tutors. They learn to meet these different criteria by applying them on different occasions and in different kinds of context;

(ix)   that a great deal of student-teachers' learning about teaching is at a level of semi-conscious trial and error learning, with 'correct' responses being shaped and reinforced by rewards and punishments from pupils. In consequence their patterns of teaching behaviour are not generally easily accessible to their awareness for critical examination;

(x)   that student-teachers' habits of scholarly reflection are not generally extended beyond the academic contexts of the university. In relation to their teaching work they learn markedly different habits of decision-making and self assessment. An example of this is that the short time-scale decision making required of a good teacher does not match the detailed examination of all the data that has been required of them as university students;

(xi)   that the developing agenda of concerns of each individual student-teacher is not necessarily closely related to the official and non-individualized agenda of the teacher education programme;

(xii)   that the criteria for the assessment of student-teachers' teaching competence and of their professional knowledge and understanding often lack clarity and may appear to be insufficiently related to one another.

Implications for Teacher Education

What then do these research-based understandings suggest we should be doing in teacher education? And in particular, how did they suggest we should make use of the collaborative framework which had been agreed for the new Oxford course?

Perhaps the most difficult implication to accept is the need to recognize that, whether we like it or not, interns will make their own judgments about what matters in teaching and about how best they can teach. Our long-term influence upon them can be greatest not so much by trying to persuade them of the merits of various practices but rather by helping them to make their judgments rationally and realistically.

The most fundamental way in which we can help them to do this is by giving them the kind of security which they greatly need in their early attempts at teaching in schools, and which they usually lack on traditional teaching practice. We can do this in various ways, for example:

(i) by trying to ensure that each of them has a secure personal relationship with a mentor;

(ii) by them being accepted in departments not as fleeting visitors but as members of these departments for the whole school year;

(iii) by them each having another intern with whom to share their responsibilities and problems;

(iv) by initially giving them only very limited teaching tasks in lessons for which their mentors take overall responsibility, very gradually increasing their shared and individual responsibilities towards those of probationer teachers. The pace at which such demands increase can vary according to the perceived needs of individuals and of pairs;

(v) by giving them structured support in the university — as the core of their university course — for the tasks which they are asked to undertake in the schools, through a jointly planned programme which carefully matches school and university tasks;

(vi) by giving them a clear indication of the range of teaching abilities they are expected to acquire, as a set of goals to structure their work in the earlier part of the year; these abilities being defined in terms of the tasks which face one in teaching, not in terms of behaviours which must be demonstrated;

(vii) by giving them effective diagnostic feedback in relation to these specified teaching abilities.

Security is probably a necessary condition if interns are to accept our help in approaching the task of learning to teach in a realistic, rational and exploratory way. It is certainly not a sufficient condition. Another important condition is that we should make it clear that, while there is a great deal of valuable knowledge available which they are likely to find very useful, the status of that knowledge, whatever its source, must be tentative. The problem here would not seem to be with what the interns will generally be inclined to do: most of them will not only be eager to pick up ideas but also will want to try these ideas out critically for themselves. The problem is rather one of ensuring that the interns understand that this is also the official agenda, endorsed and encouraged both by their mentors in the schools and by their tutors in the university. It will be only in so far as they are convinced of this that they will feel able to let us help them in their testing of our own and of each other's ideas.

Given such a shared understanding, the integrated school-university curriculum can and should be one of the explicit generation and testing of hypotheses, most typically hypotheses about what can be achieved by acting in given kinds of ways in given types of situations. Such hypotheses for testing should come to interns from various sources, including their own preconceptions about teaching, the techniques and approaches they see their mentors and other teachers adopting, and ideas suggested by their tutors and by their reading. During the early months of the year, however, so as not to undermine their sense of security, they should mostly be working to a quite carefully planned agenda within which mentors' and curriculum tutors' hypotheses substantially overlap.

Critically important in enabling interns to maintain an active and rational exploration of the tasks of teaching is the need to help them to come to terms with the different perspectives which they will inevitably encounter in schools and in the university. To some extent these differences in perspective will reflect ideological or theoretical differences among teachers and tutors; but there will also be differences in perspective which primarily reflect the different institutional positions and roles which people occupy, and the different priorities which follow from these. Thus it will for example be important for interns to reflect on how their own current perspectives have been shaped by their personal histories and especially by their temporary roles as interns. Especially important too, if we are to avoid them developing two different agendas, one for the university and one for the school, is the need to enable them to appreciate the contrasting perspectives to be expected from these two institutional positions.

We can do this by persuading them of the need to test suggested ideas and practices against a variety of criteria. These criteria should include some which reflect dominant perspectives in schools, and which can most easily be applied in schools: these might include the *feasibility* of adopting a particular approach (taking account of time, resources, and the intern's present skills, for example), the *acceptability* of the approach to colleagues, pupils and others, and the effectiveness of the approach in achieving its immediate purposes within that specific context. But there should be other criteria which reflect perspectives which are (and should be) dominant within the university department. These might include criteria of the *intellectual clarity and coherence* of the theory underlying the proposed approach, the *educational values* implicit in it, and its general effectiveness in achieving its intended purposes as reflected in research evidence.

If interns are to begin their professional careers without experiencing incompatible pressures from the university and from the schools and without thinking in terms of a crude and disabling distinction between theory and practice, we must enable them to see that the inevitably different messages which they will sometimes receive from university and school sources are not necessarily opposed. This can be done by helping them to discover that educationally valuable and effective practices which may be followed in certain circumstances may not be effective, or acceptable, or even feasible in other circumstances; and that practices which embody less ambitious educational values may have the merit that they can be implemented effectively in a wider range of circumstances. Interns, then, have to test ideas against the several criteria emphasized in each of the university and the school contexts, and they have to be encouraged and helped to reach their own tentative syntheses of the different perspectives.

If this is to happen, it is of course necessary that mentors and curriculum tutors should be seen to be collaborating in helping interns to test ideas, and this is especially important when the mentors and curriculum tutors may disagree about the ideas. Thus curriculum tutors can most effectively foster such collaboration by showing their concern for practicality criteria, by recognizing that these criteria can most effectively be applied through observation, discussion and direct personal experience in the schools, and by stressing that it is the ideas emanating from their own work with interns in the university which most need to be tested against such criteria; but at the same time they need to assert the pervasive relevance of the broader, more general and more analytic criteria which they themselves are well placed to help interns to apply. Similarly, mentors can most effectively foster the collaboration by both asserting the importance of their own practical and contextualized concerns and also explicitly recognizing that it is those ideas which interns learn through working with them in the schools that most need to be tested against the criteria emphasized in the university.

Given this concern with the testing of ideas, it hardly needs to be said that the content of a programme based on such thinking will consist primarily of ideas which the interns can test for themselves against the various suggested criteria. Application of such varied criteria of course involves very different kinds of activity, including observing, discussing, reading and reflecting. Interns, however, will quite properly give precedence to those ideas which can be tested, and those criteria which can be applied, through their own attempts at teaching. That is important, because the primary goal of the programme must be that interns should learn to teach competently. Fortunately, that need not imply the trial and error, untheorized, unreflecting process which has often characterized learning to teach in the past. On the contrary, the testing of hypothetically practical and effective procedures and the acquisition of skills can and should be closely interdependent: especially in the early stages, skill acquisition is most effective when learners seek, and are helped, carefully to analyze both the nature and the effects of their actions; on the other hand, hypothetically effective approaches to teaching can be adequately tested only when interns have acquired some fluency in using them; and finally, a characteristic of professional skilfulness is surely that the professional, even when her or his skills have become automatic, understands the nature and implications of these skills and is therefore well placed to examine, and where necessary to modify or develop, these skills.

The need to give primary importance to interns' attainment of a basic competence in classroom teaching results both from our obligation as teacher educators to ensure that this is so and also from the need discussed earlier to offer interns a secure learning environment. In their new professional contexts many interns will need to be convinced that they are competent as teachers and are recognized as being competent before they will have the sense of security necessary to examine their teaching objectively and openly in relation to their own aspirations as educators. It is therefore necessary that during the earlier part of the year, interns' investigations of teaching should be concerned primarily with finding effective ways of doing things that are specified in advance as necessary aspects of competent teaching, and that the hypotheses suggested to them by mentors and tutors should mainly be concerned with such aspects of competent teaching and should largely overlap.

However, as interns' confidence and competence develops during the year, the emphasis should shift towards more wide-ranging and more individualized investigations of teaching, with interns beginning to articulate the kinds of teachers they want to be, to investigate ways of realizing these aspirations, and to acquire the abilities needed to evaluate their own teaching. An adequate preparation for professional teaching must both enable interns to cope effectively with the heavy demands implicit in fulfilling their classroom roles adequately, and it must also provide at least the foundations of the skills and habits needed for examining, analyzing and, where appropriate, deliberately modifying their established patterns of teaching.

Practical Implementation of the General Ideas

As was indicated at the start of this chapter, the ideas that have been outlined above provide only a partial account of those that have shaped the Oxford programme. Some ideas that have been very important in the construction of the programme, such as those relating the classroom teaching of subjects to more general aspects of secondary school work, have not been considered here at all. Furthermore the ideas which have been discussed have been presented at a very general and abstract level. Clearly, a great deal of further thought and decision-making was necessary before these ideas could be realized in the practice of the programme.

Detailed planning, in preparation for the initial implementation of the programme from September 1987, has taken three main forms. First, planning groups of tutors and teachers for each curriculum area have met regularly over an eighteen-month period, as have cross-curricular planning groups more recently, to plan the integrated university-based and school-based curricula for these areas. As the mentors and professional tutors who are to be involved in implementing the programme have been identified, they have been included in these planning groups. Second, a Development Group was established, consisting of twelve experienced Oxfordshire teachers seconded for the 1986/87 year and coordinated by Anna Pendry, who until then had been an Associate Tutor working half-time as a teacher in a local comprehensive school and half-time as a curriculum tutor. The Development Group accepted a remit to explore and to provide guidance to the planning groups on how, if at all, various proposed innovative ideas might feasibly and usefully be incorporated in the programme. Third, there have been regular plenary meetings of various groups to examine, develop and achieve shared understandings of what the new programme was to involve. From the earliest stages, the OUDES's professional advisory body has met regularly to examine and to endorse successive developments in the planning; especially during the 1985/86 year, there were frequent meetings of the OUDES staff as the basic ideas were worked out; during 1986/87, these tended to be replaced by joint meetings of OUDES staff and the Development Group; and as final plans have gradually been elaborated, there have been meetings of all mentors and tutors, together with headteachers and Oxfordshire advisers, culminating in a weekend conference in July 1987 at which plans for the coming year were approved.

In relation to the concerns of this chapter, it is the work of the Development Group which is of greatest significance. It is they more than anyone who have developed the ideas outlined above to form practical plans and who have gone on to test these ideas, mostly through action-research projects. Fortunately they have on the whole concluded that these ideas are indeed viable and potentially useful.

A collection of papers reporting the work of the Development Group is being prepared for publication; all that is possible here is to indicate briefly the nature of the questions they have been investigating. Five members of the group have tackled the central issue of the feasibility and effectiveness of an approach emphasizing the provision of knowledge of different kinds from different sources and perspectives, and especially the testing of received ideas against various criteria in school and university contexts. Each of them did so in the context of a different curriculum area, focussing on one or more exemplary topics: the use of problem-solving in science teaching; the teaching of controversial issues in history; the development of pupils' oral skills in English; the use of different teaching styles (and other topics) in mathematics; and provision for special needs as a cross-curricular issue.

Each of these topics is appropriately included in the predetermined curriculum for all interns, or all those preparing to teach in a particular subject area. Typically these topics are introduced and elaborated through discussion and reading in the university context before other perspectives are introduced and critical questions asked in both university and school contexts. There are, however, other issues which cannot be planned for as common to all interns, either because they arise as distinctive concerns or problems of the individual interns, or because they arise out of what interns observe, hear, or otherwise experience in the particular school or school department in which they are placed. Effective partnership among tutors, mentors and interns will imply responsiveness to these relatively unpredictable issues as well as implementation of the common pre-planned programme; and four members of the Development Group engaged in action research to investigate aspects of this need.

One of these investigations was concerned with how interns can most effectively gain access to and use the professional craft knowledge being used by teachers they observe. A second was focussed on the interns' own teaching and on the feasibility and value of the kind of non-judgmental structured analytic discussion of it which has elsewhere been described as 'clinical supervision' or 'partnership supervision'. A third examined the problems and possibilities for mentors in supervising and collaborating with a pair of interns. And the fourth investigated the task of a mentor as manager of the diverse kinds of learning experiences sought for interns within the school subject department, including the tasks of recruiting the help of colleagues and coordinating their contributions.

Three members of the Development Group investigated issues which could better be examined by surveys rather than in the first instance through action research. One of these sought to establish the extent and nature of any consensus among OUDES tutors and Oxfordshire teachers with regard to the teaching abilities which it was most essential for interns to acquire. Another similarly examined what consensus if any there was on lesson planning practices and how student-teachers' own ideas and practices developed during their PGCE year. And the final investigation concerned the crucial role of professional tutor, who is expected both to coordinate the programme as a whole in each school and to play a major part in interns' professional education concerning whole-school issues: the survey sought, from professional tutors and others in the schools, descriptions of existing responsibilities, perceptions of good practice and expectations for the role within the new scheme.

It has been possible, then, as a result of these twelve investigations, to give appropriate shape to the abstract research-based ideas for the programme that were described earlier. There is, of course, no guarantee that all the proposed practices will be viable on a larger scale, nor that they will be fully effective in achieving the hoped for results. What can be claimed, however, is that it is a programme directed towards clear goals and based upon a theoretical understanding of research evidence. As well as being a useful programme for the interns who follow it, it should be a useful programme to study.

References

ALEXANDER, R.J. (1984) 'Innovation and continuity in the initial teacher education curriculum', in ALEXANDER, R.J., CRAFT, M. and LYNCH, J. (Eds) *Change in Teacher Education: Context and Provision Since Robbins*, London, Holt, Rinehart and Winston, pp. 103–60.

BROPHY, J.E. and GOOD, T.L. (1986) 'Teacher behaviour and student achievement' in WITTROCK, M.C. (Ed.) *Handbook of Research on Teaching, Third Edition*, New York, Macmillan Publishing Company, pp. 328–75.

BROWN, S. and McINTYRE, D. (1986) 'How do teachers think about their craft? in BEN-PERETZ, M., BROMME, R. and HALKES, R. (Eds) *Advances of Research on Teacher Thinking*, Lisse, ISATT and Swets and Zeitlinger B.V., pp. 36–44.

HIRST, P.H. (1979) 'Professional studies in initial teacher education: Some conceptual issues' in ALEXANDER, R.J. and WORMALD, E. (Eds) *Professional Studies for Teaching*, Guildford, SRHE, pp. 15–27.

JUDGE, H. (1980) 'Teaching and professionalization: An essay in ambiguity', in HOYLE, E. and MEGARRY, J. (Eds) *World Yearbook of Education 1980: Professional Development of Teachers*, London, Kogan Page, pp. 340–9.

LACEY, C. (1977) *The Socialization of Teachers*, London, Methuen.

McINTYRE, D. (1980) 'The contribution of research to quality in teacher education', in HOYLE, E. and MEGARRY, J. (Eds) *World Yearbook of Education 1980: Professional Development of Teachers*, London, Kogan Page, pp. 293–307.

McINTYRE, D., MACLEOD, G. and GRIFFITHS, R. (1977) *Investigations of Micro-teaching*, London, Croom Helm.

McNAMARA, D. and DESFORGES, C. (1978) 'The social sciences, teacher education, and the objectification of craft knowledge', *British Journal of Teacher Education*, 4, 1, pp. 17–36.

7   Expert Systems and Understanding Teacher Education and Practice

Sharon Wood

Introduction

The Expert Systems in Teacher Education project has focussed on the nature of advice given to trainee teachers concerning their classroom practice, especially the experienced teacher's knowledge regarding classroom teaching which underlies the advice given to trainees. We have set about formalizing this knowledge explicitly so that it may form the basis of a computer-based advisory system for trainee teachers — the Trainee Teacher Support System (TTSS) — for providing guidance on their lesson practice.

Our work is couched within the framework of seeing the teacher as a reflective practitioner, someone who thinks over her teaching practice, aims and objectives in an effort to improve upon them. The typical scenario between trainee and teacher tutor is one of building on the trainee's own experiences in the classroom. The purpose in building a computer-based advisory system might first and foremost be seen as slotting into this pedagogical context as a tool for prompting reflection upon the trainee's classroom teaching experience.

Through this reflection, we hope to deepen the trainee teacher's understanding of the mechanisms by which desired classroom situations may be achieved and others avoided; to fill out her understanding of the relationships between what she does, different classroom contexts, and what she hopes to achieve. We do this within a framework of explicating a model of classroom processes in the context of analysing the trainee's individual problems arising from classroom teaching practice.

In taking this approach, we are aware that the trainee often equates effective teaching with classroom control and therefore tends to assume that once control is achieved, there is little more to be done in the quest for effective teaching. To some extent this is clearly true; a happy and well-motivated class will be easier to control, and to some extent achieving this state of affairs will depend upon the pupils' experience of learning and achievement. However, we are also keen to provide a context within which the trainee might investigate how they could improve upon their teaching *per se*. Through the framework of analysis we have adopted we seek to support progression from straightforward classroom management to ways in which the trainee might improve upon her teaching methods.

The Context of Advice Giving

Trainee teachers usually receive advice about their lesson practice in the context of discussing some particular classroom experience — an event, perhaps, which troubles them. The teacher tutor will usually seek further information about the context of the situation then provide advice on how to deal with or avoid it, and explain why the problem may have arisen. For instance, in the excerpt below a student is having problems with a class's lack of incentive for a lesson. Although it is wise for the student to be clear about what she is hoping to achieve, the need to convey this to the pupils is emphasized, expressing the pupils' need to know why they are doing things and for them to have an interest in the work.

> *Trainee:* ... I had problems starting the lesson ... they want to know why they should do it ...
>
> *Teacher-Tutor:* ... it's a good idea to start by recapping on previous lessons. Outline the course and tell them the aims of the course. Also breaking down the lesson gives you confidence; knowing why you're doing what you're doing helps if you're worried about getting started. It can help in starting lessons if you can give them a reason why you're doing it; they may rather be doing something else, so you must explain aims and where the course is going. Pupils have high expectations in humanities for the lesson to be interesting. (Wood, 1984, p. 5)

In order to advise students appropriately, the teacher tutor often needs to go beyond the superficial characteristics of a situation in order to analyze what led to a particular situation arising in the first place. For instance, an uncontrolled class might either be bored with the activity or simply not aware of what the teacher wants it to do. Information about the circumstances under which the situation arose might indicate that the pupils had been working well until there had been a change in what they were expected to do. Or one might discover that the class had been occupied with the same activity for the past half hour and were becoming progressively more uninterested. In the one case, appropriate advice might be to give better explanations to the pupils about what they are meant to be doing and to be sure that they are aware when the lesson is meant to be moving on by giving clear instructions at the appropriate juncture. In the other case, the advice might be to make lessons more interesting by providing the pupils with more challenge.

Identifying the causal antecedents to a situation often requires knowledge about processes such as 'motivating' and 'communicating' which underly events in the classroom and their outcomes. For instance, in the example below the teacher tutor focusses on the process of 'comprehending' when discussing a problem brought about by a decline in the pupils' ability to understand the work whereby they are no longer participating in the lesson.

> *Trainee:* ... the first lesson went very well, but I had a struggle to keep them quiet and teach in the second lesson ...
>
> *Teacher-tutor:* ... when kids start to play up in lessons when previously they have been good, this can be because the work starts to get a bit beyond them, and their whole pattern of behaviour can change. (*Ibid*, p. 6)

Occasionally, the teacher tutor will refer directly to the underlying processes which are implicated in this way. For example, below the teacher tutor advises the student about motivating a class by constantly relating the work to their experiences.

> *Trainee:* ... as I was talking, the class started to split off into small groups which were talking amongst themselves ...
>
> *Teacher-tutor:* ... the attention span of the 4th year CSE group is not long enough for a whole lesson based around a talk; if the standard is low, you must go quicker to keep attention, and relate the content to the kids more. (*ibid*, p. 3)

In our previous studies (Wood, 1986) we discovered teachers apparently referring to a range of processes which are listed below.

> *controlling:* the process governing the extent to which a class is engaged in task appropriate behaviour;

motivating: the process governing the class's predisposition to participate in the lesson and to pay attention, listen, understand and to generally make the effort to learn;

comprehending: the process by which pupils come to understand the material presented to them; through its structure and relationship to previous knowledge, and its pacing according to the pupils' rate of comprehension;

communicating: the process by which pupils remain aware of what they should be doing and why (contrasting with content of learning materials);

learning: the combination of all the aforegoing processes which goes beyond mere rote memory of the material presented, involving its apprehension and retention as the basis for subsequent learning and application to new situations;

recalling: the process of accessing from memory what has been previously learnt in earlier lessons or over the duration of a course.

relating: describes the process underlying the relationship developing between class and teacher.

Some of the causal antecedents to changes brought about through these processes have also been identified. For instance, control is gained through ensuring the class is engaged in an activity. It is also influenced by the relationship existing between pupils and teacher, whilst the motivation of the class and effective communication with it also play a role in controlling it.

Motivation may be gained through involving the pupils in whatever activities are taking place, allowing them to play an active role where possible. Also the experience of a sense of progress, challenge and achievement in their work is instrumental in maintaining the level of class motivation. The teacher's own enthusiam for the subject matter may also influence the motivation of the class, as do appropriate levels of communication and comprehension by the class.

Comprehension, or pupil understanding of the subject matter, is affected by the structured presentation of the subject matter. It is also influenced by such factors as its level of difficulty for the class concerned and whether or not its presentation is paced to their rate of comprehension. What may be understood in a lesson may also depend on what is previously learnt and how well the class remembers this.

Effective communication with pupils requires that they be kept informed of what they should be doing and why. This depends upon not only their being told, but ensuring that they actually receive the information-especially when there are other demands upon their attention.

Counteracting the process of forgetting, requires that pupils have adequate recourse to prior knowledge. Ensuring that pupils have this knowledge to begin with, reminding them of previous work where appropriate, and including revision where necessary, helps to counter-act this process.

The relationship which exists between class and teacher appears highly dependent on the degree of respect the pupils have for the teacher. It is easily lost if the teacher demonstrates an insincere or 'couldn't care less' attitude, or seems ineffective in disciplining the class.

For pupils to learn, some combination of control, motivation, communication, comprehension, remembering and a good relation-ship are required. What the antecedents of learning are otherwise, still remains unclear in this model of classroom processes, which does not seek to model the learning of individual pupils themselves, but is concerned with the *collective learning of a class as a whole*. In a sense this is an artefact, but it is a very useful artefact and one which many teachers make use of (Bromme, 1987).

Modelling Classroom Processes as a Basis for Consultation

The processes described above have been represented within a process model which describes different situations as states and the changes from one situation to another as transitions. A description of a class's behaviour may be viewed as lying somewhere along a continuum. For instance, if looking at the degree of control a teacher has over a class, the class may be described as either doing completely what the teacher desires for the activity they are engaged in or at the other extreme nothing like what the teacher desires, with many shades of greater or lesser compliance in between. We have identified points along this continuum which distinguish between qualitatively different states of control over the class. What would be considered an appropriate response by the teacher to a situation characterized as being to the one side of this point would be different from what would be considered appropriate in a qualitatively different situation characterized as being to the other side of this point. So, for instance, a reasonably well controlled class may be kept in that state by being kept occupied with some work. A less well controlled class however may require some threat to be administered in order to gain better control of it before successfully being given some work; otherwise it may simply ignore the teacher. Once the desired state has been achieved, maintaining it depends very much upon what the teacher does next. If the class is kept occupied control will be maintained, if not then the class will again slip into a state of disarray.

The changes which may be brought about and the situations which result, then, depend partly on the initial situation the teacher finds herself in and partly on how she responds to this. In addition processes interact so that, for instance, one might anticipate a highly motivated class to be more likely to keep on task than one which is bored with the work. Similarly pupils having difficulty understanding the work will find it difficult to participate in the lesson, perhaps becoming demotivated and less likely to do what the teacher would like. In this way processes act causally upon each other.

The process model captures some of what experienced teachers know about events and their outcomes in the classroom. The model provides us with a basis for reasoning about the causal antecedents to a particular outcome in the same way that a teacher might reason about a student's difficulties and what gave rise to them. By identifying which state within the model corresponds to the situation the student describes and which state within the model corresponds to the earlier classroom context, one is able to identify the type of transition brought about during the lesson. The knowledge associated with various transitions within the model, provides a means of focussing on those actions which are implicated in giving rise to the problem situation, so that how they may have contributed to the problem situation may be investigated further.

By focussing on the context in which a problem situation has arisen the model supports analyses of novel problems. There is no way to anticipate all the things which might go wrong for a teacher in any classroom — the 'checklist' approach — nevertheless uncovering the root of a problem depends upon being able to pose the right questions. For instance an initial diagnosis might suggest a communication problem; the task is then to pinpoint how this has come about. Knowing the contexts in which communication fails enables sensible questioning strategies to be formulated. Say the problem was a shiny blackboard. Having discounted that the class had not actually been told what to do, one might then focus on the *means* of communication. Verbal instructions are known for their failings: you need the *complete* attention of *all* the class — failings of memory apart. So in a situation where instructions must be referred to over a period of time or where their importance to some operation is paramount, for example a biology practical, they are best written down somewhere — in a book, on a worksheet or on the board, for instance. These conditions are satisfied in this example, however, as the instructions are constantly accessible. One might then begin to suspect a *problem* with the medium of communication. Perhaps poor photocopying or printing which is too faint to read. With a blackboard the problem might be one of many: dark chalk on dark board; shortsightedness of class members; distance seated from the board; size of handwriting; legibility of handwriting; or *a shiny blackboard!* One does not need a checklist of possible failings however; what pinpoints the problem is knowing that questioning the medium of communication is sensible and appropriate. Similarly, had the medium involved been a book, one may discover, for instance, that a child has reading difficulties. The student can be quite creative in pinpointing a problem, once she knows what type of problem it is and what she should be looking for.

The potential exists for the process model to support advice on how to improve situations. Given a situation and a desired outcome, it may indicate how the desired outcome might be achieved by referring to the range of factors critical in teachers' decision making causally associated with the transition to be made. The model may also support commentary upon the potential of achieving a desired state from a given situation or using an intended plan of action.

We have implemented a prototype TTSS which pursues an analysis of a trainee teacher's difficulties using this approach. It presents a series of menu-based questions aimed at identifying which states in the model most aptly correspond to those the student experienced and what actions on the part of the student were responsible for bringing about that situation. Preliminary trials with the system indicate a reasonable analysis can be achieved using this approach; albeit the analysis currently supported by the process model is somewhat abstract in terms of the way situations are accounted for.

The Expert Systems Methodolgy

The TTSS has a conventional Expert System architecture. It has a knowledge base of rules, corresponding to the knowledge of the teacher tutor, accumulates a database of facts, and has a 'goal-directed' rule implementation program (inference engine) for evaluating the antecedents to rules from the knowledge base on the basis of accumulated data from the user and its own internal reasoning using the rules in its knowledge base.

Traditionally, Expert Systems have been developed in the field of medical diagnosis but there are many similarities in approach: the evaluation of symptoms, the diagnosis of disease, the recommendation of an appropriate course of therapy. In fact, an interesting classroom simulation program which simulates a class's 'vital signs' in response to teacher inputs was itself based on an early medical simulation program (Dunn, 1979).

The rationale underlying the typical Expert Systems architecture is that knowledge can be represented modularly — as independent rules — and can be gradually incremented to increase the specificity, accuracy, and variety of instances the system can respond to. However, in practice we find that knowledge is highly structured and that knowing one thing affects how we evaluate another. Making an inference that takes us nearer to a solution is partly based on knowing it is a sensible inference to pursue.

For example, a doctor may see two patients who present very similar symptoms, indicating a range of possible causes. However, he obtains the additional information that one of his patients has just returned from a trip abroad. He is more likely then, in evaluating the symptoms of this patient, to take into consideration diagnoses which are linked to diseases endemic to that part of the world just visited. Whereas for his other patient, the range of diagnoses the doctor considers will be constrained to those diseases he believes the patient could possibly have come into contact with within his locality.

The information an experienced practitioner uses when undertaking a task such as solving a problem then can have two roles: it can provide information about the problem, enabling the expert to deal with the task in hand; or it can indicate how the investigation should proceed — what information should be selected next, for instance, or whether a particular aim should be pursued. In this example, the doctor has evaluated that a particular range of inferences are not appropriate or sensible, because of the additional information he has obtained.

Similar observations pertain to teaching. Typically this knowledge would be represented as rules like:

> *Antecedent:* class is not behaving as teacher wishes; loss of control occurred during transition between activities
> *Consequent:* problem is possibly one of communication

and:

> *Antecedent:*   class is not behaving as teacher wishes; loss of control occurred during course of activity
> *Consequent:*   problem is possibly one of comprehension or motivation

This then affects the diagnosis subsequently pursued. On the one hand, a sudden change in the teacher's control over the class indicates the class no longer knows what it should be doing: a communication problem. On the other, a gradual loss of control indicates the class's lessening participation in the lesson indicating their inability to follow the work or their loss of interest: a comprehension or motivation problem respectively. There is a branch in the line of reasoning or decision making, and the system takes one path over another.

The TTSS uses metarules which control when an inference may be appropriately made or when it is sensible to pursue another scenario. Our rules look more like this:

> *Antecedent:*   class is not behaving as teacher wishes
> *Consequent:*   problem is possibly one of communication

and:

> *Antecedent:*   class is not behaving as teacher wishes
> *Consequent:*   problem is possibly one of comprehension or motivation

Whilst our metarules would look like this:

> *Antecedent:*   loss of control occurred during transition between activities
> *Consequent:*   consider communication

and:

> *Antecedent:*   loss of control occurred during course of activity
> *Consequent:*   consider comprehension and motivation

The metarules are used to constrain which ordinary rules are used in making a diagnosis — only those that may be used to infer what at that time based on the available evidence is considered to be a sensible goal. At all times, however, it is as equally valid to infer that the patient has influenza as that he has typhoid; the metarules simply specify the differing circumstances under which the doctor may prefer to pursue one hypothesis over another. This strategy does not determine the final conclusion of the system — further tests may prove one conclusion totally invalid — it simply constrains or controls the search for a solution in the same way as a doctor constrains her own reasoning.

The current phase of development of the TTSS knowledge base focusses upon the way in which the teacher tutor modifies the analysis she is making as she finds out certain key items of information from the student. There are some situations which leave a trainee wide open to particular types of problems. For instance, a real problem for trainee teachers is getting a lesson started. It is one of the major obstacles to be overcome by the trainee, very often lying at the heart of a conviction that they can't control classes. If we look very closely at the problem of starting lessons, we find what appears to be a characteristically distinct scenario to within-lesson teaching. At the heart of this distinction is the fact that the behaviour of the class is not primarily the responsibility of the teacher. The class have just come in, maybe altogether or maybe a few at a time. They may have come from lunch or another lesson which may have been boring or interesting and it may be the last lesson of the day or the first. In this very different context, the teacher's response to the fact that the children are talking to each other (or worse!) when she wants to get the lesson started is going to seem a little out of place if it is the same as her response to a class who are openly talking to each other in the middle of her lesson.

Under closer analysis, therefore, it appears that the relevance of a process to the interpretation of a situation varies in relation to other processes according to a wider contextual appraisal of events. Much of the reasoning appropriate to understanding a trainee's problem within a lesson, just does not apply to the beginning of a lesson. If the problem occurred in the middle of a lesson the tutor may be concerned with the material presented to the class and how it was presented or maybe curious about class motivation. In contrast at the beginning of the lesson there is much more focus on how effectively the trainee is communicating with the class; little else is relevant.

It might appear then that the notion of a generic process model is misplaced, accounting for only a small range of situations occurring during the middle of lessons whilst at the beginning of lessons there is a different set of states and a different range of causal antecedents bringing about those states. However communication fails at the beginning of lessons for exactly the same reasons as at any other point in the lesson. What is significant about starts of lessons is that communication problems are *more likely* to be the reason that the lesson grinds to a halt or simply fails to take off. The experienced teacher tutor knows this and therefore on learning that a problem occurred at the beginning of a lesson concentrates on communications problems first. The information about the start of the lesson is used strategically to tell the tutor what is more likely to have gone wrong for the trainee. This strategic information, used by the tutor to inform her about the interpretation being pursued, is represented therefore within the metarules of the TTSS, specifying the conditions under which particular goals are most aptly pursued. So for instance, the TTSS might incorporate a metarule rather like this:

Antecedent: It is the beginning of the lesson
Consequent: investigate communication

Consultation with our domain expert has enabled us to develop the knowledge base of the system in other ways also. For instance, failing to gain the attention of the class is currently interpreted within the process model as a special kind of failure to make an appropriate transition between two states of communication. However, we have discovered that gaining the attention of the class can itself be described quite naturally in some detail in terms of states and transitions. So that although not having the attention of a class can be a reason for a failure in communication, inattentiveness is itself a state of preparedness on the part of a class to begin a lesson or pay attention to what the teacher tells them to do next. This state of preparedness might be influenced either positively or negatively by what the teacher says or does, or by external factors. For instance, whether there is something actively distracting the class — like it's snowing outside; or whether, for instance, the teacher expects the class to put down unfinished work without the opportunity to go back to it later — the pupils will usually prefer to finish off their work while the teacher is talking, instead of listening. Attentiveness therefore appears to be an additional process which we can represent in the same way as other processes within our model. Our model now represents the fact that a cause of a particular state of communication is sometimes failing to have the attention of the class whilst communicating. In pursuing a diagnosis, we are now in a position to investigate what caused a state of inattentiveness in the same way that we explored the causes acting on transitions brought about through other processes.

We propose to continue this theoretical development of the class-room process model through its extension at a more detailed level of analysis; in order to capture the experienced teacher's understanding of classroom dynamics on a finer timescale. Through the continued formalization of the experienced teacher's knowledge regarding classroom practice, we hope to support a wider differentiation in advising trainees, as well as increasing our understanding of classroom practice. We are currently working with our domain expert on developing our understanding of pupils' comprehension of subject matter.

Summary

We have been able to identify some of the knowledge experienced teachers have about classrooms and have represented this explicitly within an expert system architecture in order to verify the model of classroom processes. We achieve this through testing the performance of the system in terms of the dialogue it pursues — the appropriateness of various questions at different points during the consultation — and the analysis and explanation brought to bear on a typical problem. Where this doesn't fit or seems inappropriate, we supplement the information contained in the knowledge base in order to modify the behaviour. We attempt to do this in a principled way — thinking through the reasons for the errors and omissions and how these affect our overall conceptualization of the domain knowledge. Very often a simple detail results in a substantial revision of the knowledge base. This may not be apparent in the performance of the system — the changes may appear very few or insignificant — but may have important repercussions for the way in which the model is developed.

We anticipate that a system of this kind will have a useful role to play in teacher education. The levels of explanation provided by the TTSS are necessarily rudimentary at present — we are applying new techniques in a novel way to a difficult area — but we propose to continue developing the knowledge base using the framework the current model provides and in time have plans to pilot the TTSS within the Sussex teacher education programme in order to evaluate its role as a pedagogical tool.

Acknowledgements

The Expert Systems in Teacher Education project is funded by the Renaissance Trust. This project has benefitted from the especial contributions of Les Coate, Ben du Boulay and Trevor Pateman to whom much is owed for the progress of this research.

References

BROMME, R. (1987) 'Teachers' assessments of students', difficulties and progress in understanding in the classroom' in CALDERHEAD, J. (Ed.) *Exploring Teachers' Thinking*, London, Cassell.

DUNN, W.R. (1979) 'Computer assisted learning programme on classroom management in the primary school', Project Proposal, Dept of Education, University of Glasgow.

WOOD, S. (1984) 'Observations of school tutoring groups', Progress Report, Cognitive Studies Programme, University of Sussex.

WOOD, S. (1986) 'Eliciting teaching expertise using videos of trainee teachers', *Proceedings of Third ISATT Conference on Teacher Thinking and Professional Action*, Leuven, Belgium.

8   Teachers' Theories about Children's Learning

Angela Anning

This research project developed from experience of working with teachers on LEA in-service courses using Open University Curriculum in Action materials (Ashton *et al.*, 1980) and of videotaping classroom practice designed to explore problem solving with young children. The teachers working through the Curriculum in Action packs found the section focussed on 'What were the pupils learning?' particularly difficult. In discussions of the question based on observations in their classrooms, responses tended to be expressed in terms of vague hunches or intuitions about children's capabilities and learning behaviour. Yet the evidence from the videotapes that I was concurrently editing indicated that the teachers' practical skills in assessing and responding to individual learners' progress and needs implied a framework for making judgments about what and how the children were learning. It was the fascination with the gap between the consummate practical skills shown on the videotapes and the inability of the teachers to articulate the professional knowledge they were demonstrating that led to this research which aimed to investigate primary teachers' ability to articulate their theories about how children learn and to explore links between their understanding of how children learn and the teaching strategies they use in classrooms.

Six primary teachers, of whom two had been involved in the Curriculum in Action courses, in an inner city area were invited to take part in the project. They were all known to the researcher and between them taught across the whole primary age range of 3–11. The methods of working with the six teachers were selected to be as 'teacher sympathetic' as possible within the constraints of the power relationship of collaborative teacher/researcher investigations.

Processes in which the Teachers were Involved

As indicated in table 1, the teachers were asked to select three groups of pupils, including a cross-section of personality type and ability range. No attempt was made to define what the researcher meant by 'personality type' or 'ability range'. Any uncertainties teachers expressed about their choices were talked through informally on the teachers' terms before the final selection was made. They were asked to plan activities for the pupil groups related to the current half-term's curriculum planning.

The teachers were then asked to write brief notes on their ex-

Table 1:   Model of the research design

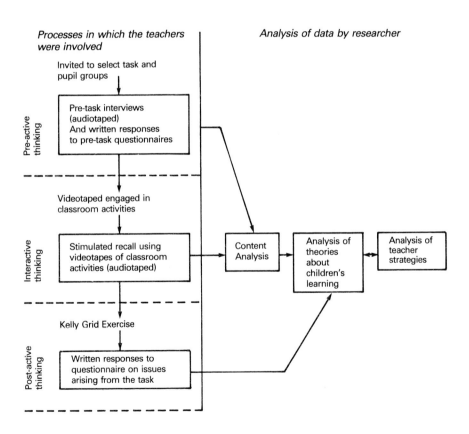

pectations of the selected pupils' responses to the specific tasks set. The notes were used as the basis of a more structured pre-task interview which was tape-recorded.

In each of the six classrooms, the three tasks were videotaped so that there would be a permanent record of evidence of the children learning and the teachers' strategies in response to the children's learning for subsequent discussions.

The post-task discussions focussed on the evidence provided by the videotaped sessions. Each videotaped recording was reviewed by the teachers and researcher three times — to gain an overall impression of the session; to look for evidence of pupil learning; and to try to identify the kind of strategies the teachers had used in response to pupil behaviour and learning. During each viewing, the tape was stopped at any point of mutal or individual interest for discussion. The discussions were recorded on audiotapes. Throughout the discussions, the researcher took a subsidiary role, leaving the teachers to make their own commentaries, but occasionally probing to explore further particular issues. This approach was in line with Patton's (1980) recommendation: 'the procedures of observation and in-depth interviewing, particularly the latter, communicate respect to respondents by making their ideas and opinions, stated in their own terms, the important data source for evaluation'.

Despite the misgivings cited by Yinger (1986) and Calderhead (1985 and 1986) about the efficacy of using stimulated recall techniques to make explicit 'knowledge in action' this method seemed to offer the teachers control over articulating their beliefs on their own terms. Moreover, it was hoped that the use of the recordings to stimulate discussion would ensure that theory generated by the teachers would be embedded in the realities of their normal classroom practices rather than the rhetoric of what they believed ought to happen there.

Once the three tasks had been extensively discussed, the teachers were asked to move to a more distanced reflection on pupils as learners. Two techniques were used. The teachers were asked to respond to a Kelly Grid procedure (Kelly, 1955). In each case, the names of all the children who had been selected for the recorded activities by a teacher were presented in triads by the researcher to the teacher. S/he was asked to consider the similarities and differences of these pupils as learners. A grid was completed relating the constructs elicited to all the pupils in the videotaped sessions. Calderhead (1985) has pointed out that highly structured methods derived from the tradition of clinical psychology might not be appropriate for probing teachers' thinking about their practice. In completing the Kelly Grid exercise the teachers constantly expressed doubts about assigning their pupils to constructs. They referred to classroom incidents in which the children had been involved which blurred the distinction between the positive or negative quality of the constructs into which they were asked to categorize the children. The process of decontextualizing the learners from recognizable classroom contexts was not a 'natural' way for these practitioners to think.

Moreover, the constructs elicited from each teacher bore no discernible relationship to either the total units of the content analysis or the separately calculated pre-task or on-task percentages of units referred to later (tables 3 and 4). It might be argued by psychologists that distancing teachers from the immediacy of classroom action focusses their attention on key issues. In this case the technique did not appear to stimulate awareness of issues which bore a relationship to classroom realities.

Finally, the six teachers were presented with twelve questions about learning and teaching in their classrooms to which they were asked to write a response. Having the opportunity to respond privately to a written questionnaire gave teachers the freedom to express their views without having to respond to the social niceties of face to face contact with an interviewer or to feel the pressure to make the kind of responses they felt that the interviewer wanted to hear.

Analysis of Data

The recorded discussions with each teacher produced about three hours of audio-taped data to be transcribed per teacher with the exception of John whose discussions lasted in total just over one hour. The decision was made to transcribe complete versions of the teacher/ researcher interviews and discussions rather than to select extracts that appeared particularly 'relevant' to the researcher.

The comments that referred to children's learning, explicitly or implicitly, were marked. These comments were used as the units for content analysis of the data, using procedures recommended by Weber (1985). The categories used and number of units coded for each teacher are listed in table 2.

It seemed evident that each of the six teachers' theories about children's learning were uniquely determined by their own particular previous experiences of teaching and learning in their classrooms. Within the context of talk about the specific three tasks and three

Table 2: Total number of units coded by content analysis

Categories for learner characteristics		Units coded into each sub-category for the teachers											
		WENDY*		JANE*		PAULINE*		JOHN		STEPHEN		SUE	
		P.	O.	P.	O.	P.	O.	P.	O.	P.	O.	P.	O.
1.1	Stage		1	1	1	1	1	1	1	1	3	3	1
1.2	Age					3	2			1	2		
1.3	Actual achievement	3	10	1		2	5	3	2	12	4	2	6
1.4	Potential achievement	5	1	1					1	3	2		
1.5	Creativity/Imagination		9		4	2	4		5			2	1
1.6	Ability to perceive links with previous learning	3	26		11		4		1	1	4		4
1.7	Ability to verbalise	10	11	2	6	2	7	2		3	2	1	4
1.8	Recall				3			1	1	2	1		
	Totals	21	58	5	25	10	23	7	11	23	18	8	16
2.1	Attitude to teacher	6	4	1	5	4			1	1	3		2
2.2	Work routines		7	3	4		4		3	8	6		5
2.3	Motivation	5	2	1	4	3	1	1		9	3		1
2.4	Participation in class	2		2	2	2			1			1	2
2.5	Independence in learning situations	2	1			1	1		2	2	7	2	4
2.6	Rule tolerance				1		1						
2.7	Risk taking	1	3		1	1	3				1		
2.8	Confidence in learning situations	4	5		4	1	3				2		3
2.9	Willingness to learn from peer group	1	1	1	3	1	1		1	2	3	1	1
2.10	Concentration/Attention to task		1		4	1	1		1	1	2		4
2.11	Deviant behaviour			3		1	1		4	3	3		
2.12	Attitude to competition			1						2		2	
2.13	Learning through doing	1								3	1		
	Totals	22	25	12	30	15	14	1	13	31	34	6	22
3.1	Self-image/self-confidence				3	2			1	1	1	1	1
3.2	Behaviour in a group	2	2	1	3	3	2	1	1	5	3	8	3
3.3	Peer group responses to learner as person					1			1	1			
3.4	Personality	1	1	6		2				8	1	5	
3.5	Gender	1								3	3	2	2
	Totals	4	3	7	6	8	2	1	3	18	8	16	6
4.1	Out of school experiences				2		1		1				3
4.2	Interests						1			1			
4.3	Home factors			2								1	
	Totals	0	2	2	2	0	1	0	1	1	0	1	3

P. = Pre-task   O. = On-task

N.B. Pre-task refers to units from transcripts of the pre-task stages of discussion and on task for the stimulated recall stage of discussion.

* Infant teachers

groups of learners were embedded references back to similar incidents or justifications/explanations based on previous experiences of class-room practice as illustrated in the example of coded transcript text given below. The point is made that teacher theory is inherent in their practice and that it is *through* their practice that it is constantly re-formulated and tested. Hence the variations in teacher beliefs will be dependent upon their varying professional experiences as well as the context in which they are working.

Texts Coded for Content Analysis

Example 1 — Pre task Discussion of Task 3 by Stephen

A: For task three you've got seven did you say?

S: Yes, seven children, Um ... I'll deal with the girls first. There's Natalie F. Do you want me to mention a bit about their personalities?

A: O.K.

S: /She's bright and bouncy, a very artistic girl./ Um, but/we feel that within school actually — and this is interesting — she's an under-achiever. She could be achieving far more.// She hasn't got a very good concentration span when she's doing anything apart from art, when she will sit quietly for hours.// But she does, yes she can produce good work/ and/ she can be quite stimulating to talk to./ Then there's/ Victoria who's very bright again and very capable and competent/ and//will love the mathematics part of this. Disproves all the theories about girls not being good at maths. She is superb./ And there's/ Michelle who is probably the neatest, tidiest, most efficient worker in the class in my opinion anyway,/and/ also bright, very bright and intelligent,/ and//is usually guaranteed to do with the minimum of instruction a very good piece of work. She catches on very quickly to what the teacher wants and expects — you know, she knows the system (laughs). And she knows how to use it./ But then there's also/ Lisa who will be talking all the way through it I can guarantee in a very loud voice./ But/ she's a very pleasant girl/and/ when she stops and thinks, again, can produce some you know quite effective work,/and she's/ — / she tends to distract herself./

There's three boys in the group. There's Alex, Michael and Paul. /Alex is a very bright lad./ Again/ I think he's slightly under-achieving.// Michael is very very intelligent — in my opinion, probably the most intelligent one in the group.// But his actual work, his presentation and his reading will be poor./ We talk about it together, you know; he has problems with that./ But he enjoys doing this. They all enjoy doing it and I just hope they will get some satisfaction out of it./ Again, /Paul, his presentation is poor./ But he's a bright lad// — very very intense — when he talks to you. /But the moment you go away (laughs) becomes very un-intense! (laughs) As a matter of fact he becomes a bit of a pest when you go away./ So it will be interesting to see how he reacts to the rest of the group. (laughs)/ He was away today and they all said, 'Isn't it lovely and quiet?'/

Example 2 — Stimulated Recall — Stephen

A: You set them off in quite a structured way didn't you, to start with?

S: /Lisa wasn't concentrating./

A: Wasn't she?

S: I've noted down here that/ she knew she could rely on Melanie. Quite often of the girls she's the one that's carried./ Yes, I noted down here that when I asked if they all knew what to do, /they appeared confident.// There was cross group consultation, but mainly between the girls.// Paul seemed unsure from the beginning and wouldn't ask for help — didn't realize how to start./ You see you said at the beginning I made it quite structured. I think with something like mapwork which is very abstract — I think it's abstract anyway what they were doing — taking a map from a map and enlarging it. I think that's quite difficult.

A: Yes it is.

S: And I've seen children make a complete hash of it before and not want to go back after an hour and do it again. And I didn't want them to fall into the same trap. We had done this once before, but we'd done it a long time ago. And Paul obviously, you see I introduced it very quickly,/ Paul obviously needed longer./ There again I assumed that because they've done it before, it would be O.K.

Table 3:   Total percentages of coded units from content analysis

	Ability	Classroom Behaviour Work Habits	Social Competence/ Personality	Out of school influences on learning in school
Wendy*	58.5	34.8	5.2	1.5
Jane*	33.7	47.2	14.6	4.5
Pauline*	45.2	39.7	13.7	1.4
John	48.6	37.8	10.8	2.7
Stephen	30.8	48.9	19.5	0.75
Sue	30.8	35.9	28.2	5.1

* Infant teachers

Although there were differences in the individual teacher's sub-category codings as shown in table 2, there were consistencies in the overall emphasis they gave to the four broad categories; *Ability, Classroom Behaviour/Work Habits, Social Competence/Personality* and *Out of School Influences on Learning in School*. The total percentages of units coded for each of the six teachers is shown in table 3.

The teachers were consistent in the overall emphasis they gave to *Classroom Behaviour/Work Habits*. These tangible and observable patterns of pupil behaviours and attitudes in the classroom appear to provide a common base-line in the teachers' views of what is significant for their understanding of how children learn. Teachers appear to be concerned with the observable learning behaviour of children rather than the abstract processes of cognition or what is going on 'inside the children's heads'. It is these observable pupil learning behaviours and attitudes that provide the evidence of learning to which teachers respond. In turn their responses shape the teaching strategies which form the basis of their craft knowledge.

In this study there were variations in the emphasis given by each teacher to particular aspects of the children's behaviour and attitudes as has been shown in table 2. Though all of the teachers emphasized the children's working routines such as their participation in class, willingness to learn from each other, concentration; and their attitudes such as confidence and motivation, there were interesting differences within this small sample between the infant and junior teachers' findings. The infant teachers more often referred to the children's attitudes to the teacher, whilst the junior teachers more often referred to independence in learning situations, deviant behaviour and attitude to competition. It is tempting to speculate that this may be a reflection of the climates of the different phases of primary education. Infant classrooms tend to be characterized by individualized teaching. Junior classrooms are areas where increasingly junior teachers are more likely to have to confront peer group rivalry as well as deviance. Independence in learning is striven for in junior classrooms but often within a more formal teaching setting.

The variations in emphasis between the teachers are more significant in the *Ability* and *Social Competence/Personality* categories. All three infant teachers, but Wendy in particular, refer more often to their pupils' abilities, whilst Stephen and Sue appear to think of their pupils more in terms of their personalities. It is an interesting reversal of what one might have expected given the previous remarks about the different climates of infant and junior school classrooms. One would have perhaps expected the infant teachers to be less concerned with ability and more with children's personalities.

Within the *Ability* category, when the teachers referred to the children's actual achievements, they defined them clearly into categories such as 'high ability', 'average' or 'poor', though euphemisms such as 'takes longer to catch on' or 'needs more help' were more often employed to describe children of below average ability. Three areas were particularly emphasized by the infant teachers — the ability to make links with previous learning, the ability to verbalize and creativity. However, the ability to make links with previous learning experiences, both within the classroom and beyond, was a significant area as far as all of the six teachers were concerned. So too was the link between language and learning.

In the *Social Competence/Personality* category, the teachers emphasized the children's attitudes and behaviour towards their peer group using such words as 'dominant', 'sensitive to others needs', 'can share', 'selfish'. Personality traits were defined in terms such as 'shy', 'extrovert', 'popular', 'a loner', 'bouncy', 'scatty'. A difference emerged between infant and junior findings in the junior teachers' preoccupation with gender issues. Boy/girl differences in learning behaviour, rather than aptitude or ability, were seen as having a significant effect on children's learning in their classroom.

The fourth category, *Out of School Influences on Learning in School*, accounted for surprisingly few units. The notion that primary teachers respond to learners in terms of their social class (Sharp and Green, 1975) was not borne out by this small sample of teachers (cf Nash, 1973). However, since all the children were in inner city, 'working class' areas, perhaps this was 'taken as read' by the teachers.

Another possible explanation is that self-monitoring, referred to below, prevented the teachers from talking overtly about class issues. Parental support was, however, mentioned as a significant factor in

Table 4: *Comparison of pre-task and on task percentages of coded units*

	Ability		Classroom Behaviour/ Work Habits		Social competence/ personality		Out of school influences on learning in school	
	pre-task	on task	pre-task	on task	pre-task	on task	pre-task	on task
Wendy*	44.7	65.9	46.8	28.4	8.5	3.4	0	2.3
Jane*	19.2	39.7	46.2	47.6	26.9	9.5	7.7	3.2
Pauline*	30.3	57.5	45.5	35.0	24.2	5.0	0	2.5
Stephen	31.5	30.0	42.5	56.7	24.5	13.3	1.4	0
Sue	25.8	34.0	19.4	46.8	51.6	12.8	3.2	6.4

N.B. Data for John was not included in this second analysis. He effectively withdrew from the project at the stimulated recall stage of the research.

* Infant teachers

pupil success as learners by three of the teachers. It may be that 'parental support' has become the new euphemism for 'a middle class background'. The children's interests, which one would have expected to be mentioned as significant in the 'child centred' primary ethos in which the six teachers were working, were mentioned in a very perfunctory manner. This brings to mind King's (1979) brilliant exposé of the 'teacher centred' bias of a so called 'child centred' ideology.

In order to explore the possibility that the kind of issues that dominated the teachers' findings about children's learning might be different at the pre-active and interactive stages, the data for the units coded at the pre-talk discussion stages was compared with the data from the stimulated recall (on task) stages of discussion. The percentages are shown in table 4.

The comparison between the pre-task and on-task codings reveal some consistencies across data from the teachers as well as some individual differences. In the pre-task discussions the teachers tended to emphasise the learners' *Classroom Behaviour/Work Habits* and *Social Competence Personality*. As soon as the teachers switched to talking about the learners in an interactive situation, there was a marked change of emphasis to *Ability* issues. It seems clear that when teachers are involved in classroom action, even in the distanced conditions of stimulated recall, they have different priorities in reacting to the learners in their classrooms.

Two hypotheses are posed for this change in emphasis. Firstly, when teachers are reacting to the mass of information about learners which assails them in teaching situations, even when working with a small group, they have to filter out the essential features which inform their decision-making (Peterson and Clark, 1978; Shavelson and Stern, 1981). The ability of the learners is often the most significant feature to inform the kind of instant routine decisions which teachers are constantly making in classrooms — when to slow down or speed up the pace of instruction, when to check on understanding, how long to sustain a working session, how long to wait for pupil responses to questions, when to introduce a more difficult task. The wider issues of children's attitudes, personalities and interests are subsumed by more easily controllable and essentially mechanistic and quantitative aspects of decision-making.

Nevertheless, it is important to remember that these mechanistic and quantitative decisions are made essentially within the context of teachers' understanding of other facets of the children's learning than ability. This wider context also informs their decision-making, and research which concentrates on one phase of teacher thinking exclusively might gain a simplistic view of teachers' interactive thinking. The teachers' statements about the particular strategies they used in relation to individual learners demonstrated that they were consistently aware of pupils' personal situations and likely emotional responses and the assumption is that this awareness had a significant effect on the types of strategies the teachers used. They demonstrated an awareness of children's social and emotional needs even within the context of an emphasis on precise mechanistic decisions based on their knowledge of children's ability levels.

Secondly, it is suggested that teachers have been sensitized so effectively to the dangers of self-fulfilling prophecies and the effects of teacher expectation on pupil performance through initial and in-service training, that they have adopted a self-censoring device which makes them reluctant to talk about the ability of pupils in 'cold', reflective situations. In the interactive phases of teaching this self-monitoring becomes less stringent as the pressure of responding instantly to children's learning needs builds up.

In this small sample, the junior teachers appeared to be less reluctant to talk about children's abilities in the pre-task discussion than the infant teachers. There is a less marked difference in the number of references to ability between the junior teachers' pre-task and on-task commentaries. They also appeared to focus more than the infant teachers on personality issues in the on-task stimulated recall discussions. Perhaps the differences between children as learners in terms of their abilities and personalities, tentatively defined at the infant stages, have become too obvious for teachers to ignore by the junior stage. The ability gaps are ever widening and the children's personalities are well and truly defined.

The Teaching Strategies

A more detailed analysis of the teachers' strategies will form a second stage of the research project. However, it is clear that the principles embedded in each of the six teachers' beliefs about children's learning were clearly linked to the teaching strategies they identified. Teaching and learning issues were consistently interwoven in the teacher talk.

For example, Wendy believed that children needed to be actively engaged in order for effective learning to take place. Children learn through an accumulation of experiences. As she put it, 'Do first, theories later'. At the same time she tempered this essentially Plow-denesque belief in experiential learning with a belief in the value of structuring learning. Providing a structure was seen as the teacher's responsibility.

Her 'image' (Elbaz, 1983) of what stages she planned for the children to go through during an activity was made explicit in her projections for a task with top infants translating data from a chart into graph form:

> The purpose of the task was to go in three stages — to first of all have the numbers that were written down counted by the children; secondly, to then transfer that information to each family to be a cube, which is quite a big step; and then, thirdly, which is a lot all in one go, to actually put that down on paper — in other words, get rid of the cubes and just have it written down, a written record. Those were my three steps — and I suppose I was quite determined to go through those steps. I was determined they were going to do it, but I had thought it would need a lot more direction from me. And I was very pleased they came up with the conclusions I *wanted* them to, without me having to prepare the way. A lot of it came quite spontaneously. The unknown to me was how much I would have to put in.

While she believed that her role as a teacher was to provide an underlying structure for children's learning, she argued that within the guidance she gave, the children should be encouraged to develop their own strategies for learning. She was aware that the moment at which the teacher intervened was critical. She described her strategy with Stephen and Gemma on the same task:

> I hadn't used the word graph at any time, but that's what I was trying to get them to do, but I really didn't want to say to them, 'This is how you can make a graph'. I wanted them to try to come to the conclusion themselves that if you're making a graph like that, that you need to do it in a vertical way — to show the difference between each particular thing that you are measuring. And the thing was that I said to them — they put their cubes horizontally — and I tried to get *them* to make some decision about placing them in a better way. But it didn't come straight away. So I didn't — I just left it at that because I didn't want to say, 'Oh no, *this* is the way you're going to do it'.
>
> When the children obviously hadn't come to what I considered the right sort of placement of cubes for a graph I just decided to continue. And I said, 'Oh alright, let's just leave it. We'll talk about that later'. Then there was quite a bit of silence really because the children did seem to be working it out for themselves. I chipped in when it wasn't going quite right.

In the first task, alphabetical ordering, she described her strategies when the children were first faced with two names beginning with the same letter:

> They found the two names that both began with 'A' and I said, 'Do you think it matters where I put them?'. I think I was trying to — instead of just giving them a rule straight away — I was trying to make them realise the *need* for a rule if you know what I mean. In that way they would realize that you've got to do something about it — and hopefully they would then remember *what* you do about it, rather than just be told. And I wanted them to try various strategies themselves, hopefully to see if they could somehow get something out of that. You know, to build on what they did rather than me just throw in something entirely new to them. I wanted *them* really to come up with the answer. I didn't want to come in straight away and correct them. Because I've often found that if you leave it long enough it evolves anyway; and if it's come from the children then they tend to remember it, rather than me, having me tell them.

Jane believed that children need a climate of emotional security if they are to learn effectively. She was particularly sensitive to the children's feelings in learning situations. She described Nicola's reactions to a task involving making a word bank:

> I noticed that Nicola was very quiet. She was watching and knowing Nicola, she probably wanted to be brought in at that time, so I brought her in, 'Nicola, can you tell me?'. Because she gets very embarrassed if she is being overlooked although she won't actually push herself forward. She jiggles her legs and I know she wants to say something.

When Daniel was stuck on a question Jane said:

> I thought rather than get him in a state, we'd offer it to someone who *could* answer. It's horrible when you've done something wrong. It makes it horrible not just for them but for that little group.

When children made incorrect responses to a direct question, she was particularly skilful at putting the child at ease, often by immediately asking the child a follow up question to which she was sure the child was able to respond correctly. She said:

> I sense there's some sort of discomfort, so I try to do something that will make them feel like — what I *think* they feel like. No, I don't like children to feel nervous, embarrassed or shy. Because you don't get anything back really, anything out of them that you want. And it makes you slightly uncomfortable really.

She was willing to discuss openly her own feelings of insecurity. She was particularly anxious about the open-ended nature of the third task when a group of mixed ability children were to dramatize, with puppets, the story of the *Three Little Pigs*:

> It seemed to me in the middle of it all — and particularly in the part where we started with the fair, the little pig at the fair, from then on it seemed to me like a melée. It just got to be — it seemed, you know, I had to have my mind on so many different things at once: different aspects of it, and directing various things — and that it just seemed completely out of hand. Things were just going haywire you know ... But since I've looked at the tape, I think it seemed very good really. They responded very very well. And I didn't look as

aggressive, or as harrassed, frustrated or whatever (laughs) as I felt at the time.

She described with great sensitivity, her reaction to being observed at work in a classroom:

> I think the other thing about that too is you think, you know, if it does break down, I've had that situation, and I just say, 'Well right'; if that's happened. I'll sit on the chair and put my legs out and say, 'Well, we can't do it anymore'. Having to put yourself in that position on camera is difficult. I mean I could have done it. And the other thing about it is even if it's not being recorded, you're always afraid that if someone comes into your classroom, advisers or whoever, or visitors even — and you are just sprawled out saying, 'Right, well if that's how it's going to be ...', they would think, 'Golly, what's going on here?' and then you have to justify yourself ... I think I'm getting better at it. I used to, when I was newly trained, I used to think that was terrible — and I would never master it all. But I no longer feel that. It took me about two years — eighteen months — before I felt comfortable no matter what happened.

Stephen believed that children should be encouraged to learn through trial and error and guess work. Consequently, his strategies often involved setting up a very open ended task for the children. Sometimes this very openness resulted in the children facing frustrations. For example, in a woodwork task the children were given very little guidance about the types of wood most appropriate for making a bicycle stand.

> I think that upon reflection, you see I felt that I perhaps left it too open for them with the wood they needed. I think again, I don't think a task should be too long if it isn't necessary and that task could quite easily, had they not been four patient children, have ended in disaster. I think I should have discussed with them the type of wood needed for this. Because they quite often picked up the wrong sort of wood, and I was biting back saying, 'Don't use that' (laughs).

Stephen wrote in the questionnaire:

> I do find sometimes that the children find great difficulty with a problem that is *too* open ended and most (not all) need a guide or even a tight structure if they are to learn at all. I

would like to do more learning based on problem solving but time always seems to run out.

He also wrote:

> Trial and error involves a *lot* of time. The effort involved in trying to ensure that understanding has been achieved is often counter-productive as it means neglect of others. Some children can work to a formula and the understanding comes later (hopefully!).

The reality of trying to reconcile the constraints of restricted time, numbers of children and external pressures in the classroom with his philosophy of teaching were well expressed in the following extract from the pre-task discussion:

> Since I've been at this school, I've decided that's the only way. When I first came in I had all these ideas that I'd got older children and was going to — I wasn't going to do what I did with infants — well, to an extent I was because the head wanted me to do that — but I was going to give them more tasks more efficiently. But then I thought, 'Good Lord, we're doing so many different things and what are they learning? I've rushed them through this and rushed them through that'. Whereas now, I'll take a whole week to concentrate on two or three points. And do them I think perhaps a lot better and give them more time. I think in the end time is irrelevant. It's so easy though just to say, 'Well, they've done some maths today and they've done some art today and we've been out and done P.E.'. It makes you feel better, but it doesn't necessarily mean that the children have *learnt* a lot. But it takes a lot to stand in the staffroom and say, 'We don't do maths every day'. You still get some looks. Like if you don't hear the readers. Somebody asked me how often I hear my top juniors read and I said it was degrading to hear them. I mean I'm trying to get them to read for enjoyment! You don't have 10 or 11-year-olds who are articulate fluent readers reading out just for the sake of filling in a record book.

Conclusion and Recommendations

It is suggested that teachers generate theory through cumulative experiences and reflection on teaching and learning. In evaluating each

Table 5: *A cyclical model of teacher thinking*

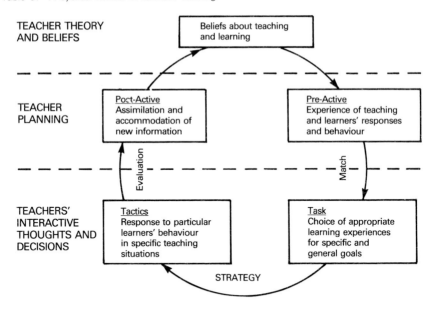

new teaching and learning event, the principles embedded in teachers' theories are further confirmed, refined or modified. This reflective cycle is illustrated in table 5.

This cyclical process of reflection-in-action, a 'continual inter-weaving of thinking and doing', was identified by Schon (1983) as the hallmark of the theory of practitioners, the kind of knowing 'inherent in intelligent action'.

It is argued that a research tradition in which theories are generated from teacher and pupil realities and needs is more likely to focus on issues of central rather than peripheral concern to practitioners. Moreover, if teachers themselves are involved in the processes of generating theory, which is then articulated in a language familiar to them, it is more likely to be shared with colleagues and translated into practice rather than to be left lying unopened in paper form in teachers' desk drawers or on library shelves.

Some implications of the nature of the teachers' theorizing may be drawn for the professional development and initial training of teachers.

1   Educational psychology courses at initial and in-service level might take teachers' theorizing as the starting point for subsequent examination of theories of learning.

2   Pedagogy should be taken as a subject for study in its own

right rather than studied through the disciplines of sociology, psychology and philosophy.

3   Intelligent action should be given equal value to theorising in teacher training programmes.

4   Teachers at both initial and in-service level should be taught the skills and confidence to analyze and articulate their thinking.

5   Teachers might share accounts of their thinking in order to clarify the terms and concepts loosely defined by their talk.

6   Teachers and researchers should strive to develop a language of discourse in which a dialogue might be encouraged.

References

ASHTON, P. *et al.* (1980) *Curriculum in Action: An Approach to Evaluation*, Milton Keynes, Open University Press in Association with the Schools' Council.

CALDERHEAD, J. (1985) 'Conceptualising and investigating teachers' professional knowledge, paper presented at a seminar on Teachers' Professional Craft Knowledge, University of Stirling, 12 April.

CALDERHEAD, J. (1986) 'Developing a framework for the elicitation and analysis of teachers' verbal reports', paper presented at the annual meeting of the American Educational Research Association, San Francisco, April.

ELBAZ, F. (1983) *Teacher Thinking: A Study of Practical Knowledge*, New York, Nichols Publishing.

KELLY, G.A. (1955) *The Psychology of Personal Constructs*, New York, Norton.

KING, R. (1979) *All Things Bright and Beautiful*, Chichester, John Wiley.

NASH, R. (1973) *Classroom Observed*, London, Routledge and Kegan Paul.

PATTON, M.Q. (1980) *Qualitative Evaluation Methods*, London and California, Sage Publications Ltd.

PETERSON, P.L. and CLARK, C.M. (1978) 'Teachers' reports on their cognitive processes during teaching', *American Educational Research Journal*, 15, p. 555–65.

SCHON, D.A. (1983) *The Reflective Practitioner*. New York, Basic Books and London, Temple Smith.

SHARP, R. and GREEN, A. (1975) *Education and Social Control*, London, Routledge and Kegan Paul.

SHAVELSON, R.J. and STERN, P. (1981) 'Research on teachers' pedagogical thoughts, judgements, decisions and behaviour', *Review of Educational Research*, winter, 51, 4, pp. 455–98.

WEBER, R.P. (1985) *Basic Content Analysis*, California, Sage Publications.

YINGER, R.J. (1986) 'Examining thought in action: A theoretical and methodological critique of research on interactive teaching', paper presented at the annual meeting of the American Educational Research Association, San Francisco, April.

9   Situated Knowledge and Expertise in Teaching

Gaea Leinhardt

In this chapter, the anthropological and psychological construct of situated knowledge is taken as a starting point to investigate the knowledge of teaching displayed by expert teachers. Situated knowledge is contextually developed knowledge that is accessed and used in a way that tends to make use of characteristic features of the environment as solution tools; it is contrasted with principled, context free knowledge. The specific focus for this chapter is on the teacher's use of situated knowledge in the selection of and use of example in explanations of early mathematical topics. If the school/classroom setting is seen as a situation in and of itself — in the same way as the storage and loading room of a dairy (Scribner, 1984), the supermarket (Lave, Murtaugh and de la Rocha, 1984), or the street trader's corner (Carraher, Carraher and Schliemann, 1983) — then several important pedagogical research findings, such as those related to the difficulty of changing teacher behavior, seem to have slightly different interpretations than previously considered.

Situated knowledge can be seen as a form of expertise in which declarative knowledge is highly proceduralized and automatic and in which a highly efficient collection of heuristics exist for the solution of very specific problems in teaching. This automation or resistance to change on the part of the teacher should not then be perceived as a form of stubborn ignorance or authoritarian rigidity but as a response to the consistency of the total situation and a desire to continue to employ expert-like solutions. Similarly, student teachers' lack of transfer of teaching behaviors from their courses to their own teaching situation can be seen as a failure of the courses to replicate some of the more significant features of the classroom situations that either trigger or facilitate actions on the part of the expert.

I take the position that a worthwhile object of study and research is the set of actions, thoughts, and functions of teachers. I assume that teachers' thoughts and actions, while not always consistent with my own, do not occur within a vacuum and that we can learn much about the art of teaching if we seriously consider the nature of the environment in which teachers work and reason. I try, on the one hand, not to romanticize teachers' behaviors, an action which would end up with finding all such behaviors quaint and 'equally correct'. On the other hand, I try to understand why teachers act as they do. When teachers teach, they tend to formulate their role and, therefore, their actions in ways that are quite dissimilar to the formulations that teacher educators, specifically mathematics teacher educators, have for them. Specifically, the teachers, especially good ones, drift towards routinization and consistency whereas university researchers and teacher educators tend to glorify spontaneity and responsiveness. We should not make this an issue of identifying who is correct, teacher educator or teacher. If we are going to make progress in working with teachers we will have to spend the same kind of energy trying to understand the reasoning and knowledge bases that teachers use when teaching as we now expend when studying how to teach students a new mathematical or scientific idea.

When teachers are successful at their jobs — that is, when they are capable of getting students to learn material that they did not already know before teaching took place — they look a lot like other experts who perform complex intellectual tasks (Leinhardt and Greeno, 1986; Leinhardt and Smith, 1985). Expertise does not refer to doing things the 'right' or 'preferred' way. Expertise is a technical term that refers to working with speed, fluidity, flexibility, situationally encoded informational schemas, and mental models that permit larger chunks of information to be accessed and handled (Chase and Simon, 1973; Chi *et al.*, 1982). Some teachers are experts because they retain large amounts of detailed information about the entities with which they work (students, content, management, timing, etc.) and they have a large repertoire of behaviors.

Much of the knowledge teachers have about teaching is situated within the context of teaching. Like other forms of situated knowledge, the situated knowledge of teaching has developed in a specific context, and within that context, is extremely powerful. This situated knowledge has ancillary knowledge attached to it. Situated knowledge connects teaching events with particular environmental features such as classrooms, time of year, individual people, physical surroundings, specific pages of text, and more abstracted subject matter knowledge. Situated knowledge is defined in part by its history. It is also knowledge which permits a specialized kind of problem solving to occur.

Situated knowledge has the property of being embedded in the artifacts of a context. Thus, in problem solving, solutions that use situated instead of generative knowledge are produced by calculating with the entities of the problem itself. For example, when a grocery shopper is comparing a smaller bag of dried noodles with a larger bag, two knowledge bases may be activated. One is the relatively context-free 'halve it' rule, by which the shopper doubles the smaller (or halves the larger) price and compares the answer with the price of the larger (or smaller) bag. The other is a size or heft test of the two bags to check the approximate correctness of halving or doubling the price. This second action is an example of the entity itself being a part of the solution process. The generative and always correct procedure (the algorithm) would be to determine weight, volume, or number of items in each package, divide the total price by the unit, and calculate a per unit cost for the two bags. The generative solution is clearly a more cumbersome, time consuming, *and* overly accurate procedure.

Situated knowledge may be contrasted with context-free principled knowledge that is applicable or accessible in any circumstance. Principled context-free knowledge is detached and generally true. It will always work and is thus very powerful, but its power comes from its across-setting generality. In some sense, situated knowledge is competitive with principled knowledge. When principled context-free knowledge exists alongside situated knowledge, the situated knowledge will be preferred in the particular situation in which it normally operates. Both the Lave *et al.* (1984) description of grocery shopping and the Scribner (1984) milkman study support this claim. In both studies, the experts (shoppers and dairy workers) knew the school mathematics appropriate for their tasks and knew how to do their problems that way, but they used alternative systems. In fact, such situated knowledge seems to be more accurately and flexibly used, and more quickly accessed than the detached but more generalizable knowledge. Usually, when we teach young adults, and maybe even children, new information we like to detach it as much as possible from specific situations, so that it will turn out to be maximally useful. Thus, for example, courses in statistics teach ANOVA, trend analysis and regression, assuming that these will be quantitative tools usable by students in many diverse settings. Users, however, often have difficulty choosing the appropriate statistical tool for specific problems.

Traditionally, situated knowledge has been seen as rather low level, bounded or limited knowledge that is rigid and clumsy, except in its special setting — in short, inelegant, although that view may be changing. The other side of this view romanticizes the 'wisdom' of the basket weaver or knitter and suggests that she truly understands in a deep way basic combinatorial mathematics because the patterns she weaves can be expressed in a mathematical formulation. I find that silly. The chambered Nautilus, for example, does not understand the beauty of its shell either mathematically or esthetically. Although knitters and weavers do have their own formalisms which permit them to share and reproduce patterns in a knowing way and which permit mappings from one system to another, they most certainly do not have generative mathematical knowledge that would let them express it outside the familiar setting.

Moving from knitters and natural mathematics to formal mathematics, let us consider two problems that have some unique features. Both problems use the same numbers but one involves fractions and the other involves ratios. What I am trying to show with these problems is the connection between context, which we know extensively influences the attack on a problem, and bodies of knowledge, which are situationally embedded. Most research has shown that with context cues, correct performance goes up (DeCorte and Verschaffel, 1985). However, the situation itself may change what *is* correct. The following problem illustrates this latter point. In the first situation, a teacher asks students to determine the total amount of pizza consumed if a class ordered two pizzas, and if they ate 11/12 of one pizza and 13/15 of the other (the same size but cut differently). The question is how much did they eat altogether? (Note that this is an illegal problem because the numbers are much larger than those usually used in elementary school fraction problems). The answer, after we convert to a common denominator of 60, is that 107/60ths or 1 and 47/60ths pizza were eaten. Both the teacher and the students would have agreed to this little charade knowing that they were not dealing with real pizzas and that they would not have solved the problem in real life that way. This is a case of *school* situated mathematics.

Now let us suppose that this problem occurred not with imaginary pizzas embedded in a mathematics lesson but with real pizzas ordered for a group of twenty-four people. Suppose that the two large pizzas arrived with one cut into fifteen slices, and the other into twelve. Suppose further that there are two clusters of tables, one with eleven people sitting at it and another with thirteen. What will happen? As this is the real world, I cannot say for sure, but most likely the

Figure 1: A fraction/ratio problem.

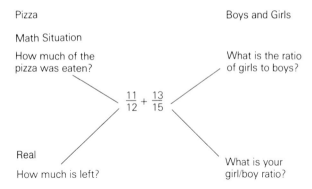

fifteen-slice pizza will go to the table of thirteen and the twelve-slice pizza will go to the table of eleven. I am fairly certain that no one will subdivide the pizza slices by four or five to get sixtieths. Also, the size difference between slices will be judged insignificant so each person will simply take a slice. When calculating how much has been eaten and how much is left over, people would likely add the number of slices (the numerators), ignoring the size difference of the two different denominators. With three slices remaining, they would probably say that more than One-and-three-quarters of the pizzas were eaten and that less than one-quarter of the pizza is left over and would ask, 'Who wants it?' So, the 'real life' pizza situation uses some arithmetic but more to the point it involves violations of some mathematical principles. It plays havoc with the unit (is it combined number of slices or the two whole pizzas?). Another feature to note is that in this case the context not only prompts or suggests solutions, it carries part of the calculation burden.

Now let us look at the same numerical problem in another way and apply it to two school based situations. The first case is one in which we consider two classrooms of mathematics students (one with eleven girls and twelve boys, the other with thirteen girls and fifteen boys). The problem is: What is the ratio of girls to boys in the two classes combined? The lesson topic is ratios and is probably quite separated from the lesson on fractions. In fact, some teachers might not attempt the question at all because it will lead to illegal moves. To answer the question, what is the ratio of girls to boys in the two classrooms combined, one practices the most common fractions bug, adding the tops and bottoms to get 24/27. Now suppose instead teachers are talking 'shop' and one asks what the ratio of girls to boys is in the two fourth grade classrooms combined. What is meant is what is the girl/boy split. S/he replies, 'Oh, about 50–50 with a couple of extra boys.' Technically speaking, s/he is imprecise by one.

What I am trying to show is that not only will we get different answers to the same problem when the problem is stated slightly differently, but we will get different problems with different answers when we make modifications of setting. These setting modifications are universally understood. In fact, when we ask children, who are accustomed to 'school' situations, to be more realistic they are often baffled. For example, in the NAEP question on school buses, students order a fraction of a school bus which is an impossibility in reality, but acceptable in school mathematics. I think this is a situational confusion, not as is claimed, a mathematical one (Peterson, 1986). Further, we will see this difference in answers from people deeply embedded in school type math. Part of this discussion can be framed in terms of issues of accuracy versus precision. In all situations accuracy is desired. The grocery shoppers of Lave's world want to make or rationalize the right decision; the real pizza eaters want to know what is left to eat; the Carraher's street mathematicians want to calculate prices correctly; the Scribner milkmen want to tally milk loads and bills correctly; but in all cases, as Scribner (1984) has pointed out, people want to reduce the mental workload. So, they generate an answer that is circumstantially correct and sufficient. In shopping, one does not need any procedure more precise than the one that will decide between the directionality of two costs. In school math, however, one must develop the most precise and most universal system, one that could be used by anyone who was not a situationally based expert.

Building an Explanation Over Time

In studying elementary arithmetic teachers, I have spent some time focussing on the type of explanations that they offer students. There are three features of the work on explanations that are useful here: a concern with what the inherent *problem* is — what is it that needs to be figured out?; a concern with the way in which the *legal moves* can be made mathematically — what is permissible?; a concern with *a referent* — a way of reasoning or a microworld in which to work. There are many other elements to an explanation but for the issue of which parts of an explanation are situationally built, these three are crucial.

To help give the flavor of situated knowledge as it affects

Figure 2: Time line scenario.

Scene 1	Scene 2	Scene 3	Scene 4
1945	1965	1966	1984
Childhood	Teacher Education	First Year Teaching	20th Year Teaching
GINN	SMSG text	Addison Wesley	Heath

teaching and learning in classrooms, I will trace over a forty-year span the hypothetical origins of a particularly effective mathematics lesson on subtraction with regrouping. To do this, I will outline four scenarios, three of which are built from slim evidence, and one of which is taken from an actual classroom observation. The four scenes will be given in chronological order. *Scene 1* occurs sometime shortly after World War II, between 1945–49, and shows a bright young girl learning subtraction. *Scene 2* shows our girl now as a young woman in the mid-1960s. As a prospective teacher she is relearning elementary arithmetic in her teacher preparation class. *Scene 3* is the day in 1966 when this same woman taught subtraction for the very first time in her own classroom as a teacher. Nearly twenty years later, in 1984, with videotapes running, *scene 4* shows this teacher teaching an excellent mathematics lesson on subtraction with regrouping. The elements to look for across the four scenes are similarity of both argument (explanation) and setting, and a sense of textual familiarity. I will present the critical portion of text and a semantic net analysis of the key passages for each scene.

Scene 1

It was late spring in 1945. Our little girl sat in a small rural parochial school. There were only eighteen students in the third grade class. The teacher was a warm, cheerful nun in her early sixties. She was, of course, single, and she was very dedicated to her students. Our little girl sat with her mathematics book on her desk. The text was considerably smaller than those we have today (about 20 cm by 12 cm) and was remarkable because of its story-like nature, having many more words than numbers per page and smaller print (5.2 characters per cm). The class had just finished two days of adding columns of five or six numbers. The students checked each page of work by adding the columns in the other direction. The teacher wrote five problems on the board and told the students to copy them over in their notebooks and to subtract. (Note that no sign for subtraction was written on the board or in the books.) Our little girl was called to the board to do the problems as soon as she has finished her problems in her own book. She did them correctly and then sat down. The teacher smiled warmly and nodded at her, indicating a correct response. Then she said, 'Today we will continue with subtraction and finding the difference.' She wrote on the board and read from the text book:

Figure 3: Text A.

SOMETHING NEW IN SUBTRACTION

Problem. Harold had 35 cents and spent 15 cents. How many cents did he have left?

This is a problem in subtraction. You have to find 'how much is left.' You do just as $\qquad$ 35
you have always done in subtraction problems. You think 5 less 5 are 0 and 3 less 1 are $\qquad$ <u>15</u>
2. Harold had 20 cents left. $\qquad$ 20

If Harold had had 34 cents, instead of 35 cents, and if he had spent 15 cents, how many cents would he have had left? When Harold started with 35 cents, he had 20 cents left. Now when he starts with 1 cent less—34 is 1 less than 35, is it not?—he will have left 1 cent less. That is, he will have 19 cents left. How can we get this answer?

34
The problem is a subtraction problem; but when you write the numbers, <u>15</u>,
you see that you cannot think 4 less 5, because 4 is already less than 5.

(Buckingham and Osborn, 1928)

The teacher then showed the class how to trade with dimes and cents. She placed three dimes in her right-hand habit pocket, four cents in her left, and a pile of loose pennies on the desk, and then ceremoniously changed one of her dimes for ten cents from her desk. She put the ten new cents into her penny pocket and then subtracted (five pennies from the fourteen) finishing with removing one more dime from her pocket. After this *one* lengthy demonstration, the students set to work on twenty subtraction problems. After completing the set of twenty in ten minutes, the class worked with the special case of zero in the minuend and did another twenty problems. Then, they talked about general subtraction problems, some requiring regrouping and some not, and worked a final set of twenty. There were no notational marks made on the problems in the teacher's demonstration or in the students' work.

Figure 4 is a semantic net showing the concepts in this short presentation. Ovals are concepts and lines represent the connections between them. Subtraction is a problem type. There are changes that can be made in the usual problems which render them unusual. The subtraction problem can be represented by money using dimes and cents to emphasize the base ten aspect of the problem. The *problem* is how to subtract in unusual cases, when the minuend is smaller in a given column (other than the left most) than the subtrahend; the *legal*

Figure 4: Scene 1.

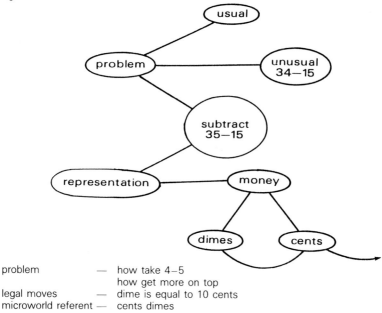

problem	—	how take 4–5
		how get more on top
legal moves	—	dime is equal to 10 cents
microworld referent	—	cents dimes

moves are to transform the units in a higher place value column and add it to the appropriate column; and the *referent* is money.

Scene 2

We see our student some twenty years later in class studying to become a teacher. She had been an English major in her small girls' college in Western Pennsylvania and was taking a one-year course to become an elementary teacher. (While rare, these fifth-year programs did exist at this time.) Her mathematics methods course was separate from her subject matter courses. She was using the 1963 edition of the SMSG text for elementary school teachers. In SMSG (Bell *et al.*, 1963) twenty-three pages are devoted to addition and subtraction. The text is 25 cm by 17 cm with an average of 5.6 characters per cm.

The general approach taken by the kindly, if diffident, male professor was to follow the text closely, to lecture, and to define subtraction in three different ways — two of which were related to sets, and one to addition — and then to build operations from each definition. The sets given in the text refer to stars, diamonds, and other abstract shapes. The text, as shown in Figure 5, reads a little like a Tom Lehrer song.

Figure 5: Text B.

First Definition of Subtraction

We can use the idea of remainder set to define the operation of subtraction of whole numbers. If *a* is a number and if *b* is a number less than or equal to *a*, we first choose a set A such that $N(A) = a$. Next we pick a set B which is a subset of A and such that $N(B) = b$ ...

Second Definition of Subtraction

This definition does not use the idea of remainder set, but uses the ideas of union of disjoint sets and of one-to-one matching. If *a* is a number and if *b* is a number, with $b \leq a$, we start by choosing a set A with $N(A) = a$ and a set $\tilde{B}$ disjoint from A with $N(\tilde{B}) = b$. ($\tilde{B}$ is used for this set instead of B to remind us that it is a set disjoint from A and not a subset of A as B was in the first definition. In both cases the use of the letter B in the name reflects the fact that the set is chosen to have *b* members.) ...

Third Definition of Subtraction

In this definition we do not use sets at all, but instead work directly with whole numbers and the operation of addition.

Our definition is:

$$a - b \text{ is the number } n \text{ for which } b + n = a.$$

Another way of putting this is:

The statements

$$a - b = n$$

and

$$b + n = a$$

mean exactly the same thing.

From this point of view, subtraction is the operation of finding the unknown addend, *n*, in the addition problem

$$b + n = a \ldots$$

Horizontal Form

$$
\begin{aligned}
342 - 187 &= (300 + 40 + 2) - (100 + 80 + 7) \\
&= (300 + 30 + 12) - (100 + 80 + 7) \\
&= (200 + 130 + 12) - (100 + 80 + 7) \\
&= (200 - 100) + (130 - 80) + (12 - 7) \\
&= 100 + 50 + 5 \\
&= 155
\end{aligned}
$$

Vertical Form

$$
\begin{array}{llll}
342 = 300 + 40 + 2 = 300 + 30 + 12 = 200 + 130 + 12 \\
187 = 100 + 80 + 7 = 100 + 80 + 7 = \underline{100 + 80 + 7} \\
\phantom{187 = 100 + 80 + 7 = 100 + 80 + 7 = } 100 + 50 + 5 = 155
\end{array}
$$

Introduction

In the preceding chapter we dealt with the fundamental connection between the union of sets and the addition of whole numbers. This fundamental connection is:

$$N(A) + N(B) = N(A \cup B),$$

whenever A and B are disjoint sets. Here N(A) is the number of elements in A or the number property of A, and N(B) is the number of elements in B.

We now come to the operation of subtraction of whole numbers. This operation is more complicated, conceptually, than addition. There are two fundamentally different approaches to subtraction. The first approach starts with set operations and defines the operation of subtraction of numbers in terms of these operations. The second approach is more abstract, and defines subtraction directly in terms of addition of whole numbers.

To make things even more complicated, the first approach, the more concrete one, can

Figure 5 (con't)
be done in two different ways, thus yielding three different ways of thinking about subtraction . . .

Remainder Sets
Suppose we have a set A and another set B which is a subset of A. Now consider the set which consists of all the elements of A which are *not* elements of B. We call this new set a *remainder set* and denote it by A ~ B. For example, if A is the set of all the children in your class and B is the set of boys in your class, then A ~ B is the set of girls in your class. Similarly, if A = { ○, △, □, ☆ } and B = { ○, □ }, then A ~ B = { △, ☆ }. Also, A ~ A = { }, the empty set. Note that removing the elements of subset B from A is indicated by the symbol '~', read 'wiggle,' and not by the familiar sign '−' which we reserve for the subtraction of two numbers.
   We now have two set operations, that of forming a union and that of forming a remainder set. The fundamental connection between them is;

$$(A \sim B) \cup B = A$$

   In words: If we first form the remainder set A ~ B and then form the union of it with B, we get back the original set A . . .
   The idea of the inverse of an operation is a very important idea in mathematics, as it is in many non-mathematical situations, and it is an idea which you will meet again and again. If we wish to put the idea in a non-mathematical situation we might ask the question, What will 'undo' taking two steps backward? . . .

(Bell *et al.*, 1963)

Note that there is absolutely nothing in the text on how to teach. There is no reference to the student at all or what might be hard or easy to learn. There is a brief verbal mapping that indicates how each definition solves a different word problem (not in the portion shown). The mathematics is elegant and powerful. The pedagogy is lousy. The explanation builds on a system of mathematical definitions of inverse, identity properties, and number systems. It is a perfect example of principled knowledge. From interviews, we know that our teacher retained a considerable amount of this information twenty years later but it was not used in the lessons she taught. This discussion is not meant to disparage the mathematical nature of this treatment, nor to laugh again at new math. I am trying to show why this information is or is not used when a teacher is in the long forty-year process of building knowledge from which to teach. In this particular case there is no connection between what the teacher came into the environment knowing — namely, the base ten number system and 'borrowing' within it and the new material. Further, as we shall see, there will be no forward connection to the texts or students with whom she will be working.

   Figure 6 is a semantic net of the concepts handled in scene 2. The two central concepts are subtraction and number. Subtraction is defined in three ways and number has two properties (i.e., that it is expressed in a base ten notation which can be expanded and that the expansions can be moved around). The *problem* is to select a definition

Figure 6: Scene 2.

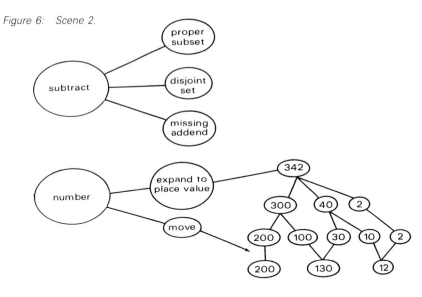

problem	—	to have at least 'as many ones in ones place' ...
legal moves	—	expand numbers by base 10 rules
		rearrange numbers by associative and commutative property
microworld referent	—	numbers
		sets of objects

of subtraction that is suitable and to have '... as many ones in the ones' place ...'. The *legal moves* involve the application of learned principles such as commutativity, and associativity, etc. The *referent* systems are the numbers themselves and sets of shapes. The assumption underlying the acquisitional process is that when properties of the numbers are clearly understood and the definitions of permissible moves associated with operations are also then procedures will fall out naturally.

Scene 3

It is late March in 1966 and our teacher has just finished teaching column addition and has had students check it by adding in the opposite direction. Tomorrow, she will teach subtraction with re-grouping for the first time. The pages of the students' text book are shown in figure 7. The text is larger than the original student text (22 cm by 17 cm), uses two colors, still has considerable writing on the page and at an average of 4.2 characters per cm, and poses the problem for the student in a similar way.

Figure 7: Text C.

Changing One Ten to Ten Ones
REGROUPING IN SUBTRACTION

Betty was trying to subtract thirty-eight from sixty-four. She did not know how to subtract eight ones from four ones. She asked Ruth to help her.

Ruth said, 'I will show you with some sticks.'

First she showed sixty-four with the sticks (see Picture 1).

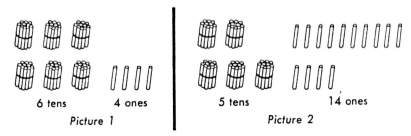

6 tens	4 ones	5 tens	14 ones
	Picture 1		Picture 2

'You cannot take away eight sticks from four sticks,' she said. 'So, take one of the tens and use it as ten ones. This gives you fourteen ones in all' (see picture 2) 'This is called "exchanging" or "regrouping" a ten. Instead of six tens and four ones, you have five tens and fourteen ones.'

'Now subtract eight ones from fourteen ones is six ones. Three tens from five tens is two tens. The answer is two tens and six ones, or twenty-six.'

Then Ruth showed Betty how to work without sticks.

Study this example. Say each missing number.

$$
\begin{array}{r}
{\scriptstyle 5\ \ 14} \\
6\ \ 4 \\
-\ 3\ \ 8 \\
\hline
2\ \ 6
\end{array}
$$

First subtract the ones. You cannot subtract eight from four. Take one of the six tens, leaving five tens. Use the one ten as ten ones, and make fourteen ones in all. Think 14 − 8 = _?_ Write _?_ in ones place.

Then subtract the tens. Think 5 − 3 = _?_ Write _?_ in tens place.

The answer is _?_.

The colored numbers usually are not written, but are kept in mind. When you find you can keep them in mind, stop writing the numbers shown in color.

Copy each example and subtract. Check by adding.

1.	62	86	75	53	97	81	61	73	74
	28	67	37	26	39	25	42	25	47

2.	91	72	85	96	84	93	65	97	62
	74	13	48	58	35	48	16	18	36

Cents are subtracted like any other two-place numbers. Remember to put a dollar sign and decimal point in each answer.

3.	$.51	$.45	$.94	$.82	$.63	$.78	$.94	$.36	$.95
	.16	.29	.26	.57	.34	.59	.69	.17	.58

Solve the following problems. Each time think of the reason why you subtract to get the answer.

4. The baker made eighty-four doughnuts. He sold all but eighteen. How many did he sell?
5. Tom's mother baked thirty-six cookies. She has nineteen left. The boys ate the rest. How many cookies did the boys eat?
6. On Monday Jack counted forty-three bicycles outside the school. On Tuesday he counted seventeen. On Tuesday there were how many fewer bicycles outside the school than on Monday?
7. Bill had $.52 in his pocket when he went out to play. He lost some of his money while he was playing. He counted what was left and found he had only $.35. How much money did he lose?

(Randall *et al.*, 1962)

In spite of the fact that the fundamental research on arithmetic 'bugs' was still more than ten years in the future, our teacher had a sense that this lesson is somewhat more important and subtle than some others and she sat down to think about how she was going to 'get through' it. We do not really know, of course, what she thought then or even if there was any time to do any thinking at all. Clearly the resources she had available — the situations, if you will, that she could call on — would come from three different sources. One, was what she remembered of her own childhood learning experiences; a second was what she remembered from her training as a student teacher, and the third was what the environment around her could offer from texts, her neighboring teachers, and students. She probably did not have experience in the teaching of subtraction during her six-week stint in student teaching. More than likely, she taught a unit on Roman numerals or measurement. Given the textbook that the teacher had to work from, she probably tried using some sticks in her demonstration. She did not introduce the sticks before she taught the lesson, but rather handed bundles of sticks to the students and had them work through the example in the book. It is also likely that she made no special mention of the difficulty that stimulates the regrouping process although the text does indicate it. That is, she may not have mentioned exactly why they had to take the rubber band off one of the bundles of ten sticks in order to solve the problem. Her explanation probably rested on demonstrating with sticks that you could get enough ones from a bundle of tens, and then went almost directly into rewriting numerals, ending with the so-called short form. She showed and the students did. I imagine that the explanation that she offered was fairly complete in the sense of demonstration and she may have even shown that there was no change in the total value of the minuend because of renaming. I am fairly confident of this scenario because, although we were not around to watch this particular teacher, in her first year we do know that most of our novice teachers behave in a similar way.

Figure 8 is a semantic net of the concepts that form the basis of this hypothesized lesson as taken from the text. The net shows that some problems are subtraction problems. They come in two types, usual and unusual. The unusual ones are those like 64−38. The *problem* is how to do subtraction when a number in a column of the minuend, other than the left most, is smaller than it its corresponding number in the subtrahend. Subtraction problems also can be *represented* using money and sticks as well as just being written out. The money is of two types, dimes and cents; similarly the sticks can be grouped as tens

Figure 8: Scene 3.

problem   — how take 8 sticks from 4 sticks
legal moves   — take 1 of the tens and use it as ten ones
microworld referent — sticks, money, numerals with cross out notations

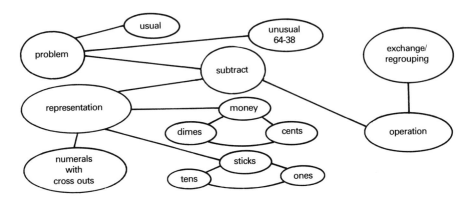

or remain as loose ones. An operation label of 'regrouping' is introduced in the text and cross–outs are shown in the written presentation. The *legal moves* are to exchange or regroup. The *referents* are money and sticks.

Scene 4

Another twenty years has passed and it was the spring of 1984. There have been several late freezes, making the roads hazardous but our teacher was, of course, there on time as she always was. She was warm, friendly and focussed on her students as a family. She was about to teach subtraction with regrouping to her class of second graders. It was a little different than in past years because a team of observers had been videotaping and interviewing her for several weeks. The team had also taken a good deal of time to interview eight of the students. The textbook had changed dramatically in twenty years. It is larger (22 cm by 17 cm), there are barely two characters per cm, there is almost no language, rather it is all numbers. However, the basic argument structure has remained the same.

In this introductory lesson, the teacher focussed considerable energy on building up several representations of the subtraction process and on delineating the class of problems known as foolers, (see Leinhardt, in press for a detailed description of lessons). While teaching, she was faced with multiple trade offs, and possible branches in her decisions of which perilous routes she should follow into the

Figure 9: Text D.

Name_____

Subtract.

Two-place subtraction, regrouping.   (one hundred forty-five) **145**

(Rucker, 1979)

161

Figure 9 (con't)

Subtract.

61	32	43	75	90
−28	−19	−27	−18	−36

74	65	62	46	81
−35	−48	−19	−38	−26

71	52	60	63	72
−53	−19	−46	−59	−26

64	85	93	83	51
−27	−36	−44	−58	−28

(Rucker, 1979)

murky lands of misconception. She could have focussed on the nature of the number system and the base ten notation, but the subtraction operation might slip away. She could have focussed on the addition and subtraction facts, but then the conceptual whole might have slid away. She could have emphasized the operation of subtraction at the expense of concept, or she could have introduced too many concrete (conceptual) systems, not one of which would quite work. All in all, it was a tough lesson to teach. She decided to start with a quick brush-up on a portion of the adding skills, a review of simple subtraction, and an identification of the set of problems she called foolers. These refreshed notions had to be available later in the lesson in order for her to get her explanation across. If she had reversed the process, her explanation would have to have been interrupted.

The teacher began her lesson with a review of adding tens to ones, moved into a review of regular two-digit subtraction and embedded in the review, two foolers, a term she had introduced previously.[1] She then had the students solve subtraction problems using bundles of sticks which the students themselves had assembled in a prior lesson on addition — a correction from her first lesson in 1965. After working with simple two-digit problems, she posed the problem, 26–8, and had the students use the sticks to generate the answer. The students found that they could unband a bundle of sticks to get more ones. The students were very familiar with the sticks, as they were with the next two representation systems that she used, felt strips and a renaming chart.

Figure 10 shows the semantic net of the concepts introduced in this lesson. Some problems are subtraction problems of which there are two types: foolers and non-foolers. Foolers have a number in the minuend smaller than its corresponding number in the subtrahend, which is the *problem*. Subtraction of foolers can be represented by feltstrip or stick *referents*. There exists a rename operation which is a move of *proven legality* that permits changing tens to ones, and so the solution of the problem.

When we consider the sets of lessons in scenes 1 through 4, we can see that certain approaches to the situation have remained consistent over the thirty-five years.

- The sticks are similar to the coins that were used in scene 1 and they are clearly present in the first lesson material from which she taught in scene 3.
- The felt strips in scene 4 are similar to the coins of Scene 1 in that their operation is to *trade*, not unbind.

Figure 10: Scene 4.

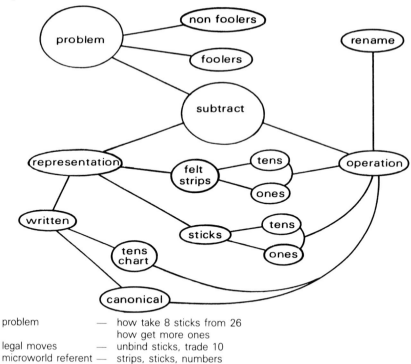

problem	—	how take 8 sticks from 26
		how get more ones
legal moves	—	unbind sticks, trade 10
microworld referent	—	strips, sticks, numbers

- The number chart and the sticks in scene 4 are present in the textbook that she is working from in 1984.
- Referents are consistent and supported by texts except for scene 2, which used sets, subsets, and principles.
- The need to show the problem or the task for which regrouping is a solution is present in scene 1. It is present in the 1966 and 1985 textbooks of scenes 3 and 4 and it is noticeably absent in the 1963 edition of the SMSG of scene 2. However, the notion of getting more (or equal) ones is consistent in all four scenes.
- Concrete base-ten referents are likewise present in the three trading scenarios but are absent in the student teacher's text, and of course, the general setting is the same in the three elementary classroom scenes.
- Legality of moves is proved by demonstrated equality of quantity in scenes 1, 3, 4 and by properties in scene 2.

If we look at the relationships between the features of the three classroom presentations we have described and the logical connection between concepts, several things emerge. The textbooks tend to present a fairly stable argument for why and how to regroup when subtracting. The microworlds or referents are similar if not identical. We can see how a full blown instructional explanation might have come to be. Further, we can see why the teacher's own text (SMSG) did not contribute to that system of thinking and why it remains isolated from the core of her instructional or pedagogical knowledge. The teacher's instructional reasoning is built around both the reality of a new mathematical activity and the joint reality of how 7-year-old students will come to understand this material. This is the situational knowledge of teachers. We can see in scene 1, a structural similarity that is present in scene 3 and scene 4 and is noticeably absent in scene 2. For example, scene 2 does not distinguish between those problems that require regrouping and those that do not. Because the *problems* are not different mathematically, it is only a matter of whether or not you apply the commutative property. The primary referent *system* is the set definitions of subtraction, a system which is not used in either the student text problems over the next twenty years *or* in teacher notes for solutions. Again, it is not that the abstractions of SMSG are bad; they or others may be excellent. However, they do not fit the situation. To make them 'fit', considerable work would have to be done.

Circles as a Counter Example

Lest all of this sound as though I believe that all early mathematics must be taught either procedurally or experientially because teachers are totally bound by how they learned it, let me describe one very convincing instance of a mathematical explanation being recommended for students. It is one which I think many teachers would readily adopt if it were offered to them. This example comes directly from an article by Ott, Sommers and Creamer (1983) in the *Arithmetic Teacher*, entitled, 'But Why Does $C = \pi d$?'. In it the authors argue that having students measure diameters and circumferences of a lot of round things does not in any way get at the heart of *why*, it just restates what *is*. In almost all textbooks, over the past twenty-five-year period, this has been the approach: Give the child a hands-on experience with circles. Ott *et al.* (1983) however, suggest that the important aspect is understanding the notion of a constant ratio and that understanding the fixed progression of the particular family of constants, namely, the ratio of the diameter to the perimeter of regular polygons, is especially relevant. They recommend doing this by having students find this relationship for squares and hexagons, etc. showing that the ratio is the same for similar regular figures and that

Figure 11: Ratio of diagonal to perimeter.

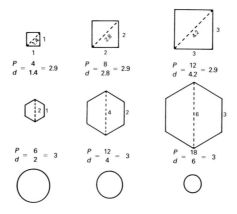

$$\frac{P}{d} = \frac{4}{1.4} = 2.9 \qquad \frac{P}{d} = \frac{8}{2.8} = 2.9 \qquad \frac{P}{d} = \frac{12}{4.2} = 2.9$$

$$\frac{P}{d} = \frac{6}{2} = 3 \qquad \frac{P}{d} = \frac{12}{4} = 3 \qquad \frac{P}{d} = \frac{18}{6} = 3$$

Source: Ott, M. Sommers D.D., and Creamer K. (1983) "But why does C = πd?"

the ratio increases as the number of sides increase. While I am certain many sixth-grade teachers have never thought of this way of working with circles, I do not think they would have much trouble changing. This is because there is a relatively simple substitution of one aspect of an activity for another and one specific portion of the explanation for another. It requires building a new system of connections but doing so by substitution rather than by constructing an entirely unique plan of attack, as was required by the explanation for subtraction with regrouping provided in the student teacher's textbook in scene 2.

Situated Knowledge as Pentimento

With apologies both to Lillian Hellman (1973) and artists in general, what we have posited here is an historical trace of the type of explanation that one teacher built up for herself over time. It is a rich pentimento in that it contains many layers of understanding and experience. It is complex in that sights, smells, sounds of important actors — whether they are former teachers or classmates or the face of the child who just couldn't understand and never got it — are present alongside, and most probably connected to, the mathematical logic this teacher uses as she teaches. It is interdependent in that aspects of the situation are themselves tools for the application of the knowledge as it is presented in lessons. A portion of this layered set of knowledge results in what Putnam (1987) has called a curriculum script; a portion contributes to the formulation and nature of the explanation a teacher offers when faced with the richly contextualized task of teaching second graders how to understand and do subtraction. When we seek to alter this teaching, we must do so not only with sensitivity and care but also with an understanding of how the nature of the teaching we are looking at came to be and why it is as it is. We must connect the new perspective to the existing one.

I hope that this does not come across as an anti-mathematical formulation of teaching because I feel that for many teachers their understanding of the mathematics was as carefully built up as their other associations. In fact, it is precisely because of that strength of their mathematical and instructional beliefs that implanting a new view becomes so very difficult.

Note

1 In our analyses of explanations, we have identified several conditions which must be met if the explanation is to work. Among these are that the subskills needed in the work are available when needed. This means that if the teacher is using an example of 37−18, when she gets to the point of showing the students that the three tens can be rearranged into two tens and how many ones, she does not want the class to have to stop and spend time figuring out what ten plus seven is equal to. After all, we are right smack in the middle of the problem and mental working space is at a premium.

References

BELL, M.S., CHINN, W.G., McDERMOTT, M., PIETERS, R.S. and WILLERDING, M. (1963) *Studies in Mathematics, Volume IX: A Brief Course in Mathematics for Elementary School Teachers*, Palo Alto, CA, The Board of Trustees of the Leland Stanford Junior University.

BUCKINGHAM, B.R. and OSBORN, W.J. (1928) *The Buckingham-Osborne Searchlight Arithmetics Teacher's Manual*, Boston, MA, Ginn & Company.

BURTON, R.R., BROWN, J.S., FISCHER, G. (1984) 'Skiing as a model of instruction' in ROGOFF, B. and LAVE, J. (Eds), *Everyday Cognition*, Massachusetts, Harvard University Press, pp. 139–50.

CARRAHER, T.N., CARRAHER, D.W. and SCHLIEMANN, A.D. (1983) 'Mathematics in the streets and in schools', *British Journal of Developmental Psychology*, 3(1), 21–29.

CHASE, W.G. and SIMON, H.A. (1973) 'Perception in chess', *Cognitive Psychology*, 4, pp. 55–81.

CHI, M.T.H., GLASER, R. and REES, R. (Eds) (1982) 'Expertise in problem solving' in STERNBERG, R. (Ed.), *Advances in the Psychology of Human Intelligence*, Volume 1, Hillsdale, NJ, Lawrence Erlbaum, pp. 7–76.

DeCorte, E. and Verschaffel, L. (1985) 'Empirical validation of computer models of children's word problem solving', paper presented at the annual meeting of the American Educational Research Association, Chicago, April.

Hellman, L. (1973) *Pentimento, A Book of Portraits.* Boston, MA, Little, Brown.

Lave, J., Murtaugh, M. and de la Rocha, O. (1984) 'The dialectic of arithmetic in grocery shopping', in Rogoff, B. and Lave, J. (Eds), *Everyday Cognition,* Massachusetts, Harvard University Press, pp. 67–116.

Leinhardt, G. (in press) 'The development of an expert explanation: An analysis of a sequence of subtraction lessons', *Cognition and Instruction.*

Leinhardt, G. and Greeno, J.G. (1986) 'The cognitive skill of teaching', *Journal of Educational Psychology,* 78, 2, pp. 75–95.

Leinhardt, G. and Smith, D.A. (1985) 'Expertise in mathematics instruction: Subject matter knowledge,' *Journal of Educational Psychology,* 77, 3, pp. 247–71.

Ott, J.M., Sommers, D.D. and Creamer, K. (1983) But why does c = πd? *Arithmetic Teacher,* November, pp. 38–40.

Peterson, P.L. (1986) 'Selecting students and services for compensatory education: Lessons from aptitude-treatment interaction research', paper presented at the Conference on Effects of Alternative Designs in Compensatory Education, Washington, D.C. June.

Putnam, R.T. (1987). 'Structuring and adjusting content for students: A study of live and simulated tutoring', *American Educational Research Journal,* 24, 1, pp. 13–48.

Randall, J.H., Fehr, H.F., Gunderson, A.G., Phillips, J. McK., Urbancek, J.J., Wren, F.L. and Wrightstone, J.W. (1962) *Learning to Use Arithmetic, Book 3.* Boston, MA, D.C. Heath and Company.

Rucker, W.E. and Dilley, C.A. (1979) *Heath Mathematics, 2nd grade.* Lexington, MA, D.C. Heath and Company.

Scribner, S. (1984) 'Studying working intelligently', in Rogoff, B. and J. Lave (Eds) *Everyday Cognition: Its Development in Social Context,* Cambridge, MA, Harvard University Press, pp. 9–40.

10 Changing Teachers' Conceptions of Teaching and Learning

Kate Johnston

Introduction

This chapter examines the relationship between the stated intentions and the classroom practice of two teachers involved in a curriculum development initiative, The Children's Learning in Science Project.

The project, which subscribes to a constructivist view of learning (Driver and Bell, 1986) has worked collaboratively with groups of teachers in the development of teaching strategies and materials in three topic areas in high school science — energy, particulate theory, and plant nutrition (see CLIS, 1987). These teaching materials take account of students' prior ideas in the topic area, and provide learning experiences which interact with these prior ideas and which aim to encourage more active involvement in learning by the students.

The two teachers under consideration here were involved in the particulate theory working group. This group of ten teachers devised a series of lessons, 'Approaches to Teaching the Particulate Theory of Matter' for 14-year-old students. The lessons followed the generalized outline suggested by Driver and Oldham:

— an elicitation phase, encouraging students to put forward their own ideas;
— a restructuring phase, providing experiences which interact with students' prior ideas and encourage them to develop, modify and change these ideas;
— an application phase, where students are provided with opportunities to try out new ideas in a variety of situations, both familiar and unfamiliar.

An outline of the particulate theory teaching scheme is shown in figure 1.

Figure 1:   Outline of the Particulate Theory Teaching Scheme.

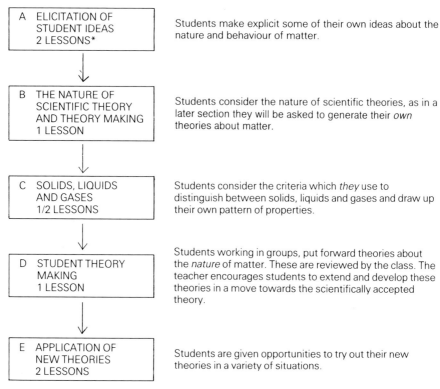

A ELICITATION OF STUDENT IDEAS — 2 LESSONS*
Students make explicit some of their own ideas about the nature and behaviour of matter.

B THE NATURE OF SCIENTIFIC THEORY AND THEORY MAKING — 1 LESSON
Students consider the nature of scientific theories, as in a later section they will be asked to generate their *own* theories about matter.

C SOLIDS, LIQUIDS AND GASES — 1/2 LESSONS
Students consider the criteria which *they* use to distinguish between solids, liquids and gases and draw up their own pattern of properties.

D STUDENT THEORY MAKING — 1 LESSON
Students working in groups, put forward theories about the *nature* of matter. These are reviewed by the class. The teacher encourages students to extend and develop these theories in a move towards the scientifically accepted theory.

E APPLICATION OF NEW THEORIES — 2 LESSONS
Students are given opportunities to try out their new theories in a variety of situations.

*1 lesson = 70–80 minutes

The chapter focusses on an analysis of the way in which the two teachers dealt with part of the student theory making lesson, which occurs about two-thirds of the way through the teaching scheme. This lesson has been selected as it illustrates one of the crucial pedagogic features of the teaching scheme, the management of open discussion.

In order to set the scene for the lesson analysis there now follows a brief description of each teacher, a short summary of the student theory making lesson, and an account of the framework for the analysis.

The Two Teachers

Teacher A has been teaching for over twenty years. He entered teaching as a non-specialist science teacher, and is now Head of

Science in a co-educational school on the outskirts of a large town. The school has 1000 students on its roll, aged between 13 and 16 years. Teacher A was aware that his initial teaching qualification (non-graduate) was not held in high esteem, so some years ago he decided to involve himself in further study. He recently completed an Open University degree.

Teacher B has been teaching for eleven years. He obtained a degree in applied science and completed a one-year postgraduate teacher training course. He is also Head of Science in a suburban coeducational school. There are 920 students between the ages of 11–18 at this school. After working with the project for two years teacher B has decided to study for a master's degree in education.

Both teachers displayed a high level of commitment to the work of the project, attending meetings of the particulate theory working group after school and at weekends. Both also displayed a willingness to allow a researcher from the project to visit their classrooms to observe their initial trials of the particulate theory teaching scheme.

The Student Theory Making Lesson

Under consideration is part of section D of figure 1 *student theory making*. Students have worked in groups to come up with their own theories as to the nature of solids, liquids and gases. They have developed these theories with reference back to discussions held in previous lessons about the properties of matter and the nature of scientific theories and by drawing on any other ideas which they might have. After discussing their theories, each group produces a poster, which is displayed on the wall of the classroom, for others to see. A nominated member of each group then reports back to the rest of the class on their poster. It is this report back session which is the focus of the analysis. The report-back, in effect a class discussion, had the following aims:

— firstly to provide opportunities for students to share their ideas with others in the class;
— to encourage students to consider how their theories might *differ* from those of others in the class and to question each other about the theories put forward;
— finally to provide the teacher with the opportunity to encourage students to make a critical evaluation of their ideas as a prelude to moving towards the scientifically accepted theory.

The Framework for the Analysis

The Data

For each teacher the following data are available:

— transcripts of audiotapes of the lesson;
— transcripts of audiotapes of discussions between researcher and teacher both before and after the lesson;
— written comments on the lesson from the teacher.

Intended Pedagogic Strategies

The working group hoped that during the student theory making lesson, teachers would adopt some of the following strategies:

— an indication by the teacher that he/she values students' own ideas;
— an acceptance of these ideas as valid alternative points of view (at least in the first part of the report-back session);
— active encouragement to students to listen to others and to value the ideas of others;
— asking questions in an open way, so that students have opportunities to put forward their own ideas rather than trying to guess the answers which the teacher desires;
— asking questions which check out the meanings which students attach to words and symbols rather than making the assumption that meanings will automatically be shared by students and teacher.

Instruments for Analysis of the Data

The bulk of the analysis has been carried out on the transcripts of lessons. In attempting to draw up a framework for this analysis the following were considered; the project's stated views on learning, the implications of such a view for pedagogy, and the list of pedagogic strategies described above which the particulate theory group itself saw as being central to the teaching of the student theory making lesson.

The analysis of lesson transcripts has been carried out in two ways. Firstly, a simple count has been made of the proportion of open and closed questions asked by each teacher. For the purpose of this analysis, open questions are defined as those which provide students with opportunities to put forward their own ideas; closed questions are intended to elicit specific responses (the teacher already knows the answer which he/she requires).

Secondly, the transcript has been examined in more detail, looking at the ways in which each teacher uses verbal interactions in attempting to achieve some of the intended pedagogic strategies. The following specific strategies have been considered:

(i)   general statements by the teacher stressing the value of student ideas;

(ii) non-critical acceptance of individual contributions from students;

(iii) strategies to open up discussion, for example, asking for more than one student's response to the same question;

(iv) positively accepting students' ideas, perhaps with development from them;

(v)   rewording/reconstructing student ideas;

(vi) asking probing questions to check meanings;

(vii) introducing teacher ideas;

(viii) simple negative responses to student ideas;

(ix) criticism of student ideas;

(x)   ignoring student ideas.

The analysis: Teacher A

Before the Lesson

During discussions with the researcher (R) prior to this lesson, Teacher A expressed some concerns about the way in which it might progress.

> The next bit strikes me as being the hard bit, generating this particulate theory. And I'm a little bit unsure here. They're supposed to discuss it, then we have to come up with a theory. How far am I supposed to do any — kind of — demonstrations to illustrate ...?

He was very concerned about spending more than one lesson on this section, partly because of the absence of practical activities:

> T: You see there's no practical work is there and (pause).
> R: So you're unhappy about running a whole lesson without practical work?

> *T:* Yes, in the sense that we don't want to lose touch with the fact that they are, that we are looking at a practical subject, and we're trying to figure out the reasoning behind the experiments. I mean the practical work is the important element.

Later he commented:

> I'm loath to spend more than one lesson on the theory making because there is no practical for them to do, and I think you do get to a point where you start — you *have* to look at some actual things and say well how do you explain. I mean at some point you have to make the transition into looking at some real situations and saying how do you explain this using the idea of atoms.

He was quite clear in his own mind before the lesson started that he would keep within the time limit. He also had a reasonably clear idea of his own role in the report-back session:

> *R:* Supposing they don't get (the theory) by the end of the lesson?
> *T:* Ah! (laughs)
> *R:* If they're not ready . . .
> *T:* My feeling is going to get stage managed so that it happens. I mean isn't that the intention?
> *R:* Yeah?
> *T:* I mean, to manoeuvre it a bit — but it doesn't want to be too heavy-handed . . .

He saw his role as that of 'stage manager', 'drawing out the threads' from the students' ideas.

> Well after the posters we want them reporting back, and for me to summarize what comes out in their posters, because I think that's the crucial bit in a way isn't it . . . and then to pull out the accepted theory from there. I mean, that's the unknown bit.

He was therefore rather concerned about what the students might put on their theory posters. Would there be enough there to enable him to operate in the way he envisaged?

> When I started to plan out exactly what I was going to do in the lesson and the next one, that's the bit that left me a bit uneasy, because I'm not convinced that they are going to come up with the theory without an awful lot of prompting.

This issue of 'what they are going to come up with' appeared to be his dominant concern just prior to the start of the lesson.

The Lesson in Outline

Teacher A was working with a class of twenty-six students, considered to be of above average ability by the school. They had just spent twenty-five minutes working in discussion groups (as shown in figure 2) putting forward their own theories as to the nature of matter. The six groups (each consisting of four or five students) had produced posters which the teacher displayed on walls around the laboratory. Students were given five minutes to walk around the laboratory to study each others' posters. They then returned to the places which they had occupied during the group discussion and teacher A stood at the front of the class, in front of the demonstration bench (figure 2). There then followed a report-back session, which lasted a total of eighteen minutes. It took the following form.

Firstly, the teacher asked a member of a discussion group to describe their poster. He then summarized the main points on the poster before turning to the next group. The six posters all referred to particulate ideas though many put forward ideas which were not 'scientific' in nature.

The teacher then summarized what he saw as the important points raised by the posters. This, though not explicitly stated by him, was his introduction of the 'scientific theory'. A homework task was set, and finally, students were given a 'particulate theory' summary sheet which had already been prepared.

The activities described above will now be examined in more detail.

The Lesson in Detail

Report-back on posters

The report-back was introduced in the following way:

> I'm going to ask somebody in each group just to say something about their ideas, very briefly. I'll try and draw some of the threads together.

and to the first group to speak:

Figure 2: Teacher A: Class arrangement for report-back session.

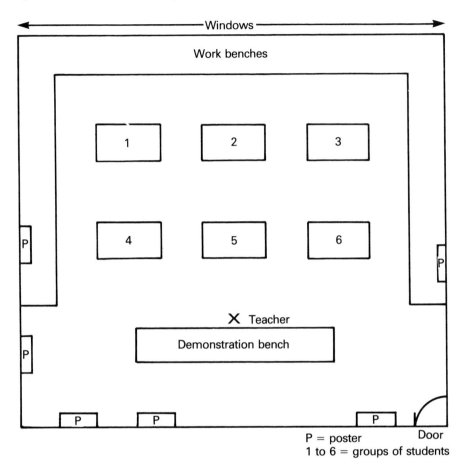

Just tell us briefly what is happening. For the rest of you —
listen to what each group has said, because there are some
common threads running around all of these.

The report-back took the following form, where

Q = question from teacher
R = student response
T = extended teacher talk

In this discussion there were no student-initiated questions or
statements.

Poster 1: Q.R.Q.R.Q.R.T.
Poster 2: Q.R.Q.R.R.T.
Poster 3: Q.T.
Poster 4: T.Q.R.T.Q.
Poster 5: T.Q.R.Q.R.Q.R.Q.R.Q.R.Q.R.Q.R.Q.R.Q.R.Q.
R.Q.R.Q.R.Q.R.Q.T.
Poster 6: T.

At any one time only the students whose poster was under discussion were involved in the question/response sessions. For posters 3, 4 and 6 students were given little or no opportunity to make an input.

In total the teacher asked twenty-two questions and students made twenty responses, most limited to a few words and some completely inaudible.

The proportion of open to closed questions was five open to seventeen closed.

The open questions were in general invitations to students to describe their understanding of an issue:

What have you decided about these atoms in order to explain?
Was there any particular experiment that made you think along these lines?

Six of the closed questions were checks on information on the posters:

You mentioned magnetism didn't you?
How did you draw your atoms in liquids?

The others were of a more probing nature, checking understanding, often in a way which forced students to make an either/or choice:

Do you mean by squashed that the atoms themselves are squashed more, or do you mean pushed closer together?

An examination of the verbal strategies used by teacher A, with reference back to the list on p 6–7 reveals the following:

Little was said explicitly about the value of students' ideas, [Strategy (i)] though the teacher did ask the class to listen to each group at the start of the session, and also commented on group 2's poster:

I'm not really too concerned about where they got that idea from; what they've been able to do is to relate it to what we are doing here. Don't feel that knowledge gained from somewhere else mustn't be used. I mean the whole point is trying to bring together things that you already know about.

When students put forward ideas in the discussion, the teacher's response to them could be a neutral acceptance, phrases like 'right, go on', or 'I'm happy with your spacing idea, that seems reasonable enough' being used. [strategy (ii)]. However as most of the report-back on the posters came from the teacher himself, in his 'drawing some of the threads together' he was able to select only those aspects of each poster which he thought reasonable, thus obviating the necessity to make negative comments [strategies (viii) and (ix)].

As the teacher was making the greatest contribution to the report-back, there were many opportunities for him to pull out ideas from students' problems and develop them [strategy (iv)].

Right, so one of the key things they're talking about is the packing of the particles, and it does say on their sheet about diffusion, that in liquids diffusion can take place because the atoms are less tightly packed together than they are in solids, and when I talked to them, they were talking about them (atoms) going in between each other and that in a gas it can take place very quickly because they're spaced further apart.

An example of strategy (v), which illustrates the teacher introducing words which students had chosen not to use, occurs in this short discussion of what holds molecules together:

S1: Everything — all the molecules are joined up by energy of some sort.

S2: Energy.

T: Actually when I was talking to you, you didn't use the word energy, you were talking about bonds and forces.

S1: Oh, yes, magnetic fields.

S2: Some sort of force of some sort.

T: They were not sure what kind of force it was but they were talking about magnetism and electricity, and you can seen even from a distance that they've drawn lines between their atoms. Now they did make it quite clear to me that the lines are not things. The dots are the things ... molecules or atoms. The lines were just representing the fact that there was something holding them together, and they have introduced the idea of forces of some kind.

While the teacher was putting forward this explanation, one of the students who had produced the poster was muttering to a friend, 'It's energy, it's *energy*.'

There was one extended question/response section (poster 5) in which the teacher attempted to explore the meaning which a group of students had given to the word 'squash' in relation to 'atoms being squashed together in solids'; an example of strategy (vi).

> *T:* You said, can I just be clear about something on yours, you said on the sheet, that in a solid they're squashed. Now I'm not quite sure what you mean by squashed. Do you mean by squashed that the atoms themselves are squashed more, or do you mean pushed closer together?
>
> *S:* Squashed and . . .
>
> *T:* You mean both?
>
> *S:* Yes.
>
> *T:* So that they get closer together and they get smaller?
>
> *S:* Yeah.
>
> *T:* What made you suggest that they might get smaller as well as pushed closer together?
>
> *S:* I dunno.
>
> *T:* You mean it's just an idea with not much reason to it?
>
> *S:* No.
>
> *T:* Was there any particular experiment that made you think along those lines?
>
> *S:* (Whisper)
>
> *T:* Well, I think it's something we need to consider a little bit, about the idea of the particles themselves getting smaller.

Many of the questions were posed in an either/or way so that the student had the choice of responding 'yes' or 'no'. At one point the teacher cast some doubt on the students' thought [strategy (ix)]:

> You mean it's just an idea with not much reason to it.

and the discussion ended on an inconclusive note as far as the students were concerned.

As mentioned above, teacher A very rarely refuted students' ideas directly, though he did express doubts about some suggestions:

> So I'm wondering if this bit about squashing atoms is particularly useful.

Instead he tended to ignore ideas which he did not consider useful [strategy (x)] and many suggestions were in this way rejected by him when he summarized the 'theory'.

Student participation in this report-back session was limited. At any one time, only the group whose poster was being referred to, plus three or four interested students sitting at the front of the room seemed to be actively involved (in the sense that they were listening to what was being said). By the time the third poster was being considered some students were becoming restless, talking quietly among themselves. At no time were students invited to comment on each others' posters, and no student chose to intervene.

The summary of the theory

By making selections from the posters, the teacher had been summarizing the theory throughout the report-back. He then spent a few minutes presenting a condensed version of the 'particulate theory' of matter, in which he used the words 'atoms' to describe the particles. He started by praising the students for their efforts:

> Now I think, when you look around all these, that you've done really remarkably well, because between you, you seem to have come up with a theory, which as far as I can see is capable of explaining most of the things that we've got on that problem there.

('that problem' refers to the students' version of the pattern of properties which considers differences in density, strength, compressibility etc. between solids, liquids and gases.)

He then ran through a series of issues such as differences in density, compressibility, movement, strength, using the particulate theory of matter to explain each in turn. Few of these issues had been directly addressed by students on their posters; most were introduced by the teacher. No 'visual aids' or notes were available for students to refer to at this point, nor were they invited to ask questions or comment. At the end of his summary, the teacher commented again on how well the class had done.

The lesson ended with three homework questions being set, and a printed summary sheet being handed out.

After the Lesson

Teacher A's feelings about this lesson were positive. He had ended up where he'd planned; presenting the class with a scientifically correc version of the particulate theory of matter.

He came back to a point which he'd raised in the pre-lesson discussions; would the students come up with ideas which would enable them to make links with accepted scientific theory?

R: Well how do you feel about it?
T: Relief! (laughs) I wasn't at all sure what was going to come up on the posters this time.
R: And that was your major concern.
T: Erm, yes, because I did feel by this stage — the thing *ought* to be showing some progression forward, and I was a bit uneasy that we might end up on square one again.

His main interest was in the posters which students had produced and the aspects of 'correct' theory which had been put forward. He had little to say about the report-back session except that it was 'reasonable'. Nor did he wish to pursue a discussion on the management of the report-back session. He felt that it had gone well. His stated aims prior to the lesson had been:

Well, after the posters we want them reporting back, and for me to summarize ... and then to pull out the accepted theory . . .

These he felt had been achieved.

When compiling a short written report on the lesson, later the same day, his only comment on the report-back session was:

Reporting back was a little brief — could be extended a little by reducing poster production time.

As in the post-lesson discussion mentioned above his written comments focussed on the content of the posters, in particular the fact that they had all contained particulate ideas:

Relieved that the groups were able to produce a theory without too much prompting.

Quite surprised at the coherence of ideas (at least superficially — probing did reveal some weaknesses).

The Analysis: Teacher B

Before the Lesson

Teacher B had, like teacher A, initially intended to spend one double lesson on pupil theory making. At the last minute however he decided to allow the pupil groups more time for discussion and production of posters, and devoted the double lesson entirely to this activity. This provided him with the opportunity to examine the posters which had been produced, and to review the ideas which groups of students had come up with. Much discussion with the researcher therefore focussed on the range of theories (scientific and alternative) and ways of dealing with them. Teacher B was reasonably happy with the ideas that students had put forward.

> In the event, with this class, it's not going to be their putting their theories up and me putting up another one. It's just going to be a sharing of ideas, and I think we will fairly quickly come round.

There was much agonizing over which student ideas were acceptable and which were not. Should the teacher discard ideas which were not absolutely scientifically correct, or should he be ready to accept theories which contained some flaws.

> T: This business of models, using models which are appropriate to the clientele that you've got. Now I've no qualms at all about er ...
> R: Lying? (Laughter)
> T: Well — er — putting forward information which 'proper' scientists could construe as not quite correct or something like that. And you would agree. Er ... I'm not one for academic rigour (laughter) not in schools anyway ... Science is just a series of models. Science education is all about introducing pupils to increasingly sophisticated models, according to where they're going.

Another concern was the management of an open discussion. Just before the start of the lesson, when the posters had been displayed on the walls, teacher B looked at them and said:

> If I get them to say something about all of this, it will take absolutely ages, won't it? Mm ... I will just get each group to say a *bit* about their poster.

He was also concerned about the pupils' ability to participate in open discussion.

> T: I don't expect *them* to be able to handle it.
> R: Well ... it's in the scheme so we may as well have a go.
> T: Mm ... yes. The role that I shall *attempt* to take is more that of chairman — sorry, chairperson.

Although he started the lesson with several doubts about how it would proceed, and with no clear ideas about its timing, his overall mood was positive.

> I don't know what this lesson will be like, but at this stage I'd quite willingly defend the scheme. I'm quite impressed by how it's gone so far.

The Lesson in Outline

Teacher B's class consisted of twenty-five students, considered by the school to be of about average or just below average ability. Six theory posters had been produced by the end of the last lesson, and of these four contained some particulate ideas. The ideas put forward were very sketchy, and all students who had mentioned particles had suggested that there must be air between the particles in liquids and gases.

The teacher had no clear idea in advance how long the report-back session would last. He envisaged that it would take the form of an initial reportback on each poster, followed by a general discussion on the issues which had arisen. He had prepared the apparatus necessary to carry out some diffusion demonstrations if time allowed at the end of the lesson. In the event there was no time, as the report-back and discussion lasted for thirty-five minutes (this was a short lesson).

The laboratory was arranged as shown in figure 3. The teacher had chosen to sit amongst the students as he said he wanted to 'focus the students away from the teacher and on to the posters'. As the discussion proceeded he had to turn around so that he was facing the students.

The discussion was still in full swing at the end of the lesson. No concluding remarks were made, and no summary sheet was given out. The report-back on the posters, and the general discussion are now considered separately.

Report-back on posters

Teacher B explained that he'd decided to put the posters up on the wall so that everybody could see them. He explained that firstly he would like somebody from each group to say a little about their poster:

Figure 3: Teacher B: Class organization for report-back sessions

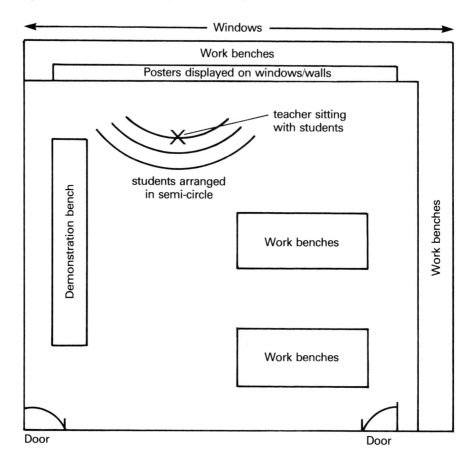

Within this lesson what I want to get at is a sharing of ideas. Within your smaller groups of say four people, four or five people, then it was very interesting in the diaries to see people writing that they'd found out what other people had thought and that what others had thought was not necessarily what they were thinking themselves. Somebody said that within our group so-and-so had all the ideas but I think that I agree with them. What I want to do now is to extend that so that we find out what the other groups were doing.

In terms of numbers of questions asked the report-back part of the lesson (which lasted about eighteen minutes) looked similar to that run by teacher A. (Again, Q = question from teacher, R = student response, T = extended teacher talk.)

Poster 1: Q.R.Q.R.Q.T.
Poster 2: Q.R.Q.T.
Poster 3: Q.T.Q.R.Q.R.Q.R.Q.R.Q.R.Q.R.Q.T.
Poster 4: Q.R.Q.
Poster 5: T.Q.R.T.Q.
Poster 6: Q.R.Q.

The style of questioning was, however, quite different from that of the reportback of teacher A. Of the nineteen questions asked, seventeen can be categorized as open questions and only two as closed. The most common question asked was along the lines of 'Would anybody else from that group like to add anything?'

In the case of two posters, teacher B did say something about what was written down on a poster before allowing members of the group to comment on it. In both cases however he simply read from the poster without altering any of the words or making any comments. Another strategy which he used was to ask groups to comment on ways in which their poster was different from those of others:

> It seemed to me actually ... it's purely by accident that they've ended up side by side here, but you can certainly see similarities there. Are there any differences there at all from what you've said? Those two groups — can you spot any differences in the kind of thing that you've been saying?

Some of the verbal strategies used are now examined in more detail. Teacher B made several explicit references to the value of students' ideas, [strategy (ii)], by asking students to listen to each other, by reminding them of the importance of *listening* when some members of the class found their concentration wandering (this happened once during the reporting-back session) and by thanking individuals for their contributions.

> *T:* Yes, you're quite right, it does say molecules there. Thank you Gary. Well go on Gary, what do you think a molecule is?
> *G:* It's them little bits.
> *T:* So the little bits are molecules. Darren?

This also illustrates his use of questions which check on students' understanding [strategy (vi)]; in this case of the word molecule. He did not, however, follow this up at this stage, but simply asked another member of the group (Darren) to comment [strategy (iii)]. As already noted above this was teacher B's main strategy for opening up discussion in the report-back.

At no point during this initial report-back did teacher B introduce ideas of his own [strategy (vii)], negate or criticize anything said by a student [strategies (viii) and (ix)] or ignore any idea which was put forward [strategy (x)]. Apart from one lapse of concentration towards the end, most students seemed to be involved in the session, and appeared to be listening to each others' ideas with interest.

The general discussion

This discussion, which lasted for about seventeen–eighteen minutes was quite complex in terms of the verbal interactions which occurred. Teacher B introduced it in the following way:

> What I want to do at this stage with all of you getting involved here and trying to think is to consider whether we can pull some of these ideas together and come up with, if you like, an overall theory which we should all be agreeable with . . .

A full analysis of the discussion is not provided here as it is rather complex. A brief consideration of this analysis does show however that there are a range of verbal interactions occurring, including questions from the teacher (twenty-nine open and twenty-three closed), student responses to these questions, extended periods of teacher talk, student comments and a few questions from students. The discussion is therefore much more than simply a question and answer session.

The discussion was opened by a student asking a question, and this question set the agenda for the next fifteen minutes or so.

T:	Could anybody give us any lead on this, about any aspect of these that they are not happy about? Darren?	Strategy (i)
Darren:	On that gases. They say they're further apart. What's in between them?	
T:	Anybody care to answer the question? I'm just an innocent bystander. Craig?	Strategy (iii)
Chris:	Is it just concentrating on one type of gas?	
T:	I think it's a good point. You know these things here, it says solid, liquid, gas, it	Strategy (iv)

	has to be true of any gas whether the gas is oxygen, air or carbon dioxide or anything. Now if it works for any gas, the question remains, and as you say it has to work for any gas, what is there between the gas bits, these gas particles or gas molecules or whatever you want to call them. Any ideas on this at all? Sean, what do you think?	Strategy (iii)
Sean:	Little germs and flies.	
Chris:	You can't see anyway — little microbes.	
T:	Germs, flies, microbes, specks of dirt, things like that. Thank you.	Strategy (ii)

This interchange is quite typical of the discussion which followed. After a student answered an initial question, teacher B would focus the issue and throw the question open again. Again, as in the report-back session, teacher B accepted and acknowledged the contributions of most students, and usually asked more than one student to comment on any question. However, he now started to pick up on certain ideas put forward by students and to develop them further, as in this exemplar:

T:	So you could have these air particles all over and what would be between them?	Strategy (vi)
Sarah:	Nothing.	
T:	What do you think would be between them?	Strategy (iii)
Chris:	Nowt.	
T:	Nowt he says.	Strategy (ii)
Gary:	If they were square you wouldn't need gaps.	
T:	Just a minute. Go on.	Strategy (x)
Sean:	If they all went together — if there were a lot of them around and they all went together they'd turn into a solid . . .	

He then used Sean's comment to enable him to develop some ideas about the spacing of particles in air. Again, as in the report-back session, there are examples of teacher B asking probing questions, and encouraging students to be more explicit about their ideas. There are also examples of the teacher choosing to ignore comments from students as if they do not move the discussion in the desired direction:

> T: If there was nothing at all between
>   particles, would that help in explaining
>   any of the experiments that were done
>   so far . . . Which one do you think it
>   would help if you believed there was
>   nothing there at all? What do you think,
>   Sarah?   Strategy (vi)
> *Sarah:* Solids.
> T: In what way?   Strategy (vi)
> *Sarah:* Particles way.
> T: OK you say solids — what does
>   anybody else think?   Strategies (ii)
> *Janine:* Syringes   (iii)
> T: Why do you say syringes, Janine?   & implicitly (x)

In inviting another answer teacher B was looking for a student who would provide him with 'syringes'. This enabled him, in an extended session of talk, to develop some of his arguments further.

Finally there are two other ways in which the teacher's style differed from that in the report-back. He introduced his own ideas [strategy (vii)] via two 'stories', one about what would happen to a fish in distilled water, and the other about travel in outer space, where there is no air, in order to further focus students' thoughts on issues concerned with the existence of a vacuum between particles.

He also challenged students directly on the issue of the existence of particles, in a way that seemed critical, in order to encourage them to defend their viewpoints:

> T: Somebody else has just said why are we bothering with
>   particles. I mean look — six groups have been working here
>   — 1,2,3,4,5,6. Four groups have started drawing these little
>   circles. I didn't say draw circles — don't blame me. So why
>   have you started drawing the damn things on the posters?
>   It's your idea, not mine. I feel quite emotional about this,
>   third year. Why have you started drawing these? We're
>   coming round to saying why have we got those on the
>   posters. You tell me. You tell me Sharon, why did you start
>   drawing round things like that?
> S: Because . . .
> T: Joanne?
> J: Because we thought that's what they looked like inside,
>   inside solids and liquids and that, and if you cut them in half
>   that's what we thought they look like.

As in the report-back part of the lesson, most students seemed to be actively involved throughout the discussion, and arguments were still being put forward as the lesson ended. No firm conclusions had been suggested as to a final theory, and students were still putting forward a wide range of alternative ideas.

After the Lessons

Teacher B's expectations for the lesson ('a sharing of ideas, and I think we will fairly quickly come round ... ') appeared in retrospect to have been somewhat optimistic. Immediately after the lesson, the following conversation took place.

> *T:* You can't say that I didn't try everything — every trick in the repertoire.
>
> *R:* You did very well. I thought it was very interesting. I wouldn't be negative about it.
>
> *T:* Jokes, puns, anecdotes. Self-humiliation, feigned aggravation, lies, deceit, everything went in. Did it move them to — it just moved them to more obscure positions by the moment. I tried to give the last word to a child — what did the child do? Came up with the most obscure thought of the day.
>
> *R:* It was a very good lesson. I enjoyed it tremendously. I did actually — I thought it was great. So what are you going to do on Tuesday? How can you follow that one? I think perhaps ...
>
> *T:* There's only one way out — emigration.

Later that day, when he had more time to reflect, he wrote in his diary:

> I didn't want to dominate the proceedings — lab furniture was rearranged to decentralize the set-up — but it quickly became apparent that teacher input was needed to help focus upon the issues ... It was certainly helpful to have thought up the 'stories' beforehand. By the end of the session I felt I had ranted and raved, told stories, indulged in self-mockery and ... by the end of the session alternative theories were MANIFOLD! 'If there is nothing between gas atoms why don't they just fall together?', etc. etc. EXCELLENT!! What happens next??

A few days later, when discussing his plans for what would happen next with the researcher, teacher B began to express doubts about pursuing the students' own ideas much further.

> R: Anyway, you were saying ...
>
> T: Er, yes, I was just thinking that when they have thrashed ideas around as much as they have already I can't see much wrong at this stage of er of almost bringing in accepted theory lock stock and barrel. I mean it could be written down on a page, and they might as well be asked what they think of that. Because I mean they've been assassinating everybody else's ideas without much — without any qualms.
>
> R: Mm?
>
> T: I'm almost thinking that it would be counter productive at this stage to encourage more feedback from the class, do you know what I mean. I'm almost inclined to try to order it all up as it were. Because within that last lesson they were talking about particles in nothingness weren't they?
>
> R: Some of them.
>
> T: Right at the end they *were* willing to admit that you could have gas particles in space then I mean the response that — oh God, the last response — that they would all fall together if there was nothing there!

Although he continued to attempt to justify to himself the necessity of 'making an input now', teacher B finally decided that this was not the way forward. He in fact spent another two lessons in working with the class towards a consensus view of the particulate theory of matter, before presenting them with a written 'summary sheet'.

Summary

Members of the teacher group had assumed that they had a shared understanding of what was involved in the pupil theory making lesson, as it had been jointly designed and discussed in detail prior to its implementation. As can be seen from the above analyses, however, two members of the group interpreted it in rather different ways. Some of the reasons for this are now examined.

Though caution is necessary when attempting to generalize from such brief extracts of classroom activity, some of the general issues which emerge include:

— the relationship between each teacher's views of learning and his classroom practice;
— each teacher's perceptions of his role as a *science* teacher;
— the reactions of each teacher when dealing with an open learning situation (problems such as time constraints, forward planning versus flexibility, and issues of control of the class).

Each teacher is now considered in turn in relation to these issues.

Teacher A

In discussions about learning, within group meetings and with the researcher, teacher A often commented that students' prior ideas *were* important.

> You look at what *they* know and you start from that, wherever it may be and you give *them* a chance to say what they *do* know ... this seems to be the whole thesis of this teaching scheme doesn't it, that you are prepared to accept what they say, without saying this is right or this is wrong.

He also felt that pupils would benefit from being actively involved in the learning process.

> It seems, on the face of it, to be a better way of approaching teaching simply because it *involves* the pupils more ... and if they have to *say* what they are thinking they have to *think*. The trouble with a lot of other teaching is they can be as passive as they like and get away with it, as long as they write neatly!

Indeed, in group meetings teacher A often acknowledged that 'the learner must take final responsibility for his/her own learning'.

In talking about his classroom practice however, teacher A expressed doubts about students 'being able to think it all up for themselves' (this being his interpretation of a constructivist view of learning). The view of learning which he espoused was of a 'guided discovery' type. With the help of the teacher, students could discover for themselves some of the theories of science. At times he expressed doubts about whether he was giving students *enough* help and guidance.

> The first lot of posters they did I don't think I gave them enough guidance about *how* to do them, and they spent a lot of

time writing out long sentences that were either unnecessary or in some cases irrelevant instead of highlighting key words and phrases.

The statement highlights one of the dilemmas in which teacher A found himself. He wished to value students' ideas, but often these ideas seemed to him to be irrelevant to the task in hand, which he saw as providing students with the required answers, so that they might pass their examinations.

Although teacher A's *own* views of the required answers were based on a relativist view of scientific knowledge (he saw scientific knowledge as something which evolved and changed with time, rather than a series of 'ossified' facts), his role as a teacher led him to believe that he must provide students with 'what they needed' to succeed at school. This raised some doubts in his mind about the effectiveness of the particulate theory teaching scheme.

The 'but' that I must admit is nagging away in the back of my mind is — *will* they, at the end of the day, be more *proficient* at explaining the things around them than they would have been if I'd done it by the traditional method.

In practice, the views considered above found expression in the way in which Teacher A managed the discussion session. He tended to ask questions which restricted the range of student responses, so that ideas were rarely explored in depth. Although working with a group of able students, he felt that they lacked confidence, and were in need of his help and guidance.

One of the main practical concerns expressed by teacher A was that he was spending too much *time* on the teaching scheme. In the words of a colleague he 'ran a very tight ship'. He insisted that other members of his department finished their syllabi on time and tried to set an example (he already felt that he'd made too many allowances for this new scheme). Coupled with this concern about time constraints, Teacher A preferred to have his lessons well planned. Before starting to teach the scheme he had remarked to the researcher, 'I had to sit down and write myself a *proper* lesson plan — you know, twenty minutes on this, ten minutes on that'. Once his lesson plans were written he felt that he had to get to certain points by the end of each lesson. So for example in the case of the report-back lesson, students *must* have the summary sheet by the end of it.

These concerns about timing and lesson structure, as well as his need to retain control of the report-back session, can be related to his belief that students depended on his guidance in order to learn the required scientific ideas. In conclusion teacher A's approach to teaching the particulate theory scheme might be summarised as:

> Let *them* put forward their ideas then my job is to 'pull the threads together', fill in the missing bits, put it all in the correct order and tell them what the answer is. My job as a teacher is, after all, to help them succeed (pass exams).

Teacher B

Teacher B also subscribed to the view that students' ideas were important, and acknowledged that he was actively having to rethink his teaching because of his involvement with the project.

> I'm now firmly convinced that the ideas that children have in their heads *are* important — that we ignore them at our peril ... the other thing that's really prodded me, that's made me feel uncomfortable was the idea that I've been teaching for eleven years and it wasn't until the last year that I've even *considered* what I'm actually doing and how children learn.

He espoused a belief in the role of the individual in learning, and in lessons often encouraged students to take responsibility for their *own* learning.

> There's a point where you have to invest a bit of your *own* brainpower here, and this is what I want you to do, and *think* about the issue.

His espoused views of learning seem to be reflected in his classroom practice. He felt that his students had interesting ideas to offer. He was conscious of time constraints, but was prepared to let lessons develop, and to change his plans at short notice. This adaptability was due in part to the fact that he did not see the teaching scheme as a discrete series of lessons but as a continuum. His teaching was not however unplanned. He made strategic decisions (such as postponing the report-back sessions so that he could read each poster and plan his responses) which enabled him to evaluate pupils' ideas at each stage of the scheme in order to plan the next stage accordingly.

Though he had a strong commitment to a constructivist view of learning, and to the particulate theory teaching scheme, teacher B, (like teacher A) also felt a responsibility towards his students.

> We're not just in the business of just getting at their ideas. My job as a teacher is to help them appreciate some of the scientific ideas.

His view of the nature of these scientific ideas was that they were not a series of 'facts' about reality, but a set of models, of varying levels of complexity; using models that are appropriate to the clientele.

Having reflected on the way in which the report back had gone teacher B did feel that it might be appropriate to present the class with one of these models 'lock stock and barrel' and 'written on a page'. This concern, that students should finish the teaching scheme knowing something about the accepted theory, became more important to him as the scheme progressed.

A summary of teacher B's approach might be:

> Let them put forward their own ideas so that they become aware of the problems and we can explore them together. But this approach seems to lead to even more problems being exposed — how can they be resolved? Students' ideas *are* important but somehow I have to help them to appreciate the scientific ideas as well.

Conclusion

Osborne and Gilbert (1985) suggest that 'all teachers have views of learning, which are implicit in their practices, but are rarely articulated even to themselves ...'. Teachers have prior knowledge and ideas about the teaching/learning process, which they use to make sense of classroom experiences. It is suggested by Driver and Oldham (1986) that when teachers are involved in implementing new teaching approaches in classrooms, such approaches may challenge their underlying views of teaching and learning.

For some teachers, such challenges to their beliefs may be quite problematic.

Promoting changes in teacher behaviour may be further complicated by the disparity which may occur between a teacher's 'espoused theories' about teaching/learning and his/her 'theories in action' (Argyris and Schon, 1976). Some of the constraints which teachers perceive as operating on them within classrooms may mean that the changes in practice which are required of teachers involved in curriculum innovation (changes which teachers themselves may wish to make) are quite difficult to achieve.

The Children's Learning in Science Project has as one of its aims the improvement of students' understanding of science. It hopes that the teaching strategies and curriculum materials which it has developed in collaboration with teachers will encourage students to change their conceptions about science. The project acknowledges that this may be a difficult and time-consuming process.

It may be, however, that the pedagogic strategies which the project wishes teachers to use in promoting conceptual change in students place conceptual demands on *teachers* themselves. Such changes in practice, which may require teachers to restructure their *beliefs* about teaching, learning and the nature of science, can be as problematic, time consuming and personally threatening as the changes which we ask our students to make in restructuring their views of the world.

References

ARGYRIS, C. and SCHON, D.A. (1976) *Theory in Practice: Increasing Professional Effectiveness*, San Francisco, CA, Jossey-Bass.

CLIS (1987) *CLIS in the Classroom: Teaching Schemes*, Leeds, Centre for Studies in Science and Mathematics Education, University of Leeds.

DRIVER, R. and BELL, B. (1986) 'Students' thinking and the learning of science: A constructivist view', *School Science Review*, March, pp. 443–56.

DRIVER, R. and OLDHAM, V. (1986) 'A constructivist approach to curriculum development in science', *Studies in Science Education*, 13, pp. 105–22.

OSBORNE, R. and GILBERT, J. (1985) 'Some issues of theory in science education' in OSBORNE, R. and GILBERT, J. (Eds) *Some Issues of Theory in Science Education*, Waikato, New Zealand, Science Education Research Unit, University of Waikato, Hamilton, New Zealand.

11 Management Knowledge: Its Nature and its Development

Michael Eraut

Introduction

The stimulus for this chapter comes from combining the author's theoretical interest in problems of professional learning with practical experience of designing and running mid-career courses for head-teachers, deputies and heads of department. A cardinal principle in our mid-career professional courses has been the need to build on the existing experiences of participants and to enhance their confidence in and control over their own further professional development. Our capacity to do this is limited by our epistemological frameworks, by both our own and our course members' ability to describe or map the nature of our knowledge: neither of us knows what we know. It is also reasonable to suggest that there might be a relationship between types of knowledge, modes of acquisition and approaches to its further development.

At the same time we became aware that many of our misgivings about common patterns of management training could be traced back to epistemological assumptions. It tended to deal with a relatively narrow range of knowledge, chiefly management concepts, theories and skills; and to give that knowledge too 'hard' a profile, i.e. allow too little room for its personal and situational interpretation. Thus it became urgent for me to take up the challenge of developing a map of school management knowledge to guide the next stage in our thinking about management learning.

This map is still in an early stage of development, consisting merely of six knowledge categories. So I must begin with several provisos; few management tasks involve only one category of knowledge; the categories are interdependent in a complex variety of ways; some might benefit from further sub-division; and it might be better to map the categories in Venn diagram form as sets of over-lapping circles. However, I would make two positive claims. The map covers a much greater range of territory than is common in management education; and the typology serves as a powerful heuristic for thinking more deeply about the nature of a school manager's experiential knowledge and how it might best be further developed.

My six categories are as follows:

Knowledge of People	Conceptual Knowledge
Situational Knowledge	Process Knowledge
Knowledge of Educational Practice	Control Knowledge

These will each be further defined below. At this stage I will merely explain the last four. Knowledge of educational practice could be described as knowledge of a repertoire of policies and strategies, of actual and proposed practices in schools. Conceptual knowledge is theoretical knowledge of education and management, concepts and frameworks for thinking. Process knowledge is knowledge of how to get things done and also incorporates what are sometimes called management skills. Control knowledge is a cybernetic not a manage-ment concept: it comprises self-knowledge and metacognitive skills, the control and use of one's own knowledge.

Knowledge of People

Management behaviour is strongly influenced by knowledge of the people involved. We are also aware that some managers' knowledge appears both to participants and to impartial observers as more authentic, more thorough and more insightful than others. It is an area where there is always scope for improvement, but not one in which managers are offered much practical help. The territory has been explored by psychologists but the results of such exploration have not been translated into the field of management education, except in areas where current concerns with gender and racial stereotyping have been prominent.

Knowledge of people is largely acquired unintentionally as a byproduct of encounters which have other purposes. These may be direct encounters with the person concerned or involve the exchange of accounts which provide information about that person, often only incidentally. The information presented by these encounters will be filtered during acquisition by such factors as the manager's knowledge needs at the time, the contexts of the encounters (varying from personal interviews to large meetings), the manager's views of people presenting 'third party accounts', the saliency of particular events, and the manager's existing constructs or schemas for organizing information of this kind. Thus knowledge of another person is normally constructed in a manner that is largely intuitive, but occasionally reflective; is based on a sample of that person's behaviour which is often extremely unrepresentative of their daily professional lives; is characterised by typifications which necessarily oversimplify; and is often confirmed during further interaction in a way that is essentially self-fulfilling (Nisbett and Ross, 1980).

How then is a manager to change or develop their knowledge of people and what should be their learning goals? Their knowledge is likely to be changed by seeing a person in different contexts and situations, by encounters designed to enhance their knowledge of a person, by consulting with other witnesses and by greater awareness of the nature and precariousness of their own assumptions. Relevant learning goals are as follows:

— Awareness of the above analysis, of one's own categories and assumptions, and of the effect of one's own behaviour on interpersonal encounters.
— Development of skills in acquiring knowledge of people in a more reliable and reflective manner (this is process knowledge).
— Experience of changing one's mind or greatly expanding one's knowledge about one or two particular persons (important for future attitudes).

Situational Knowledge

The domain of situational knowledge is extremely complex, comprising many different types of information relating to different aspects of the situation. In practice much of this information will not be used, some because it has never been perceived as relevant, some because it has not been selected out as having special importance. In most educational situations, classrooms included, there is more information potentially available than can be processed on any normal occasion; so the way in which information is selected and organized has a critical influence on decision-making. Such organization will include underpinning concepts and schemas, procedures for resolving contradictions and associations with knowledge of other situations deemed to be similar in some important aspect.

Situational knowledge is constructed in a manner that is partly accidental and partly purposive; involving some discussion and deliberation but also a lot of intuitive assumptions. Thus its conceptualization is partly explicit and partly tacit. This is illustrated by the ways in which people may generalize from one situation to another. Here there is a useful distinction to be made between intuitive generalization and conceptual generalization. Intuitive generalization involves treating one situation as similar to another without stopping to consider the nature of any similarities and differences: it is typical of rushed, unreflective, heat of the action, decisionmaking. Conceptual generalization involves thinking about the similarities and differences between the two situations and then consciously deciding that an interpretation of or decision about one can be properly transferred to the other: it closely relates to the phenomenon which psychologists call 'transfer of learning'.

Situational knowledge is likely to be changed by acquiring new information and new perspectives, by becoming more aware of one's own assumptions and by being in a familiar situation in a different role or for a different purpose. Learning goals in this area might include the following.

— To bring situational knowledge under critical control.
— To see how others see a situation.
— To acquire a wider range of interpretative concepts and schemas (conceptual knowledge).
— To develop the ability to improve one's own situational knowledge (this is process knowledge).
— To experience changing one's view of one particular situation as a result of such improved knowledge (important for future attitudes).

Implications for Management Courses

Management courses, which take the above learning goals seriously and aim to enhance their members' knowledge of people and situations, will need to include a number of appropiate school-based

activities. I have used the following activities as bridging tasks between course blocks: staff interviews, mini-evaluations, observation,
studies of a particular issue. More elaborate tasks can be used on
longer courses or award-bearing courses, for example, a department-
al profile, an organisational analysis or a course evaluation. These
activities need careful preparation, involving planning, discussion,
negotiation and skills training (for interviewing and observation);
then reflective discussion after they have been completed.

Other course-based activities contributed to the goals, but work
best when supplementing the more experiential school-based activities. These include sharing situational analyses with colleagues; introducing new perspectives through readings and/or outside speakers;
and explicit discussion of situational knowledge, its nature, its role
in management and how to improve it.

Knowledge of Educational Practice

Unlike the previous categories knowledge of educational practices is
acquired deliberately and consciously. Written sources are important
in maintaining awareness of what is happening elsewhere and of new
and proposed practices. But so also is networking, finding out what is
going on through social interaction between peers and colleagues and
pumping wandering visitors for information. The main danger from
the learning point of view is that knowledge of other practices is often
limited to the level of conversational facility; because it requires some
persistence and determination to probe much further. A deeper and
more practically useful knowledge of practice in a particular area
would have to go beyond knowledge of approaches used in different
schools, or others about to be introduced, to encompass the following: the rationales for each approach; its strengths and weaknesses
as perceived by a range of opinion; its appropriateness for particular
contexts; the implementation problems encountered; and the key
issues and arguments in deciding which is best.

The domain of such knowledge is large because it includes every
aspect of education and schooling — classroom practice, assessment,
curriculum, pastoral systems, organizational patterns, staffing patterns,
external relations, etc. But no one person is expected to be knowl-
edgeable in every part of the domain. Thus learning goals related to
this category are:

— Awareness of management's role in developing knowledge
of practice in the school as a whole.

— Recognition of a good brief.
— Developing the capacity to get oneself briefed (this is process knowledge).
— Enhancing one's knowledge of practice in certain priority areas defined by oneself and/or the course.

Course activities relevant to these goals might include the collection of information sources which map practice; groupwork on the development of briefs to be shared with other participants; and planning the use of visits and outside speakers so as to obtain the maximum useful information.

Conceptual Knowledge

The domain of conceptual knowledge is taken to include concepts, values, principles, ideas, theories, schemas — the building blocks for thinking about and interpreting experiences and proposals for action. As already discussed many of the concepts and ideas which underpin knowledge of people and situations are acquired incidentally and implicitly — they are in use but not under critical control. Others are acquired in academic contexts, in training, by reading or on courses. These are more likely to be under critical control but less likely to be used. Then thirdly, concepts, theories and ideas may be developed during the course of job-related inquiry and reflective discussion in ways which give them considerable personal significance whatever their original form and source. These will be both in use and under critical control.

I have explained elsewhere how conceptual knowledge is understood according to how and where it has been used; and that transfer of learning between academic, school discussion and classroom action contexts is difficult (Eraut 1985a and 1985b). Sometimes concepts are not used to aid thinking but to block it, because they carry certain positive or negative connotations that cannot be challenged; individualization (positive) and accountability (negative) are words commonly used in teacher discourse to avoid coming to terms with difficult problems. Indeed the use of conceptual knowledge is something that teachers rarely think about, but is necessary if they are to take more responsibility for their own learning.

Learning goals in this area are best expressed in general terms and have to include both knowledge classified as evaluation and knowledge classified as management. They include:

— To bring one's conceptual knowledge under critical control.
— To develop knowledge of one's own conceptual learning.
— To expand one's conceptual repertoire.

Many possible course activities are relevant to these goals, but I would particularly recommend the following: giving certain concepts the 'treatment' in order to explore how they are used and the positive range of interpretations; a thorough working out of the implications for personal practice of certain management ideas, using examples and case studies; and discussion of personal learning and the role of concepts therein.

Process Knowledge

Process knowledge is knowledge about how to get things done, and is a major element in management courses. It is often linked with conceptual knowledge about management and knowledge of management practice in themes like decision-making, team building, leadership, management of change. More particularly educational processes are curriculum development and evaluation and staff development. When one examines these processes more closely, one sees that more than one type of knowledge is involved. For example processes need to be conceptualized and planned in a manner that defines stages, procedures, tasks, personal roles and problems; and they need to be coordinated and monitored. But they also require a set of complex skills: interpersonal skills for interviewing and groupwork; communication skills, oral and written, for a range of formal and informal contexts; and logical skills in such operations as timetabling and budgeting. Finally these various kinds of knowledge have to be integrated in practice in order to make things happen.

Most process knowledge is probably acquired informally but deliberately. However, interpersonal skills and oral communication skills are normally exceptions. Although both these types of skill can be developed by special workshops, they are mainly developed in a highly intuitive fashion.

One of the greatest problems with trying to develop process knowledge on management courses is the artificiality of the course context. This poses considerable problems in transferring experience gained on course back into the school context. People's awareness of the conceptualization and planning aspects can be further developed by case studies of processes, including some taken from participants' own experience. Skills can be usefully developed within the course content by practice with feedback. But we find a need to take that back into the school context. For this we have used Action Learning Groups (Revans, 1982) in which small groups meet regularly during and after the course to discuss progress on an action task on which each member has chosen to work in their own school. These must be real tasks and are usually of considerable importance for them. Another approach which needs further exploration is mutual observation by pairs of course members in their normal school settings, so that they can provide feedback for each other on performance in real contexts.

Control Knowledge

The domain of control knowledge incorporates forms of knowledge that are important for controlling one's own behaviour, including one's own learning. These include self-awareness and sensitivity; self-knowledge about one's strengths and weaknesses, the gap between what one says and what one does, and what one knows and does not know; self-management in such matters as the use of time, prioritization and delegation; self-development in its broadest sense; and the metacognitive skills one uses in organizing and controlling one's thinking.

A major barrier to the development of self-knowledge is believing in or being presented with unrealistic, idealized models of managers who somehow seem to have everything organized and under control. This often creates a lack of confidence and thus inhibits any self analysis. Yet the presentation of such models is common practice in many management courses. One has to start with mutual recognition of problems and difficulties, so that people begin to feel more secure; and to create an atmosphere of group support from peers, who are not immediate colleagues and therefore not too threatening. It then becomes possible to begin to examine some of these delicate but vitally important issues and to introduce activities that bring back information and lead to deeper analysis of problems. At a relatively early stage one can plan discussions of self-management problems and begin to collect diary information for analysis of time-management. Then later there are various forms of self-development workshop, and it may be possible to collect information from colleagues on one's own role and one's relationships with them.

Throughout this chapter there has been a strong emphasis on

better understanding the nature of one's own knowledge, in order to bring it more under critical control and to establish a platform on which to base further professional learning. Thus continuing on-course discussion of the nature of management knowledge and its acquisition is an important way of developing control knowledge. Perhaps in time, our teachers might even want to read and criticize this chapter?

References

ERAUT, M. (1985a) 'Knowledge creation and knowledge use in professional contexts', *Studies in Higher Education*, 10, 2, pp. 117–33.

ERAUT, M. (1985b) 'The Acquisition and Use of Educational Theory by Beginning Teachers', UCET Conference Paper, April.

NISBETT, R.E. and ROSS, L. (1980) *Human Inference: Strategies and Shortcomings of Social Judgement*. Englewood Cliffs, NJ, Prentice-Hall.

REVANS, R.W. (1982) *The Ongoing and Growth of Action Learning*, Bromley, Chatwell-Bratt.

12   The Ownership of Change as a Basis for Teachers' Professional Learning

Jean Rudduck

Preface

The phrase 'the ownership of change' has become part of a democratic rhetoric as in-service provision becomes more school-based. It is associated with so-called 'bottom-up' initiatives after the 'top-down' models of the 60s and 70s. But it may be that behind the democratic front (see Gordon, 1987) there are complex structures of control, and teachers may be just as much 'puppets dangling from the threads of someone else's invention' as Marris (1985) puts it. Against this background, the chapter looks at a way of interpreting the concept of 'ownership' at the level of the individual teacher. It reports on our attempt to link 'the biographical approach', 'professional development' and 'curriculum change' — arguing that in order to commit themselves to change teachers must reflect on their own experience of schooling, higher education and teaching, and on the view of knowledge that these experiences have yielded. The teachers who can claim to 'own the problem of change' are those who recogize a potentially creative dissonance that they are prepared to confront and deal with. I suggest that professional development may be most dynamic when personal commitment to change is strong and when its basis is understood by the teachers concerned.

Professional Practice and Professional Learning

We deal with people's lives — not only the lives of young people but of teachers ... We deliberately try to change them and seldom exactly as they would change themselves. We interfere with their lives convinced we are helping them to something better. (Stake, 1987, p. 58)

One way into the arena of teachers' professional learning is the theory-practice avenue. Carr (1980) suggests that we challenge the 'dubious assumptions on which the ... divide is based' (see also Smyth, 1987) and his claims are bold:

> There are no 'educational phenomena' apart from the practice of those engaged in educational activities, no 'educational problems' apart from those arising from these practices and no 'educational theories' apart from those that structure and guide these practices. (Carr. 1982, p. 20)

The only task that educational theory can legitimately pursue, he argues, is 'to develop theories of educational practice that are intrinsically related to practitioners' own accounts of what they are doing'. Such theories can help teachers to improve their practice by transforming the ways in which practice is experienced and understood; but this transformation depends on teachers' capacity for critical reflection. The problem is to help teachers to 'see' what is happening in the everyday world of their classrooms in order to reflect.

The cycles of routine that the rhythms of institutional life seem to require inevitably lead practitioners to reconstruct each day in its own image, making it difficult to step back, and to look, even briefly, with the eyes of the stranger (Greene, 1981). They see what they expect to see. Bruner (1986) also talks about the need to make the familiar strange 'so as to overcome automatic reading' (p. 22):

> ... the nervous system stores models of the world that, so to speak, spin a little faster than the world goes. If what impinges on us conforms to expectancy, to the predicted state of the model, we may let our attention flag a little, look elsewhere, even go to sleep. (*Ibid*, p. 46)

This seems to be the malaise of professionals, who, as Schon (1983) says, tend to encounter the same situations again and again and again so that in the end they 'no longer find anything in the world of practice to occasion reflection'. Consequently it is difficult, as Garver (1984) points out, to learn 'the art of problemation'. Blind habit, he says, is a strategy for avoiding deliberation, 'for living in a practical world without in fact acting practically upon it'. Practitioners can easily lose their sense of vision or their capacity for constructive discontent. An important dimension of professionalism is the desire to go on extending one's knowledge and refining one's skills. Both vision and discontent can provide a stimulus to improvement. Teachers who are in search of excellence (to borrow a phrase) are likely to be those who are committed to sustaining their own professional learning.

The situation in the late 80s is made more complex because we are dealing not just with the normal occupational hazard of routinization but also with the problem of a widespread and profound sense of disorientation and deprofessionalization among teachers. Visions are likely to be elusive, discontent uncreative. Preliminary discussions of the findings of an ESRC Teacher Education Project (Poppleton and Riseborough) suggest that there is a disturbingly high level of dissatisfaction among teachers with more than a few years service. The survey data are confirmed by data from individual and group interviews. There is a strong sense of teachers being pinned against the wall by accusations that education has betrayed the nation, and of being exhausted by the demands of multiple initiatives whose coherence and whose relationship to their own values they haven't the time, and sometimes the energy, to work out. They speak of themselves as a core of veterans who are being used as work horses, set to plough the public allotment of the curriculum rather than expertly to cultivate its secret gardens. The pressures could result in what Poppleton and Riseborough called, in a recent talk, 'a militant conservatism', characterized by perspectives that are both anti-bureaucracy *and* anti-innovation.

In contrast is the self-image and spirit of new entrants to the profession (including of course mature entrants) who have a strong sense of professionalism, who see themselves as doers, innovators, new blood, and who are committed to new pedagogies and collaborative modes of working. This group appears to be career-oriented (as an alternative, perhaps, to alliance with their world weary colleagues?), and also pro-innovation. I recently interviewed a number of our own PGCE students who, at the end of their one-year's training, shared this spirit and attitude while acknowledging the low morale that they had encountered in staff rooms but that had not deterred them from entering the profession. They felt a sense of mission — they thought that they had a lot to offer to pupils and even to longer-serving teachers. Experienced teachers, in contrast, have a strong sense of being conscripts in the government's 'innovative' campaigns. The situation is, ironically, much as Scheffler (1968) described it in the era of teacher-proof curricula: teachers have the role of 'minor technician within an industrial process' where the 'overall goals ... are set in advance in terms of national needs' (pp. 5–6).

Change and the Individual Practitioner

Real curriculum development, that is, in the present climate, development that allows itself to engage with the fundamental values of equality of opportunity and independence of thought, will not be achieved by teachers who feel so used and acted upon. They have got to feel some control over the situation and in order to feel a sense of control they have to recognize what it is in schools, classrooms and in themselves that makes change difficult to accomplish. They also have to understand, at the level of principle, what they are trying to achieve, why they are trying to achieve it, and how any new possibilities might match the logic of their analysis of the need for change. It is not easy, however, to help teachers to arrive at such complex understandings. First, the teaching profession does not often allow time for, and its culture does not normally support, either communal reflection on practice or discussion of basic philosophies. As Nias (1984) reminds us: 'Many of the profession seem to receive little significant assistance in the working out of their own professional values' (p. 14). Moreover it is difficult to get an analytic grip on a situation which we have been so effortlessly socialised in to. Indeed, as Grumet (1981) says, we are not only part of it, but we are also responsible for it through our constant reconstruction of it:

> It is we who have raised our hands before speaking, who have learned to hear only one voice at a time and to look past the backs of the heads of our peers to the eyes of the adults in authority. It is we who have learned to offer answers rather than questions, not to make people feel uncomfortable, to tailor enquiry to bells and buzzers.

If we accept that practitioners' own sense of self is deeply embedded in their teaching it should not be surprising to us that they find real change difficult to contemplate and accomplish. They are more likely to seek to extricate themselves from the complex webs of habit if, as Sarason (1971, p. 36, quoted by Fullan, 1982, p. 18) says, they are 'hurting' because of the existing curriculum or pupils' response to it. Without 'hurting' as a stimulus to changing the situation, individuals may feel that they are too implicated in past perspectives and present practices to move.

Dealing with the individual's reaction to the possibility of change is not something that has attracted much attention in the literature of educational innovation. We have to go outside education to find any sustained exploration of what change means for individuals — to

Peter Marris (1975) for instance who describes the sense of loss in change as an experience akin to bereavement. Bereavement removes part of the substance and structure of one's familiar and reassuring personal world:

> Occupational identity represents the accumulated wisdom of how to handle the job derived from their own experience and the experience of all who have had the job before or share it with them. Change threatens to invalidate this experience robbing them of the skills they have learned and confusing their purposes, upsetting the subtle rationalisations and compensations by which they reconciled the different aspects of the situation.

In order to cope with the disorientations and upheavals that threaten professional status and confidence, individuals need to feel that change is not something that happens to them, and which they cannot control, like bereavement, but instead something which they are in principle seeking and welcoming. Fullan (1982) points out how in the initial stages of imposed innovations, teachers are often more concerned with how the change will affect them personally than about its educational justifications (pp. 28–33). On reflection, although this preoccupation might seem irritating to those bent on speeding the process of change, the teachers' reactions are understandable. They may not have been helped to prepare themselves for change and to work out in what ways they are or are not receptive to it and what it might offer them or do for them.

I would want to argue that most teachers, given the opportunity to reflect on their experience, would find some 'hurt' that routine or overload leads them to endure rather than to seek to eliminate. Consciousness of the hurt is most likely to recur as teachers refocus their professional values and goals, admit their political consciousness, and recognize any disturbing gaps between aspiration and present experience. The hurt may be expressed in simple, but nonetheless forceful terms.

Take for example three teachers who came to work with us recently on a project that looked at the development of biotechnology in the secondary curriculum. Each one opted to join the team because he or she had, it turned out, already experienced the 'hurting' although they had not all, until interviewed, articulated the basis of that hurt. All three were from comprehensive schools. One said that his science teaching was reaching only a few pupils and that most of those were very able and going on to higher education. He thought that science was elitist and serving the needs of only a minority of those in secondary schools. For most it wasn't anything that would stay with them and serve them in their later lives. He said that he tried to be the best showman in the world, 'would sweat blood' to entertain them and involve them, but that when he assessed the pupils' performance it was often poor. Another teacher said that he was becoming increasingly frustrated because some children were not responding to his approach: it was either going over their heads or they were just not switching on in his lessons. Things that had once been successful were not so any longer. He felt that 'something was adrift' in his science teaching. The third said that he was burning up so much energy but seeing so little satisfaction in the children. He wanted them to get involved in science in ways that would not destroy their autonomy and their capacity to develop independence of thought. He wanted them to see the consequences of science for themselves and for society. He wanted kids also to see that there is controversy at the heart of science and that science is not always a subject that is 'right' and that is 'objective'.

If we are interested in substantial curriculum change, we may need to find structures and resources to help teachers (see Aspinwall, 1985) to re-examine their purposes, as these teachers did (see appendix), slough off the sediment of socialization, and feel more in control of their professional purposes and direction. Some sense of ownership of the agenda for personal action is, in my view, a good basis for professional development and professional learning. Smyth (1987) and his colleagues have suggested that one's career can be seen as part of 'an open-ended search for identity': as such it can be useful to sort out one's values, beliefs, motives, abilities, for 'new perceptions of experience' may lead to 'altered conceptions and reconstruals' of aspects of the art of teaching (pp. 28–9). They conclude that revisiting and reflecting on one's professional experience 'seems an important entry to a deeper understanding of educational innovation and change'. Through such reflection and revaluation the teacher may gain a clearer sense of the way in which the past shapes and informs possibilities for action in the present (Strauss, 1969, p. 104).

The Contribution of the Biographical Approach

The interviews that I conducted with the teachers on our biotechnology project were not sufficiently penetrating and prolonged to constitute a good example of 'the biographical method' (see Woods,

1985) but they did, I think, help each teacher to organize his or her own thoughts and feel in command of the problem of change and, later, committed to exploring the particular strategy for change that emerged from their deliberations. The interviews provided an opportunity for what Apple (1975) describes as 'a serious in-depth search' for alternatives to what is seen with 'the almost unconscious lenses we (normally) employ' (p. 127). The interviews were a way of both legitimizing the teachers' search and of marking their progress in the enquiry. Thirty years ago, Polanyi (1985) wrote:

> Having made a discovery I shall never see the world again as before. My eyes have become different; I have made myself into a person seeing and thinking differently. (p. 143)

This feeling was echoed by one of the teachers who said this just before the end of his period of secondment:

> I feel that having had time to talk and stand back, I now see the important things that are going on in school more clearly than I did when I was right in the thick of it. I think these are lasting perceptions. They are not going to disappear.

In the biotechnology project we shall use the biographical framework as a way of helping other teachers to identify with the teachers who undertook the preliminary experimental work — not as a way of leading other teachers to the same outcomes but as a way of encouraging them to ask the questions that these teachers asked about their own past and present teaching and values. Our theory of change suggests that teachers might often be encouraged to analyze their own need for change if they can be in touch — even through print — with teachers who have gone through the process of review and reconstruction of their teaching. This perspective owes much to literature of course:

> Characters in stories are said to be compelling by virtue of our capacity for 'identification' or because in their ensemble they represent the cast of characters that we, the readers, carry unconsciously within us. (Bruner, 1986, p. 4)

We shall try to offer other teachers convincing accounts of the *process* of change, viewed 'not through an omniscient eye ... but through the filter of the consciousness of protagonists in the story' (ibid). In drawing on the tradition of biography in educational research, we are exploring our own version of what Stake (1987) calls 'an evolutionary view' of staff development.

There is a particular strength of the biographical approach that I have not so far mentioned but that is important. Whereas even grounded theory presents its understandings through generalizations and anonymizations, the biographical method is, as Grumet (1981) says, 'a process of restitution' that returns experience 'to the person who lived it' (p. 110). As Aspinwall (1985) points out, focussing on the individual teacher requires an interesting modification of a traditional perspective: the education system is dominated by two powerful hierarchies, the hierarchy of status and the hierarchy of knowledge production, and the classroom teacher is often at the bottom of both hierarchies (p. 67). The biographical approach therefore helps the teacher to feel some sense of individual power at the centre of the action.

This focus on the individual is also important because individualism in teaching has tended to be associated with privacy (see Anderson and Snyder, 1982) and privacy can, of course, be a cover for conservatism. Moreover, our dealings with pupils reveal how difficult we find it, despite our speech-day rhetoric of 'helping each pupil develop his or her potential to the full', to honour individuality. We have, as Linda McNeil points out, a remarkable commitment to 'teaching to sameness' and to 'thinking-in-groups'. When teachers talk about differences between pupils they comment on 'girls' and 'boys'; they recall pupils who cannot read, who are slow, who have trouble writing. Pupils, on the other hand, talk about how the curriculum seems not to relate to them *personally*. McNeil continues:

> Students rarely see themselves as part of a collective group . . . (when teachers) did attend to student differences, it was not to the kind of differences which students felt important to them as individuals . . . instead, the differences which teachers paid attention to tended to be those which were behavioural and procedural . . . which arose within and because of the instructional context rather than those that were brought to it. (pp. 106–8)

Similarly, I would argue that we need to give attention to the behaviours and attitudes that individual teachers bring to the innovation context, not just those that arise within it. Teachers need to understand the structure of their own readiness for change, or the basis of their own resistance to it.

To focus on the individual is not to deny the importance of the working group in effecting change (see Rudduck, 1984 and 1987). In a working group that accepts the task of change there will inevitably be a degree of shared concern: as Ionesco said: 'dreams and anguish bring us together' (quoted by Pratt, 1987). But within such a group each individual must, in my view, be there because he or she has a grasp of the basis of his or her own commitment that has deeper roots than the obvious commonalities within the group. The group spirit may, through the sense of obligation and loyalty that it generates, keep the individuals going when the task of change proves difficult, but strength must also derive from the individual's growing sense of personal understanding and control. As Bruner (1986, pp. 13–14) said, the teacher facing change needs simultaneously to construct two landscapes, the landscape of consciousness, which is essentially about personal meanings, and the landscape of action, where some corporate sense of the political struggles needed to bring about change can be a source of strength. What I am proposing is that we help teachers with the task of constructing their own landscapes of consciousness.

In this chapter I have proposed a particular view of 'the ownership of change'. I see it as bringing about a motivation towards change that is personally founded, and I see it as being about meaning that is explored in relation to the self as well as in relation to the professional situation. Professional learning is, I think, more likely to be powerful in its engagement with fundamental issues in education if teachers have constructed their own narrative of the need for change. This view of the basis of professional learning reaches across to conceptions of critical theory as a basis for professional learning, and recognizes that in situations where routine and the reproduction of sameness are prevalent, practitioners need help in getting a grasp of the worthwhile problematics of teaching. A comment by Berlak (1985) is apposite:

> People are liberated to the extent that they are, at the same time, increasingly free to choose from a range of alternative perspectives of themselves and their social worlds. This freedom of choice requires the ability to see one's own views of what is good or right, possible or impossible, true or false, as problematic, socially constructed (and) subject to social and political influence. (p. 2)

And, as Smyth (1987) says, if teachers can achieve and sustain such a perspective, they may take on the role of powerful 'intellectuals' rather than be merely 'minor technicians' in the curriculum battles that are now being played out (p. 23).

Notes

1 The interviews referred to in this chapter are reproduced in full as part of the Biotechnology in Secondary Schools Project, published by the Division of Education, University of Sheffield, 1987.
2 Poppleton and Riseborough's work on the ESRC Project, Teacher Satisfaction, is based in the Division of Education, University of Sheffield, and will shortly be published.

References

ANDERSON, R. and SNYDER, K. (1982) 'Why such an interest in clinical supervision?', *Wingspan* (the Pedamorphosis Communique), 1, 13, pp. 1–10.
APPLE, M. (1975) Scientific interests and the nature of educational institutions, in PINAR, W. (Ed.) *Curriculum Theorizing: the Reconceptualists*, Berkeley, CA, McCutchan.
ASPINWALL, K. (1985) *A Biographical Approach to the Professional Development of Teachers*, unpublished MEd dissertation, University of Sheffield.
BERLAK, A. (1985) Back to basics: liberating pedagogy and the liberal arts, paper presented to the American Educational Research Association annual conference, Chicago.
BRUNER, J. (1986) *Actual Minds, Possible Worlds*, New York, Harvard University Press.
CARR, W. (1980) 'The gap between theory and practice', *Journal of Further and Higher Education*, 4, 1, pp. 60–9.
CARR, W. (1982) 'Treating the symptoms, neglecting the causes: Diagnosing the problem of theory and practice', *Journal of Further and Higher Education*, 6, 2, pp. 19–29.
FULLAN, M. (1982) *The Meaning of Educational Change*, Ontario, OISE Press.
GARVER, E. (1984) 'The arts of the practical: Variations on a theme of Prometheus, *Curriculum Inquiry*, 14, 2, pp. 165–82.
GORDON, D. (1987) 'Autonomy is more than just the absence of external constraints', in SABAR, N., RUDDUCK, J. and REID, W. (Eds) *Autonomy and Partnership in School-Based Curriculum Development*, University of Sheffield Division of Education Publications (in press).
GREENE, M. (1973) *Teacher as Stranger*, Belmont, CA, Wadsworth.
GRUMET, M. (1981) 'Restitution and reconstruction of educational experience: An autobiographical method for curriculum theory' in LAWN, M. and BARTON, L. (Eds) *Rethinking Curriculum Studies, London,* Croom Helm, pp. 125–148.
McNEIL, L. (1987) 'Talking about differences, teaching to sameness', *Journal of Curriculum Studies*, 19, 23, pp. 105–22.
MARLAND, M. (1986) 'Appraisal and evaluation: chimera, fantasy or practicality?', *Educational Management and Administration*, 14, pp. 169–89.
MARRIS, P. (1975) *Loss and Change*, New York, Anchor Press.
NIAS, J. (1984) 'Learning and acting the roles: in-school support for primary teachers,' *Educational Review*, 36, 1, pp. 3–15.

POLANYI, M. (1958) *Personal Knowledge*, London, Routledge and Kegan Paul.

PRATT, D. (1987) 'Curriculum design as humanistic technology', *Journal of Curriculum Studies*, 19, 2, pp. 149–62.

RUDDUCK, J. (1984) 'Introducing innovation to pupils' in HOPKINS, D. and WIDEEN, M. (Eds) *Alternative Perspectives on School Improvement*, Lewes Falmer Press, pp. 53–66.

RUDDUCK, J. (1986) 'Curriculum change — management or meaning?', *School Organization*, 6, 1, pp. 107–14.

RUDDUCK, J. (1987) *The Meaning of Curriculum Change*, Sheffield, University of Sheffield Division of Education Publications.

SCHEFFLER, I. (1968) University scholarship and the education of teachers, *Teachers College Record*, 70(1), pp. 1–12.

SCHON, D.A. (1983) *The Reflective Practitioner*, London, Temple Smith.

SMYTH, W.J. (1987) *A Rationale for Teachers' Critical Pedagogy: a Handbook*, Geelong, Deakin University Press.

STAKE, R (1987) 'An evolutionary view of programming staff development', in WIDEEN, M. and ANDREWS, I. (Eds) *Staff Development for School Improvement*, Lewes, Falmer Press.

STRAUSS, A.L. (1977) *Mirrors and Masks: The Search for Identity*, London, Martin Robertson.

WOODS, P. (1985) 'Conversations with teachers: Some aspects of life history method', *British Educational Research Journal*, II, 1, pp. 13–26.

Appendix: Longer extracts from three teachers' narratives of the growth of their acknowledgement of the need for change

All three teachers had one-day-a-week release in the first term of the biotechnology project; teacher A then had a one-term secondment, teacher B a two-term secondment and teacher C a three-term secondment to continue working on the project.

Teacher A

I was doing research before I went into teaching, bench work mainly, pretty repetitive bench work and I got into this kind of rut working on this research, very isolated. I went straight into it. I never really questioned the whole momentum. I was on a sort of conveyor belt really. So I got out of that and into teaching. Now my teacher training more or less taught me basic strategies of control. What they were saying to me was that without these skills there won't be enough order for you to get the subject across. But it just didn't work in my first school. I went in with a mixture of rules of thumb that I'd got from the teacher training, plus my own visions, and it was just inappropriate. It just wore me down. I got to the point where I realized that there had to be a much deeper understanding of the relationship between me and the kids. I was burning up so much energy and seeing so little happiness and satisfaction and well-being amongst the kids.

A lot of my lessons would be very loud. I had this notion of a graded reprimand, so I'd start off with a fairly quiet reprimand, but it wasn't particularly friendly, and that would quickly escalate into me actually shouting at the kid and it would put all the other kids on edge; it would make them all defensive and it would very quickly create a sort of polarisation of me against them. There had to be another way of operating. I guess that started to dawn on me.

One of the things that happened was I realized that I actually liked kids. Just that simple. I'd been so bound up in the mechanics of teaching that I'd not really had the leisure to reflect on why I had gone into something which I thought was less isolating. I realized that if I operated within the same framework that I had done before, I was going to be just as isolated, and the realization that I actually liked kids made me want to explore that relationship and find teaching strategies that would support that relationship. I started to experiment a bit — doing more active work on environmental issues, me working with them, them working with me, having to team up with one another physically over jobs like erecting a fence.

And so from having been teacher as controller, I went to the other extreme, teacher as facilitator role. It helped me quite a lot with individuals, but I found it didn't help me with the group situation much. It was as though I was relating to the group as fragments. The group obviously had a sense of insecurity in the school as a whole: they were shifting from one lesson to another, from one style to another. I was trying to negotiate with the kids outside of any framework for negotiation and I was trying to throw the existing mode of control out of the window, and nobody could cope with that.

I think I was probably trying to move towards a relationship with the kids where I wasn't dominating them — some sort of relationship where we were cooperating in finding out something. But it was complicated. I didn't know a lot about it and I didn't understand very much about me. I just knew that I had previously disregarded things about me and what I'd done for a living that had led to trouble, and so I stuck with this new approach.

I suppose what I was beginning to feel was that as an individual I'd been absolutely swamped by all the pressures that the education system had put on me. I couldn't take any more. I realized that it was leading me up blind alleys and I felt that I didn't want to lead kids up the same blind alley. In other words I was looking for ways to get involved in teaching science with kids and yet not at the same time destroy their autonomy. The thread had to be that we could explore scientific ideas, but it had to be in a framework where it wasn't simply me telling them. There had to be a possibility of them developing autonomously — not just as scientists but as people, and I felt that if that didn't happen, I was doing them a profound disservice really.

Science for me has now come to mean a way of looking at the world which has got practical usefulness. You've got to look at it in terms of the whole planet and the way science is used in our society and all the consequences of it — right? Now how do you convey that to kids? We live in a society, it seems to me, where God and religion have just been replaced by the paradigm of science and technology. For me, that's incredibly dangerous, because you're simply taking one defunct ideology and slapping another in there. So how do I translate that into practical teaching approaches to kids? Well try and extract general principles I suppose, like autonomy, and then translate that into practical strategies. Problem solving perhaps. I'm not going to stand at the front and say 'This is the way to do it'. Instead, I'll maybe try and present a secure framework — I've learnt that you've got to have a secure framework — but within that framework have sufficient open-endedness to allow some sort of exploration.

The notion of what I'm about has changed. I've stopped shifting from one paradigm to another — being authoritarian and then being non-authoritarian — just reacting against the previous image. I think I've now reached the point where I feel secure enough to be prepared to constantly reassess and re-evaluate what I'm doing. I've not got a mixed set of models that I'm sure will work, that I'm always going to stick to. I'm flexible — that's one of the main things I've learned.

Teacher B

I started at my present school thirteen years ago — and I'm still there! I didn't go straight from teacher training to teach. I went to work as a research technician for two years, but I decided I really wasn't getting anywhere. I started as a physics teacher, but within two years I moved into biology and was immediately given the responsibility for the department. My first year was exceptionally difficult. I was given mainly bottom classes. It was around the time of ROSLA and a lot of kids deeply resented being in school.

I learned very early on, in teacher training, that when you get into difficulties the very worst thing you can do is to try to emulate the science teacher who'd taught you in school.

I started off feeling that I was trying to make information attractive — information was the all important thing — and involving children in the activity; this was the other key. And I think that stayed with me for a long time until I began to have a number of misgivings without quite knowing what those misgivings were. I wanted to get over certain skills and certain information but at the same time I also felt that good teaching was busy children and busy children were thinking children. There was something there that didn't quite fit and I think part of that unease has only begun to unravel itself in this last term when I've had the chance to think more about things.

My unease reached a stage where I felt that something had got to be done about that — we'd got to analyze the way children think. At best I was reaching a few pupils for whom I would say science had succeeded — most of those were very able and going on to higher education. For a very large number of children, the very best I was achieving was a sort of benign tolerance of what they'd gone through in science. It wasn't something that was going to stay with them. At worst there was a clear antagonism. They weren't enjoying it — it was going to be of no use at all in later life and as far as making them scientifically competent in the modern world, it certainly wasn't achieving that. In that sense it was failing and I had a gut feeling that something needed changing. But quite frankly I didn't know what.

If things are not going well, there is a natural inclination to try to make your activities more teacher directed. I would sweat blood. I'd try to become the best showman in the world, try to entertain the children, but in the end I would assess pupils' performance and it was often very poor and I was very disturbed by it. I discovered that what I was doing was to transfer my assessment marks to a piece of paper and as soon as they became a set of numbers, I would play with them, I would draw normal distributions and it was just a big get out! You feel very safe as soon as you play with numbers but you lose sight of the pupils.

One of my strengths is that I'm quite a creative person — I can 'think' activity for children. If I look back on some of the things I created I think they were embryonic problem-solving tasks. So it was evolutionary — I started in a crude sort of way, almost unconsciously, and since I've been on the project I've recognized what it was I was trying to do.

I went to another Sheffield comprehensive as a pupil and I found the experience up to sixth form level dire in the extreme. It was unproductive. I went into the sixth form on the point of failing educationally. I just scraped in, did three sciences and loved every minute of it! I learned to love science. To me it was the acquisition of information about the nature of the universe and everything to do with it that made a good scientist — with the associated skills. And still at university I thought it was about soaking up information. I don't think it even began to enter my head that solving problems had any real value. Most experiments that we had to carry out were not experiments — they were what I would recognize now as demonstrations.

Quite early on in the project, when we were coming in just one day a week and we started to trial the very first approaches in my school, a number of things occurred that really convinced me that I was at last on the right road. Firstly I think the children were enjoying it. They were smiling more than they normally smile, and they were talking about science. They were much more engaged than they had been before. Secondly, there was a continuity from one lesson to another; they seemed to remember the things that had gone on in earlier lessons — for many of the less able children that was something that had not normally happened. For the first time I actually got them to talk rather than just write up an experiment — they talked in an open forum for the first time, and listening to them questioning each other about each other's projects and seeing this ownership of their project, for the first time I began to realize that children — these children — had begun to understand at a level that was far deeper than I think I'd achieved before.

I'm having to change my mind quite a lot about fundamental things, but the principle is there that children don't just see science as something that they learn at school: they must see that it has a context and within that context there is responsibility. That was my starting point. Beyond that I began to think that if you try to teach responsibility, you become involved with the education of caring, and that is a fundamental tenet for me. The fact that I hadn't got it right in my lessons doesn't change that tenet — caring must lie somewhere at the heart of what I'm trying to do.

I think more than anything this new style of teaching is frighteningly involved, and I don't know whether, to be frank, I could sustain it on a regular basis. It challenges what I would normally do in the classroom. There is always a feeling, and it's something I've heard many teachers say, that as a teacher you've got to 'teach'; it's about getting up and doing something yourself. You feel this responsibility to somehow 'do' it. What is required is the confidence, once you've created an activity, to let it run.

It's going to bring with it problems.

Teacher C

I didn't do any teacher training. I sneaked in through the back door really. When I left school, I'd done 'A' level physics, chemistry and maths. But I was a bit of a rebellious pupil, and I was just fed up with studying. I wanted a job and I went into insurance — my maths background seemed to suit that. And I learned very quickly that it was deadly boring working in an office with about fifty other people about the same age as me. So I did some tuition in my second year of work, just a few Saturday mornings helping a youngster with some maths and I enjoyed doing it, so I thought 'I know, I'll teach'. But then, of course, I had to go on to further education. I lived in London, so I applied locally and went to the Regent Street Poly to do an external degree. Biology had always been my favourite subject at school, but I'd dropped it at 'A' level, so I decided biology for me — and I wanted to teach.

I used to be able to do biology exams in school without any revision whatsoever. I just used to sit and listen to the teachers talking about it and it used to go in and I never had to think about it again. It was very old-fashioned stuff. It was the only way we were taught. ... At the Poly it was an incredibly old-fashioned style of teaching as well. I just accepted it.

I started teaching at a London comprehensive in 1973. I had had no previous experience at all of teaching anybody other than on an individual basis. The first class I ever took was a fifth year CSE group. I'd been told by the Head of Biology that if I had any problems at all just sling them out and he'd deal with them, so I went in fairly confident — I was innocent of what could happen. The lesson started off okay, but one lad played me up fairly early on, so bearing in mind what the Head of Biology had said, I just slung him straight out. What I hadn't realised was that this particular lad was on his final warning — if he misbehaved once more in anybody's lesson he would be expelled. That made my reputation with the kids — you know — OUT and he was never seen again! Basically I found the kids incredibly easy to get on with and I had no discipline problems at all. I just felt at home with them because they were the sort of kids I'd grown up with, and I hadn't been out of school myself that long.

I was never quite sure what the kids were taking in. I suppose I didn't have the experience to say 'Stop, let's talk about it'. I just let it continue and I used to find that very unsettling — you know — *are* they actually taking it in? But the exams came up and they seemed to be doing all right, so I thought it must be working and I didn't look at it any closer than that! If things seem to be going okay, I tend to look at them rather superficially and allow them to carry on. It's only when things go wrong I start looking at them.

Then I moved to Yorkshire and things went quite well for a while but I found that I was beginning to get very frustrated with teaching: I found that some kids were not responding to my approach as well as they used to, but some were, and I used to find that in the end, I was getting to know those few very well and they'd get to know me very well, but there were a number within a class that I was not communicating with. They didn't seem to want to, and it was beginning to rattle me. It was either going over their heads or they just weren't switching on to my lessons. I wasn't getting through to them at all and I used to try to talk to some of them about it but they just didn't want to know.

I felt I was still teaching in an interesting way, trying to get something from them, but it was getting less and less effective and even areas of work that I'd introduced several years ago that had been a tremendous success when I first started, even they were failing and I was beginning to think 'Well, I'm going to have to change this'. And I couldn't understand why if I was doing the same thing, using the same material that was successful seven years ago, why it wasn't successful now. That had really begun to bug me.

I found that I was having to put more pressure on the pupils to keep them in line whereas before I never had to bother about discipline. Something was definitely going adrift somewhere and I think it was about that point that I started coming here, on the Fridays, for the biotechnology project. Actually, the adviser who told me about the project, did say that it would involve my being videoed teaching which sounded interesting, but it worried me a bit. I'd never had anybody in my lesson at any time in my entire teaching career, so to go beyond somebody just sitting there to actually having a video operating was a giant step, but I thought 'I'll tackle that one when I come to it'. That was the only thing that worried me about it. I also wasn't quite sure what biotechnology was when he first mentioned it. From a purely selfish point of view it has been absolutely superb for me, because it's the first time I've actually been able to sit down and think about what I'm actually doing in teaching. I've gone through basically ignorant of the philosophies behind what I was actually trying to do. I've not really sat down myself and thought 'Why am I teaching this particular area — why am I using that approach?' I just played it by ear, I just worked on instinct most of the time.

There obviously had been problems building up at school for which I was blaming various things, but to actually sit down with other people who obviously were thinking far more about what they were doing while they were doing it than I tend to — that was great! I dream about things and daydream. I tend to be a quiet person anyway, and this term has really changed that for me. I feel far more able to think something out and verbalise it to other people and argue a point through. It's enabled me to focus far more on what possibly has been going wrong in my teaching.

Now, after this term of secondment, I'm going to be able to think about what I'm trying to do, what approaches can be used, and certainly when I went back into school to trial the materials, I definitely felt really comfortable and happy again with teaching — the first time for quite some time. I was asking more from the kids and asking them to, in a sense, control their own destiny in the lesson, but in doing that it actually built communication between myself and the kids. They felt I was coming round to help them with the problem *I'd* given them, which they might feel wasn't theirs. The communication came back with a rush and I suddenly realised why I enjoy teaching, and all the old enjoyment, all the old feelings and pleasures were there again.

Notes on Contributors

Angela Anning is Lecturer in Education, University of Leeds, England.

Hilda Borko is Associate Professor in the College of Education, University of Maryland, USA.

Hugh Busher is Senior Lecturer in Education at Edge Hill College of Higher Education, Ormskirk, England.

James Calderhead is Lecturer in Educational Research, University of Lancaster, England.

Stephen Clarke is Lecturer in Education, University of Leeds, England.

Michael Eraut is Professor of Education at the University of Sussex, England.

Kate Johnston is Project Coordinator on the Children's Learning in Science Project, University of Leeds, England.

Fred A.J. Korthagen is Associate Professor of Mathematical Education, University of Amsterdam, The Netherlands.

Gaea Leinhardt is Professor of Educational Psychology, University of Pittsburgh, USA.

Carol Livingston is Research Officer in the College of Education, University of Maryland, USA.

Joseph McCaleb is Associate Professor in the College of Education, University of Maryland, USA.

Donald McIntyre is Reader in the Department of Educational Studies, University of Oxford, England.

Linda Mauro is Research Officer in the College of Education, University of Maryland, USA.

Jean Rudduck is Professor of Education, University of Sheffield, England.

Tom Russell is Associate Professor in the Faculty of Education, Queen's University, Ontario, Canada.

Laura Taggart is Research Officer in the School of Education, University of Leeds, England.

Sharon Wood is Research Fellow on the Cognitive Studies Programme at the University of Sussex, England.

Name Index

APU, 57
Abelson, R. 55
Alexander, R.J. 100
Anderson, R. 212
Anning, A. 6
Apple, M. 211
Argyris, C. 194
Ashton, P. 128
Aspinwall, K. 210–2

BERA 2
Baird, J.R. 33
Baratta-Lorton, M. 18
Bell, B. 169
Bell, M.S. 154–6
Berlak, A. 213
Berliner, D.C. 65
Book, C. 52
Borko, H. 5, 80
Bromme, R. 119
Brophy, J.E. 101
Brown, A.L. 49, 60
Brown, S. 102
Bruner, J. 206, 211, 213
Buchmann, M. 65, 81
Bull, D. 33
Busher, H. 5
Byers, J. 52

Calderhead, J. 51, 57, 66, 80, 86, 130
Carnegie Foundation, 1
Carr, W. 85, 206
Carraher, D.W. 146, 151
Carraher, T.N. 146, 151
Chase, W.G. 147
Chi, M.T.H. 147
Clandinin, D.J. 54

Clark, C.M. 138
Clarke, S. 5
Connolly, F.M. 54
Corcoran, E. 35
Creamer, K. 165–6

DES 1
DeCorte, E. 149
de la Rocha, O. 146
Desforges, C. 102
Doyle, W. 56
Driver, R. 169, 194
Dunn, W.R. 122

Elbaz, F. 54, 139
Elliott, J. 85
Eraut, M. 7, 201

Feiman-Nemser, S. 65, 81
Festinger, L. 85
Freeman, D. 52
Freudenthal, H. 38
Fullan, M. 208–9

Garver, E. 206
Gibbs, G. 49
Gilbert, J. 194
Good, T.L. 101
Goodman, J. 35
Gordon, D. 205
Green, A. 136
Greene, M. 206
Greeno, J.G. 65, 81, 147
Griffiths, R. 103
Grumet, M. 208, 212

225

Subject Index